THE PSYCHOLOGY OF BLACKS: AN AFRICAN-CENTERED PERSPECTIVE

Thomas A. Parham, Ph.D.
University of California, Irvine

Joseph L. White, Ph.D.
University of California, Irvine (Retired)

Adisa Ajamu
Howard University

How Does the Media Influence black culture
• Beauty • friends • style
• cultural acceptance (James Brown)

Prentice Hall
Upper Saddle River, New Jersey 07458

Library of Congress Cataloging-in-Publication

Parham, Thomas A. (Thomas Anthony)
The Psychology of Blacks : an African-centered perspective / by Thomas A. Parham, Joseph L. White, Adisa Ajamu.
p. cm.
Rev. ed of: The psychology of Blacks / Joseph L. White. 2nd ed. 1990.
Includes bibliographical references and index.
ISBN 0–13–095946–4
1. Afro-Americans—Psychology. I. White, Joseph L., 1932– . II. Ajamu, Adisa. III. White, Joseph L. Psychology of Blacks. IV. Title.
E185.625.P355 2000
155.8'496073—dc21 99–24474
CIP

Editor-in-Chief: *Nancy Roberts*
Executive Editor: *Bill Webber*
Assistant Editor: *Jennifer Cohen*
Managing Editor: *Mary Rottino*
Production Liaison: *Fran Russello*
Project manager: *Pine Tree Composition*
Prepress and Manufacturing Buyer: *Lynn Pearlman*
Art Director: *Jayne Conte*
Cover Designer: *Bruce Kenselaar*
Cover Art: *"Spiritual Healing" by Shirley D. White Shockley*

This book was set in *10/12 Garamond* by Pine Tree Composition, Inc., and was printed and bound by *Courier Company*. The cover was printed by *Phoenix Color Corp.*

Printed in the United States of America
10 9 8 7 6 5 4 3 2 1

ISBN: 0-13-095946-4

Prentice Hall International (UK) Limited, *London*
Prentice Hall of Australia Pty. Limited, *Sydney*
Prentice Hall Canada, Inc., *Toronto*
Prentice Hall Hispanoamericana, S.A., *Mexico*
Prentice Hall of India Private Limited, *New Delhi*
Prentice Hall of Japan, Inc., *Tokyo*
Pearson Education Asia Pte. Ltd., *Singapore*
Editora Prentice Hall do Brasil, Ltda., *Rio de Janeiro*

Contents

NOTES

Dedication

This third edition of *The Psychology of Blacks: An African-Centered Perspective* is dedicated to the memory of Mrs. Sadie F. Parham. She transitioned from this world in July of 1998, after an extended illness. While we, her family and friends, ache with grief at her departing, we take comfort in knowing that her suffering has ended, and she has gone to be with God, the Angels in heaven, and our community of Ancestors.

In the course of my exposure to, reasoning about, teaching, and writing about African-centered perspectives in psychology, I have come to know more fully what this discipline represents. African-centered psychology is about the illumination, understanding, revitalization, and liberation of the human spirit. The spiritual essence (energy and life force) is reflected in all that we are, and in all that we do. Thus, you can find the principles and practices articulated in this text reflected in the daily life experiences of African-descent people everywhere.

Through this dedication, I want to illuminate to each of you a bit of my spirit, the spirit of my late mother, and the spirit of mothers everywhere. Although the circumstance constitutes a certain level of pain for me, the self-disclosure and the catharsis it represents provides a meaningful interpretive vehicle through which to view the power and passion of a vibrant African psychology. The emotional vitality, interdependence, respect for elders, law of reciprocity, and the manifestation of spirit are all reflected in this story. Further, I hope that this dedication, the disclosure of my "Healing Space," and the "Afterword" at the end of this text will in some small way capture that transformative power of the human spirit as it is confronted by life's circumstances. Although we give praise to our fathers and the men in our community, we honor through this scholarly work my mother and mothers everywhere. How blessed I am that the Creator chose her as the instrument to guide my life, feed my soul, and nourish my spirit.

A SON'S "HEALING SPACE"

The time is 4:15 A.M., Tuesday morning, much too early for most people to even consider abandoning their early morning dream states. But my spirit is aroused. Holding her hand, as I bend over her body lying in the bed, I whisper the few things my heart, mind, and spirit have aligned themselves to say in this moment of heightened tension, pain, and sorrow.

I mention to her "Let's say our prayers," and I begin with a sequence of "Our Fathers" and "Hail Marys" as she listens to them through the sounds of her labored breathing. Once done, I wipe my own tears, and one from her, as I thank her for a wonderful life and tell her how much I love her and know she loves me. In acknowledging that she has fought a long and hard fight against the diseases that ultimately consumed her body, I give her the verbal permission she really didn't need to let go and allow herself to go be with God and experience the rewards of heaven she lived all of her life to achieve. In doing so, I promised her in the most assuring voice I could muster, that I and we will be all right, despite missing her tremendously.

With a brother and sister sharing her hospital bedside with me and another brother on the phone, we are hurting, but blessed to be with our mom in her last moments on this earth. How ironic that the family composition that characterized our life would be one of the strongest supports in these waning moments. Her breathing is now sporadic at best, and the pulse and oxygen saturation monitors are telling us the end is close, as she takes her final breath and exhales to release her spirit to join the Creator and the community of ancestors. The time is now 4:40 A.M., the room is quiet, but for the sounds of our pain and tears, and I and we have just said goodbye to our mother, Sadie F. Parham, as she passed away.

No amount of preparation can ever truly prepare one for the pain and emptiness associated with losing one so close and dear. And yet, it is a bridge we all must cross one day, however difficult it is to imagine. And so, in a subject we brothers (and even sisters) rarely talk about, I want to share my pain with you on these pages in the hope that you understand just how special our mothers are, how strong our young mothers of today must be, and how imperative it is to let them know this each and every day while they are still among us.

The sentiments behind the expression "They don't make mothers like that anymore" come close to expressing my admiration for a woman whose life was a model of self-sacrifice. Raising four children by yourself is a challenge to be sure. But to do so without an ounce of regret about the marriage she separated from, the social life she never pursued, or the personal luxuries and even necessities she could never afford is to me the essence of strength and character. Four grown adult children, two with Ph.D.s, another college-educated, all four with parochial high school educations, with no one on drugs, in jail, or on the streets doing wrong is a tremendous legacy for a woman who never went to college herself, nor earned more than $18,000 per year during her 32+ years of civil service.

Admittedly, I sometimes have to catch myself from smirking and shaking my head at young mothers, be they single- or two-parent families, who moan and groan about the modern-day trials and tribulations of parenting even one child, let alone four. Don't they know it can be done with more confidence than they think they possess? I'm living proof of what the power of that maternal spirit and the strong belief in God can do.

In acknowledging a mother's special place in our lives, I wonder if they really experience the reciprocity they deserve for the love and care they provide? Oh sure, we won't bring just any young lady or woman home to meet them, nor will we usually forget to acknowledge them on Mother's Day or birthdays. For those of us who are more athletically inclined, we even will share our parade time before a local and national television camera at a sporting event with an acknowledgment of mom. But is that all our mothers deserve or expect? Not Sadie! No matter how many times people applauded her for my professional accomplishments, status, or awards (or those of my siblings), she usually tempered her pride with the simple desire that we be basically self-sufficient, God-loving, hard-working adults who are responsible, productive members of our community, and strong leaders of our families.

Having mastered (hopefully) these simple requisites, it was my desire throughout my formative and adult years to move beyond these markers of success to even greater demonstrations of thanks for her sacrifices. Beyond the reasonable grades in school and respect and deference shown her in our house, I simply couldn't bring myself to violate her trust by engaging in any behavior too inappropriate as to bring any semblance of shame to reflect on her parenting. Though my spirit could never allow my responses to life's circumstances to move too far left of what was considered socially and morally appropriate, I am grateful for the experiences that instilled in me an emotional obligation to not let my mother's sacrifice be nullified by my engaging in any scandalous behavior. Looking back on growing up now, how grateful I am for that emotional and spiritual nurturance, which continues to sustain me even today.

In this moment of reflection, I am troubled, however, by what I perceive as a collective failure on the part of some Black men to conduct themselves with appropriate deference to the struggles made on our behalf by our mothers. Certainly, many of us are very responsible, productive men in the roles we play as youth and adults. But the statistical profiles of our group compare poorly against the sacrifices made and time invested in trying to secure our futures. Too many of us perform poorly in school. Countless others submit to the temptation of the streets by yielding to gang participation, substance use and abuse, and criminal activity. Some of us even have the nerve to allow our mothers to take care of us as adults, when the role and responsibilities of caretaker should have been reversed years before. How fortunate we are that our mothers continue to love us in spite of the ways we fall short as men. But don't be fooled into believing that you will have forever and a day to appropriately thank her. Our mothers leave us all too quickly, and the contemporary realities of heart disease, stroke, hypertension, and breast cancer among Black women are chipping away at the life expectancy clock. My own mother died ten days shy of her 76th birthday. But even that time was far too short.

Having now moved past her death and the marvelous celebration of life we (my sister and brothers) planned for her funeral, I transitioned into what I call my "healing space." This is a place where the pain of her loss begins to lessen with each passing week, and my recognition of my mother's spiritual presence begins to grow each day I call her name or remember her fondly. And as I focus on my personal struggle, I am clear that my healing is being facilitated by an inner voice of comfort that reminds me of how I supported and acknowledged my mother's sacrifice while she was alive by managing my personal and professional affairs with integrity and righteous character.

There is nothing I wanted to say to or do for mom that went unspoken or undone. No place I wanted to send her that I didn't, especially trips we made together. She and I had a relationship built on mutual love and support, caring, trust, and admiration. Even during those times my schedules, professional obligations, and other family and personal priorities seemed to dominate my agenda, I always found time for a phone call or a visit. Likewise, she would stretch out to me with a phone call if she perceived that the time and distance since our last "personal time" was too great. Even now, I smile at the memory of her playful scolding if she thought I was being too generous with a spontaneous gift, or too sensitive in quickly responding to an item I thought she needed, whether she requested it or not. Indeed, how blessed I am to not have to couple the pain of her loss with the tragedy associated with a mountain of regret for wishes and hopes that were never realized or fulfilled. How many of us are prepared to say the same?

Ultimately, I hope that this sharing of my story will inspire others to acknowledge the mothers (and other women) in our life's for the wonderful ways they nurture, support, protect, and quietly correct our manhood. The contributions extend far beyond their giving us life; they are the very essence of the best in each of us as men. The sacrifices that they make allow us to be better siblings to our families, nurturing parents to our children, devoted husbands to our wives, strong and responsible African-American men in our communities, and divine manifestations of what the Creator has in store for us. Certainly, we can commit ourselves to these endeavors while never missing an opportunity to thank them personally for their love.

And so, in tribute to my mother, Sadie F. Parham, and women everywhere who sacrifice to make our lives as men better, I offer this poem/presentation entitled "A Son To His Mother" as acknowledgment that her and your sacrifices have not gone unnoticed or unappreciated. I wrote it the day before her funeral service and shared it with her and the many family and friends gathered to celebrate her life. It can be found in the "Afterword" section of this book.

Thomas Parham
July 20, 1998

NOTES

Foreword

Life is a journey, along different paths, through many transitions, marked by an individual, but certain tempo. It is a journey of the spirit, as it is of the body and mind. What we make of it is truly not known until the inevitable end of it. And then, it is revealed in the quiet moments of the final transition. Until that time we are ever searching for the meaning of those experiences from our chosen pathways, forever tied together from one day to the next into a life map of our transitions.

Reading the third edition of *The Psychology of Blacks* by Thomas Parham, Joseph White, and Adisa Ajamu is like being equipped with a guide and compass for that journey through life's transitions. They help us find our way through the forest of experiences as a person of African descent. So often the complexities of life leave us standing amidst the proverbial trees not realizing which part of the forest we are in. In other words, we may be aware that we are among people of African descent but not know that we are of African descent. In this respect, the book helps us to mark our location, get oriented, and moves us along a path of understanding about being of African descent.

Although the book uses the focus of psychology to guide our comprehension of life as an African American, it is far more interdisciplinary in its actual scope. This is deliberate. The authors want to convey that to study and fully begin to grasp the human experience our inquiry must be reflective of the scope of that experience. Therefore they advocate for a holistic perspective, an expanded conceptualization of what psychology should be. This has been a product of the authors' own evolving thoughts. We can chart the growth and maturing of their thinking starting with the first edition of the *Psychology of Blacks* with its conceptual focus challenging assumptions about Blacks, the Eurocentric models of interpretation, and providing an early representation of the Black experience. In the second edition the emphasis shifted more towards presenting the African American perspective and emerging explanatory models by a growing critical mass of psychologists of African descent.

This third edition extends our thinking further to embrace a larger perspective that links the context of African American life to the traditions, values, and spiritual essence of our African ancestors. Not any less important is the authors' belief in the necessity for African Americans to build upon an African worldview and traditions that are intrinsic to our manner of living. It is as much an acknowledgment of the African worldview as it is recognition that this perspective can assist the African American community in addressing some of the challenges we face in the 21st century. This is why in this third edition, the subtext is learning from "An African Centered Perspective".

In my opinion an ultimate goal of this book is to promote a worldview and way of life for African Americans as represented by the African perspective they offer in the text: "I am because we are and because we are therefore I am". This speaks about responsibility and commitment, two values that thematically permeate the book. It is reflected in the authors' persistence in scholarship and excellence to further our knowledge about theory, research, and applications of a Black Psychology from the first edition to this third edition.

It is further reinforced by how responsibility and commitment get represented in the mentorship of the authors. The very values of family, collectivism, and communalism so central to the authors' African centered perspective are modeled in the sharing of authorship. Joseph White after the first edition enlisted the assistance of his student and protégé Thomas Parham, and in turn, Parham's protégé Adisa Ajamu has joined the partnership for the third edition.

Mentorship and continuity is also the essential component in the evolution of an African centered perspective in the study of African Americans. Using both Dr. Wade Nobles and Dr. Thomas Parham's presidency in the Association of Black Psychologists the authors discussed how these leaders furthered the destiny of the organization in its response to the persistent outcomes from racism and historical treatment of people of African descent (i.e., the Maafa). In the transition of the Association there is a model of appropriate carrying out of destiny. We not only must pursue our destiny, but its integrity must represent a greater congruence between what we say we are, and what we actually are. It is at the heart of the identity quest not only for a professional association but also for people of African descent. It is central to how we contribute through our scholarship and service.

Therefore this book very much tackles our continuing efforts to achieve consensus in our identity as African people. It very much looks at the many facets of behavior we observe in our communities, amongst our young brothers and sisters, among our men and women as role models, and within the functionality of our family systems. A principled way of living and being, as represented by the character building tenets of MAAT is promoted as a standard for collective subscription towards living and being together as people.

The authors clearly see education as a keystone in this endeavor. Their observations about the importance of appropriate knowledge continue to echo the prophetic voices of G. Carter Woodson and W.E.B. DuBois. Statistics that might discourage or sow doubt about current trends in schools and for Black students are balanced with optimism contained with growth in other areas. Clearly, education of our youth and the growth of female single headed households, the disempowerment of African American males, and the dysfunctional patterns in our communities are recognized. The authors present clear analysis of what in their views are the determinants and strategies for confronting these challenges in our communities. One outstanding model for developing leadership in our youth is detailed in a rites of passage, mentoring, and leadership development program called, *Passport to the Future Program,* developed by Thomas Parham for the 100 Black Men of America's Orange County Chapter.

Programs like the above are another example of a main objective of the authors. They put as much emphasis upon identifying appropriate applications in meeting the challenges for people of African descent as they do to provide the proper perspective for those applications. In this regard, credit is also given to a major effort by the authors to expand how to approach providing awareness, knowledge, and culturally competent skills in working with African Americans in a therapeutic context.

We also must understand how a geopolitical and global economy still establishes inequities in status and quality of life for people of

African descent. As we enter the 21st century it is important to consider seriously the many areas of our lives that will be effected by numerous transitions within the new millennium. We must decide in what way do we become not just active, but effective agents in our own destiny. We must decide how we take charge of the socialization of our young men and women, how we promote our families and communities. We must reach back in the symbolism of Sankofa, learn from our history, retool our resilience, connect with our spiritual center, respect the wisdom of our elders, and develop a proper worldview in order to go forward. What Parham, White, and Ajamu do in *The Psychology of Blacks* is focus us for this task. They give us a way to understand and approach transitions in the development of the soul and the human spirit as manifested in our cognition, affect, and overall behavior. They give us a means for understanding life.

No where is this more exemplified than in the touching words and reflections by Thomas Parham about his late mother, Sadie, in the Book's opening segment "A Healing Place," and again in an Afterword, "Remembering Sadie: A Son to His Mother." Contained in these passages is the essence of the book's messages. As people of African descent we must not lose touch with our spiritual center, what builds character, what responsibility and commitment builds as values.

Thomas Parham's mother lived a life that truly is a study of Black Psychology. She embodied the resilience, values, and a sense of self in the world—a personal destiny—that manifested the legacy bestowed by our maternal and paternal African ancestors. Her life was a testament to faith. Hers was a faith that transcended her life circumstances, the fragility of her body, the uncertainty of her future. In her faith is confidence that her children will keep the faith, and pass it along to the next generation. Towards this goal is a manifestation of her faith, Dr. Thomas Parham, a committed son, husband, father, author, mentor to the next generation, and visionary. Sadie Parham didn't worry about articulating the principles of character discussed in *The Psychology of Blacks;* she just lived them.

And thus in one life is captured the lessons of this book. We must live life in a principled way, with values reflecting our intrinsic African centered worldview. Like our ancestors, and Like Sadie Parham, we must keep our eyes focused on the real prize, and no matter how much others, or circumstances, may try to crush the spirit, we must believe in the words of Maya Angelou, "and still I rise."

A.J. Franklin

Preface

The discipline of African-American psychology has changed considerably over the last decade. The plethora of research and scholarship now available within the field is quite impressive, particularly in light of its range and versatility. One of the most fundamental changes or transitions made in the field involves the shift in perspective. The discipline seems to be moving away from the practice of merely critiquing the principles and practices of European-American psychology to one where more time and energy is directed at illuminating the specifics of an African-centered worldview. Thus, the energy historically devoted to deconstructing Euro-American psychology is now used to create, develop, and articulate a clear vision of African-centered principles.

This third edition of *The Psychology of Blacks: An African-Centered Perspective* aligns itself with that focus and direction. It represents a collaboration of three generations of African-American psychology professionals and a student who have continued the legacy of intergenerational support, mutual trust, and peoplehood that characterizes our struggles as African-American men.

Chapter 1 of this third edition has been updated with a clear articulation of the principles of African-centered psychology including scientific colonialism, the persistence of the African-American worldview, African-centered values, and an extensive discussion about how the principles and practices of African-centered psychology becomes operationalized and institutionalized through the National Association of Black Psychologists.

Chapter 2 provides some of the latest research on Black family development, including a new section on how to build strong healthy families. Chapter 3 of this third edition continues with a discussion on issues of identity development in African-American people and also has been extensively revised and updated.

Chapter 4 discusses the psychological issues and the education of African-American people and has been updated with new data on academic profiles and the correlates of achievement. Chapter 4 also includes a discussion of the educational challenges in the new millennium, with a specific emphasis on the need to resocialize African-American youth. In addition, we highlight, through our discussion of "promising practices," how the principles and constructs of African-centered psychology are being utilized in communities across America in helping to reeducate our youth.

Chapter 5 is new in this edition, with a discussion of contemporary approaches to developmental psychology. In it, we discuss traditional approaches to developmental psychology, limitations and conceptual pitfalls, the importance of culture in understanding African-American psychological development, and future challenges and considerations. Chapter 6 has been updated and revised to include some of the latest data on mental health issues impacting African-American people. Of significance in this chapter is the new section on cultural competence and the need to train service providers to work more effectively with African-American populations.

Chapter 7 is a new addition wherein we discuss the theoretical and methodological considerations necessary in doing research in African-American psychology. Likewise, Chapter 8 is a new addition, discussing a new set of emerging issues confronting the African-American community. Here, specific attention is given to issues of coping with racism and oppression, confronting the social pathology of the American workplace, and the psychosocial experiences of African-American women, which was provided for us, by Dr. Helen Neville of the University of Missouri—Columbia. The text concludes in Chapter 9 with some summary remarks and the addition of an annotated bibliography, which includes some readings we consider essential for those serious about the study of African-centered principles in psychology.

Although we are very proud to offer you this third edition of *The Psychology of Blacks,* we are also mindful that the extensive nature of the work that has gone into writing and revising this text must be reflected both within the content contained on each page, as well as the outer cover. Indeed, outer garments often reflect the substance within. In this regard, we are grateful to Ms. Shirley Shockley, whose rendition of a print she first entitled "Recentering African Descendants . . ." so spoke to Dr. Parham that he had to have it adorn the cover of this text. We hope you will enjoy this third edition and that this contribution will make your study of the principles and practices of African-centered psychology more productive and beneficial.

NOTES

Acknowledgment

No project of this scope and magnitude can be completed in isolation. Indeed, it requires a great deal of mutual support and commitment. Within the many months it took to complete this project, we have attempted to give you our best thinking as it relates to the principles and practices of African-centered psychology at this time. However, our ability to give was inextricably bound up in our capacity to receive support, encouragement, and love from some significant people in our lives. In the spirit of reciprocity, we would like to acknowledge their contributions to this third edition project.

Thomas A. Parham, Ph.D.
In all things, I am grateful to the Creator and the Ancestors who have blessed me with enormous gifts and attributes. In addition, I am grateful to my wife Davida, daughters Tonya and Kenya, and father-in-law David Hopkins, for their love, support, and willingness to allow their needs to go neglected while I completed this task. Finally, I would like to thank my administrative assistants Ms. Peggi Cummings and Ms. Carla Gladman whose professional expertise and technological diligence prepared this manuscript in draft and final forms.

Joseph L. White, Ph.D.
In all things, I am grateful for the love and support of my wife Lois, who walks with me every step of the way as I navigate the landscape into later adulthood.

Adisa Ajamu

If Black psychology is about learning to love African people in ways that are human, healing, and profoundly powerful, then I consider my parents Evelyn and John L. Mackey to be the first Black psychologists under whom I studied. Their daily examples of good character, self-affirmation, and self-determination have been a source of perpetual inspiration. I love you both. I would also like to extend my deep love and appreciation to my extended family parents: Baba, Ifagbemi, and Iya Vera Nobles, as well as Baba Vulindlela and Iya Nozipo Wobogo, thank you for reminding me that "*Amandla Wamadlozi Ngawethu!*" (the power of the Ancestors is ours). No discourse on Black psychology is ever complete without mention of Dr. Joseph L. White, "the God Father" of Black psychology; his genius and commitment to African people continues to revitalize us astoundingly.

And lastly, it is no over statement to say that almost every good thing that has happened to me, either directly or indirectly, in the last seven years has been as the result of the contributions of one man: Dr. Thomas A. Parham. "Dr. P," as he is affectionately called by his students, is one of those rare people who actually strives to achieve a "*maatian*" balance between their words, thoughts, and actions. He is a model husband, father, scholar, and teacher. His shining example serves as a beacon that illuminates the path to African manhood for African males wandering through the forest of European cultural hegemony and Eurocentric privilege aimlessly in search of manhood. In this spirit, no person could ask for a better friend, and certainly no student has ever had a better example to follow. I love you, *Adupe'O* (thank you).

About the Authors

Dr. Thomas A. Parham is Assistant Vice-Chancellor for Counseling and Health Services, Director of the Counseling Center, and adjunct faculty at the University of California, Irvine. He is a Distinguished Psychologist in the Association of Black Psychologists, a Fellow in the American Psychological Association (Division 17 & 45), and a past president of the Association of Black Psychologists.

Joseph L. White, Ph.D. is a retired Professor of Psychology and Comparative Cultures at the University of California, Irvine. He is a founding member and Distinguished Psychologist of the Association of Black Psychologists. Dr. White has served as an academician and practicing clinical/counseling psychologist for over thirty-eight years.

Adisa Ajamu is the founder and director of the Atunwa Collective, an African family development think tank in Washington, D.C. He is a graduate of Concordia University in Irvine, California, where he holds a Bachelor of Arts degree in sociology. He is currently a graduate student in developmental psychology at Howard University.

1

African-Centered Psychology in the Modern Era

In the first and second editions of *The Psychology of Blacks* (White, 1984; White & Parham, 1990), the authors used as their guiding theme the premise that there exists a unique, coherent, persistent psychological perspective or worldview that is uniquely African-American. Accordingly, the African-American perspective can be seen in the behaviors, attitudes, feelings, expressive patterns, and values of Black people. Furthermore, it provides African-Americans with a way of interpreting reality and relating to others, as well as a general design for living. The third edition continues to hold to those same assumptions.

Some who question the need for a culturally specific psychology do so on the premise that the theories and constructs of the discipline are or should be universally applicable to the majority of the population. Others will argue that an African-centered perspective and movement in psychology is both divisive to the discipline and seeks to advance an anti-White agenda. Neither of these perspectives is accurate or true. In fact, it is our belief that the value of an African-centered perspective in psychology can only be genuinely understood if one is able to take a critical look at self. There most of us will discover how our own biases and assumptions about the nature of people have been influenced in ways that devalue and/or otherwise denigrate any perspective that differs from that on which we have been traditionally trained. After all, one of the cornerstones of a Eurocentric worldview is the application of a "difference equals deficiency" logic to those things that deviate from the traditional norms established by society.

DEFINITIONS

Those who have not had the benefit of reading the first or second editions of *The Psychology of Blacks,* or who are otherwise unfamiliar with the concept of a Black psychological perspective, may be asking themselves "What is this discipline called Black or African-American psychology?" As such, perhaps the most logical place to begin this third edition is with a definition of the construct (psychology of Blacks) and with a discussion of why an African-centered psychological perspective is necessary.

Nobles (1986) reminds us that in its truest form, psychology was defined by ancient Africans as the study of the soul or spirit. He writes:

> A summary reading of our ancient mythology reveals that ancient Egyptian thought can be characterized as possessing (1) "ideas of thought" which represent the human capacity to have "will" and to invent or create; (2) "ideas of command" which represent the human capacity to have "intent" and to produce that which one wills. Parenthetically these two, will and intent, are the characteristics of divine spirit and would serve as the best operationalization of human intelligence. (Nobles, 1986, p. 46)

Nobles further asserts that the psychology that was borrowed from Africa and popularized in Europe and America (so-called Western psychology), in some respects represents a distortion of ancient African-Egyptian thought. What the ancients believed was that the study of the soul or spirit was translated by Europeans into the study of only one element of a person's psychic nature, the mind.

In a similar vein, Akbar (1994) has persuasively argued that the Kemetic (so-called Egyptian) roots of psychology bear little resemblance to the modern-day constructs. Akbar explains, for example, that the term *sakhu* represented in its original form illumination and enlightenment of the soul or spirit. However, this perspective lost its meaning when the Greeks reinterpreted it to mean behavior and created a discipline to quantify, measure, and materialize the construct objectively.

Thus, the term psychology (in a Western context) is constructed from the words *psyche* (meaning mind) and *ology* (meaning knowledge or study of) and is generally assumed to be a study of human behavior. As previously noted, psychology has been around for thousands of years and dates back to ancient KEMET (sometimes illustrated as KMT) (African-Egyptian) civilizations (Nobles, 1986). However, as a discipline, psychology, like history, anthropology, and many other fields of study, has fallen victim to the attempts by many to both: (1) destroy and/or otherwise erase its historical connections to ancient Africa, and (2) transplant its roots into European civilization. Traditional psychology, as we know it in this country, was assumed to extend back only as far as the laboratories of Wilhelm Wundt in Germany around 1879. In its simplest form, traditional psychology was an attempt to explain the behaviors of the Europeans from a European frame of reference. After becoming popularized in America, Euro-American scientists began to engage in the same practice of defining and understanding the behaviors of various Euro-American peoples.

In their attempt to understand the mind and behaviors of their people, many European and Euro-American scholars began to develop theories of human behavior (i.e., Freud, Jung, Rogers). Theories are sets of abstract concepts that people assign to a group of facts or events in order to explain them. Theories of personality and/or psychology, then, are organized systems of belief that help us to understand human nature and make sense out of scientific data and other behavioral phenomena. It is important to realize, however, that theories are based on philosophies, customs, mores, and norms of a given culture. This has certainly been true for those theories that emerged out of the Euro-American frame of reference.

In their attempt to explain what they considered to be "universal human phenomena," Euro-American psychologists implicitly and explicitly began to establish a normative standard of behavior against which all other cultural groups would be measured. What emerged as normal or abnormal, sane or insane, relevant or irrelevant, was always in comparison to how closely a particular thought or behavior paralleled that of White Europeans and/or European-Americans. For many White social scientists and psychologists, the word *different* (differences among people) became synonymous with deficient, rather than simply different.

The presumptive attempt at establishing a normative standard for human cognition, emotion, and behavior was questionable at best for obvious reasons. The philosophical basis of this body of theory and practice, which claims to explain and understand "human nature," is not authentic or applicable to all human groups (Nobles, 1986). White (1972) in his article "Towards A Black Psychology," speaks to this issue clearly when he contends that "it is difficult if not impossible to understand the lifestyles of Black people using traditional psychological theories, developed by White psychologists to explain White behavior." White further asserts that when these theories are applied to different populations, many weakness-dominated and inferiority-oriented conclusions emerge. The foundation for an authentic Black psychology is an accurate understanding of the Black family, its African roots, historical development and contemporary expressions, and its impact on the psychological development and socialization of its members. One has only to examine the psychological literature as it relates to Black people to appreciate White's point.

Appreciation of White's (1972) perspective is enhanced when one looks first at the so-called science of psychology and then at the resulting conclusions that emerge from these research practices. In commenting on the science of psychology, Boykin (1979) argues that there are inherent biases and subjectivity in the investigation and application of scientific principles despite their claims to the contrary. Thus, he believes that biases inherent in Eurocentric perspectives render research investigations and resulting conclusions invalid at most, or at least, inappropriate.

It is important to note, however, that questions of bias could be dealt with in *less confrontive* ways if one believed the intent of scientists and psychological scholars to be honorable. When one considers that scientific intent was and is supported by racist ideologies (Guthrie, 1976; Hilliard, 1996), then challenging and confronting those biases becomes even more important. As such, one can now better appreciate the critique of science and psychological (scientific) inquiry provided by Nobles (1986), who argues that research has been used as a tool of oppression and represents a form of "scientific colonialism."

The term scientific colonialism then represents the political control of knowledge and information in order to advance a particular group's agenda and/or prevent another group from advancing its own. According to Nobles, scientific colonialism is operationalized in several ways. These include:

> *Unsophisticated Falsification:* deliberate attempts to erase and/or otherwise disguise an idea's African origins or the historical contributions of African people,

Integrated Modificationism: assimilation of a known concept into existing ideas such that the result is a distorted version of the original meaning and intent, and

Conceptual Incarceration: where all information is viewed from a single perspective to the exclusion of other world views or frameworks.

As a consequence of this biased and inappropriate method of inquiry, research and scholarship written by European-Americans about African-Americans is severely tainted. Let us now turn our attention to the outcomes and resulting conclusions of that science.

HISTORICAL THEMES IN PSYCHOLOGICAL RESEARCH

Historically, research on minorities in general and Blacks in particular has shifted focus several times. In fact, Thomas and Sillen (1972) and Sue (1978) concluded that it is difficult to fully understand and appreciate the status of ethnic minority research without reference to several general themes or models. These models include: (1) the inferiority model; (2) the deprivations/deficit model; (3) the multicultural model. Table 1–1 provides a conceptual outline of these research trends, and a brief review follows.

TABLE 1–1 Historical Themes in Black Psychological Research

	Inferiority	Deficit-Deficiency	Multi-Cultural
Definition	Blacks are intellectually, physically, and mentally inferior to whites	Blacks deficient with respect to intelligence, cognitive styles, family structure	All culturally distinct groups have strengths and limitations.
Etiology of Problem:	Genetics/heredity, individual	Lack of proper environmental stimulation; racism and oppressive conditions, individual	Differences viewed as different; lack of skills needed to assimilate.
Relevant Hypothesis and Theories:	Genetic inferiority, eugenics	Cultural deprivation, cultural enrichment	
Research examples:	White (1799) Morton (1839) Jensen (1969)	Moynihan (1965) Kardiner and Ovesey (1951)	J. White (1972) Nobles (1972; 1981)

Inferiority Models

The inferiority model generally contends that Black people are inferior to Whites. Its focus emerges out of the theories of genetics and heredity, which contend that the development of the human species is determined by heredity and views this process of development as "in the blood" or encoded in the genes. This model apparently afforded for some a scientific basis for viewing Blacks as inferior. Examples of these assertions of racial inferiority, as reported by Clark (1975) were heard as early as 1799 when Professor Charles White spoke of the Negro as being "just above the ape in the hierarchy of animal/human development, having a small brain, deformed features, an ape-like odor, and an animal immunity to pain." These inferiority assertions continued into the mid-1800s, when studies on cranial capacities showed that a European skull held more pepper seed than an African skull, and thus concluded that Blacks have inferior brains and limited capacity for mental growth (Clark, 1975). These assertions of racial inferiority continued well into the 1900s and were promoted by many leading Euro-American psychologists. In fact, a comprehensive examination of the literature related to the history and systems of psychology would reveal that in every decade encompassing 1900-1970, there was a prominent American psychologist (many of whom were presidents of the American Psychological Association) who was a proponent of the genetic inferiority hypothesis (Guthrie, 1976). Although such facts may be new information for many students in psychology, certainly most students and laypersons are aware of the well-publicized assertions of racial and intellectual inferiority by Arthur Jensen (1969).

Deficit-Deficiency Model

The deficit-deficiency model began to emerge around the late 1950s to early 1960s, and suggested that Blacks are somehow deficient with respect to intelligence, perceptual skills, cognitive styles, family structure, and other factors. Unlike the inferiority model, the set of hypotheses suggested that environmental rather than hereditary factors were responsible for the presumed deficiencies in Blacks. The deficit model arose in opposition to the inferiority model and was formed by more liberal-minded psychological and educational researchers who sought to place on society the burden for Black people's presumed mental and intellectual deficiencies. For example, it was somehow concluded that the effects of years of racism and discrimination had deprived most Black people of the strengths to develop healthy self-esteems (Kardiner & Ovesey, 1951) and legitimate family structures (Moynihan, 1965). From this deficit model came such hypotheses as "cultural deprivation," which presumed that because of the inadequate exposure to Euro-American values, norms, customs, and life-styles, Blacks were indeed "culturally deprived" and required cultural enrichment.

Implicit in the concept of cultural deprivation, however, is the notion that the dominant White middle-class culture established that normative standard discussed earlier in these writings. Thus, any behaviors, values, and life-styles that differed from the Euro-American norm were seen as deficient.

By and large, the model of the Black family that has received the most attention has been the deficit-deficiency model. This model begins with the historical assumption that there was no carry over from Africa to America of any sophisticated African based form of family life in communal living. The assumption further indicates that viable patterns of family life either did not exist because Africans were incapable of creating them, or they were destroyed beginning with slavery in the separation of biological parents and children, forced breeding, the slave master's sexual exploitation of Black women, and the cumulative effects of three hundred years of economic social discrimination. The deficit-deficiency model assumes that as a result of this background of servitude, deprivation, second-class citizenship, and chronic unemployment, Black adults have not been able to develop marketable skills, self-sufficiency, future orientation, planning and decision-making competencies, and instrumental behaviors thought to be necessary for sustaining a successful two-parent nuclear family while guiding children through the socialization process.

A variation of the deficit-deficiency model was the Black matriarchy model. In a society that placed a premium on decisive male leadership in the family, the Black male was portrayed as lacking the masculine sex role behaviors characterized by logical thinking, willingness to take responsibility for others, assertiveness, managerial skills, achievement orientation, and occupational mastery. In contrast, the Black female was portrayed by this model as a matriarch who initially received her power because society was unwilling to permit the Black male to assume the legal, economic, and social positions necessary to become a dominant force within the family and community life. Having achieved this power by default, the Black female was portrayed as being unwilling to share it. Her unwillingness to share her power was presumed to persist even when the Black male was present and willing to assume responsibility in the family circle, since she was not confident of the male's ability to follow through on his commitments. Confrontation over decision making and family direction was usually not necessary because the Black male was either not present in the household on any ongoing basis, or he was regarded as ineffective by the female when he was present.

Multicultural Model

The rise in the multicultural model has been stimulated by the contention that behaviors, life styles, languages, etc., can only be judged as appropriate or inappropriate within a specific cultural context (Greer & Cobbs, 1968; White, 1972; Pedersen, 1982). The multicultural model assumes and recognizes that each culture has strengths and limitations, and rather than being viewed as deficient, differences among ethnic groups are viewed as simply different. Although the multicultural model is the latest trend in research with respect to minorities in general and Blacks in particular, and is certainly a more positive approach to research with culturally distinct groups, it is by no means immune to conceptual and methodological flaws that have plagued psychological research efforts both past and present.

In some respects, this new emphasis on ethnic pluralism has helped researchers to focus on culture-specific models in a multicultural context. Black psychology has been the forerunner of an ethnic and cultural awareness in psychology that has worked its way into the literature on child development, self-image, family dynamics, education, communication patterns, counseling and psychotherapy, and mental health delivery systems. The blossoming of Black psychology has been followed by the assertion on the part of Asian-American (Sue & Wagner, 1973; Sue, 1981), Chicano (Martinez, 1977) and Native American (Richardson, 1981) psychologists that sociocultural differences in the experiential field must be considered as legitimate correlates of behavior. The development of an ethnic dimension in psychology suggested that other non-White Americans wanted to take the lead in defining themselves rather than continuing the process of being defined by the deficit-deficiency models of the majority culture. The evolution of the ethnic cultural perspective enlarged the scope of psychology. It served as a corrective step that reduced psychology's reliance on obsolete and inaccurate stereotypes in defining culturally distinct people.

Black Behavioral Norms

Given the negative conceptions of Black people and Black behavior that emerged from the Euro-American frame of reference, it was clear that an alternate frame of reference was not only appropriate, but absolutely necessary. Whether one considers the awarding of Sumner's degree in 1920, the establishment of the Association of Black Psychologists in 1968, or the era in ancient KMT, as the marker for the establishment of the discipline of Black psychology, is an interesting debate (Nobles, 1986). What is undebatable, however, is the recognition that general psychology had failed to provide a full and accurate understanding of the Black reality. As such, the discipline of Black psychology and the new emergence of an African psychological perspective can be defined as a discipline in science (continuing to evolve) that is attempting to study, analyze, and define appropriate and inappropriate behaviors of Black and African people from an Afrocentric frame of reference.

A second point made by White (1972) in his article is that Black psychology as a discipline should emerge out of the authentic experiences of Blacks in America. On the surface, White's contention seems absolutely logical. However, I believe this premise requires closer scrutiny.

For years, Black psychologists in the discipline of Black psychology have concerned themselves with trying to combat negativistic assumptions made about Black people by White society in general and traditional psychology in particular. In doing so, many of the writings have been reactionary in nature in their attempts to combat the racist and stereotypic assumptions perpetuated by the Euro-American culture. In that regard, Black psychology has served a vital purpose in the evolution of thought about the psychology of African-American people. In their attempt to negate the White middle-class norm and to assert the necessity for analyzing African-American behavior in the context of its own norms, Black psychologists have been attempting to establish this normative base that is uniquely Afrocentric. In developing that norm, however, new questions are now being raised about whether or not the behavior of Black people in America constitutes a reasonable normative standard of what appropriate and/or inappropriate behavior should be. In fact, if one examines the research related to Blacks, the normative standard that developed emerged for the most part from the analysis of behaviors and attitudes of Southern-born, working-class, ghetto-dwelling Black people (Akbar, 1981). Although this norm was certainly more valid than the Eurocentric perspective, it introduced biases against large numbers of Blacks who did not fit the newly developed stereotype of what a "real" Black person should be. Figure 1–1 attempts to illustrate how ghetto-centric norms are indeed based on a relatively small sample of Black people, and is influenced by a Eurocentric perspective of what Black normative behavior should be.

One can readily see the problem in adapting this ghetto-centric norm to all Black people in the criticism that was being leveled at TV's "The Cosby Show" during the late 1980s and early 90s. Much of the negative press about "The Cosby Show" that has emerged from the Black community has to do with the assumption that the characters and/or the show itself is not "Black enough." Many assume (inappropriately so) that you cannot be Black, middle-class, have two professional parents working, and have a loving family that displays caring concern, strength, and character, all in a single episode.

Apparently, many Black psychologists are now recognizing the difficulty that this shortsighted perspective has created for Black people. Akbar (1981) has suggested that this "Black norm" has two major limitations. First, it validates itself in comparison to a White norm. Secondly, the norm assumes that the adaptation to the conditions of America by Blacks constitutes a reasonable normative statement about African-American behavior. Akbar (1981) had the unique vision to recognize that oppression, discrimination, and racism are unnatural human phenomena; as such, these conditions stimulate unnatural human behavior. Thus, many of the behaviors displayed by Blacks as they attempt to adjust and react to hostile conditions in America may be functional but often prove self-destructive. For example, one who perceives her or his employment options as limited or nonexistent (because of discrimination) may turn to a life of crime in order to provide himself or herself with what are perceived as basic necessities. Such an individual might be seen selling drugs for profit, burglarizing a local establishment, engaging in prostitution or pimping, or other illegitimate endeavors. The problem with the ghetto-centric norm is that it legitimizes such behavior.

Because of these questions, many psychologists are now suggesting that statements about normative behavior should emerge from the values, norms, customs, and philosophies that are Afri-centric. Truly, this debate about what constitutes normative Black behavior is likely to rage on within the discipline of Black psychology for many years. Readers may ask, however, "What is this Afri-centric norm, and how

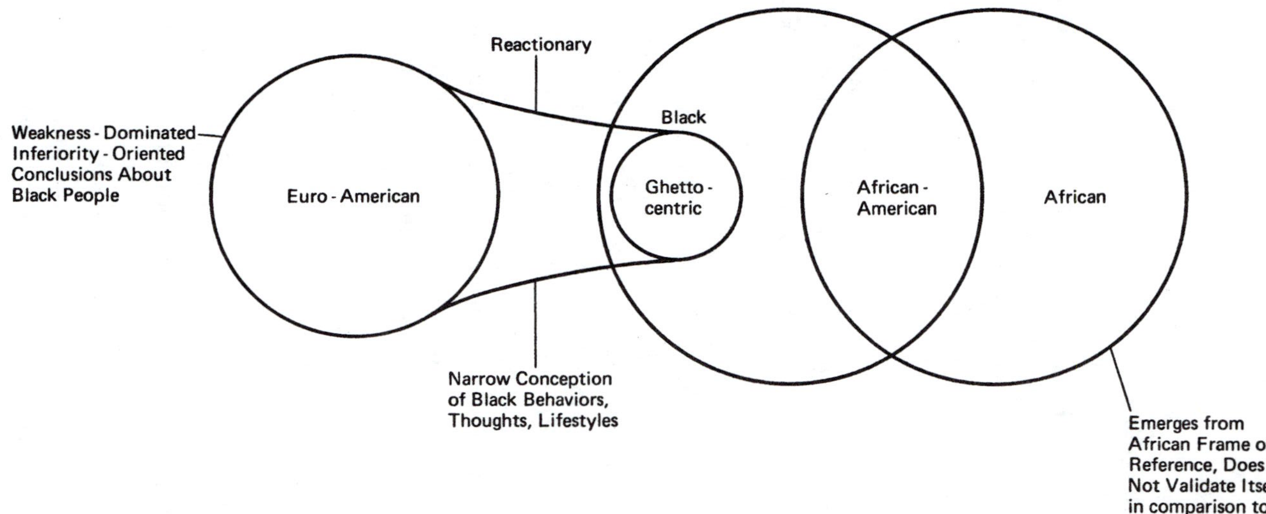

FIGURE 1–1 Need for a Worldview that Emerges from an African Frame of Reference

does it manifest itself in the Black community?" In the first edition of *The Psychology of Blacks,* White (1984) offers an excellent synthesis of the Afri-centric value system.

THE AFRICAN WORLDVIEW

White (1984) views the holistic, humanistic ethos described by Nobles (1972) and Mbiti (1970) as the principle feature of African psychology. There appears to be a definite correspondence between the African ethos and the Afro-American worldview in terms of the focus on emotional vitality, interdependence, collective survival, the oral tradition, perception of time, harmonious blending, and the role of the elderly. Some have questioned the utility of an African normative base, given the enormous tribal and geographical variability among African people. However, to discount the presence of an African norm because of differences is analogous to missing the forest for the trees. Certainly, these are individual differences, but there are more commonalities than differences, and it is those common themes that provide the foundation for the African worldview.

The African worldview begins with a holistic conception of the human condition. There is no mind-body or affective-cognitive dualism. The human organism is conceived as a totality made up of a series of interlocking systems. This total person is simultaneously a feeling, experiencing, sensualizing, sensing, and knowing human being living in a dynamic, vitalistic world where everything is interrelated and endowed with the supreme force of life. There is a sense of aliveness, intensity, and animation in the music, dance, song, language, and life-styles of Africans. Emotions are not labeled as bad; therefore, there is no need to repress feelings of compassion, love, joy, or sensuality.

The basic human unit is the tribe, not the individual. The tribe operates under a set of rules geared toward collective survival. Cooperation is therefore valued above competition and individualism. The concept of alienation is nonexistent in African philosophy since the people are closely interconnected with each other in a way of life that involves concern and responsibility toward others. In a framework that values collective survival, where people are psychologically interdependent on each other, active aggression against another person is in reality an act of aggression against oneself (Nobles, 1972). The idea of interrelatedness extends to the whole universe, arranged in a hierarchy that includes God, humans, animals, plants, and inanimate objects in a descending order.

People are linked in a geographical and temporal frame by the oral tradition, with messages being transmitted across time and space by word of mouth or the drums. Each tribe contains a *griot,* an oral historian, who is a living record of the people's heritage. The spoken word is revered. Words take on a quality of life when they are uttered by the speaker. In the act of *Nommo* the speaker literally breathes life into a word. Nothing exists, including newborn babies, until a name has been uttered with the breath of life. When words are spoken, the listener is expected to acknowledge receiving the message by responding to the speaker. This is known as the call-response. The speaker sends out a message or a call, and the listener makes a response indicating that he or she has heard the message. The speaker and the listener operate within a shared psycholinguistic space affirming each other's presence.

Time is marked off by a series of events that have been shared with others in the past or are occurring in the present. Thus, when an African talks about time in the past tense, reference points are likely to be established by events such as a daughter's marriage or a son's birth, events that were shared with others. When an African is trying to make arrangements about meeting someone in the immediate future, a specific time, such as three o'clock, is avoided. The person is more likely to say, "I will meet you after I finish milking the cows." The primary time frames in African languages are past and present. There is no word in most African languages for the distant future. The distant future has not yet happened; therefore, it does not exist. In this fluid perception of time there is no guilt about wasting time. Time is not a monetary commodity but an experience to be shared with others.

Time is also considered to be repetitive. The major events used to designate points in time, such as conception, birth, the naming ceremony, puberty, and marriage, repeat themselves throughout the life cycle. There is a cyclical, rhythmic pattern to the flow of events—the coming and going of the seasons, the rising and the setting of the sun, and the movement through the stages of life. Nature's rhythms are believed to have been put in order by God, who knew what He/She was doing. The essence of life is to be able to move harmoniously with the cyclical rhythms of the universe's internal clock. The goal is not to control or dominate the universe, but to blend creatively into the tempo and pace of the seasons of life. Life is broken down into a series of stages beginning with conception, followed by birth, the naming ceremony, puberty, initiation rites, marriage, adulthood, and old age. Death is seen as a stage of life. The living dead are still members of the tribe, and personal immortality is assured as long as one's memory is continuously passed down to each generation by the tribe's oral historian. Since immortality is guaranteed by the passing of one's memory forward, there is no pervasive fear of old age and death. The tribal elders are valued because they have accumulated the wisdoms of life's teachings. In the hierarchical arrangement of the cosmos, they occupy a position just below that of the Supreme Being and the living dead.

PERSISTENCE OF THE AFRICAN-CENTERED WORLDVIEW

In order to better grasp the worldview that emerges from an African reality, it is first necessary to understand, and in some cases reexamine, the notion of culture. Culture has been inappropriately equated with a number of superficial variables like food, music, clothing, and artifacts. Although each of these items is a representation or a manifestation of culture, they are not culture in and of themselves.

Culture is a complex constellation of mores, values, customs, tradition, and practices that guide and influence a people's cognitive, affective, and behavioral response to life circumstances. In essence, culture provides a general design for living and a pattern for interpreting reality (Nobles, 1986). Thus, in seeking to clarify and understand the African-centered worldview, the relevant question becomes: How do African-Americans construct their design for living and what patterns do they use to interpret reality?

One of the clearest expressions of an African-American cultural manifestation in psychology was provided by White (1984) in the first edition of *The Psychology of Blacks.* White believed that the African ethos helped to create a collective psychological space for African-Americans independent of their oppressors where they could generate a sense of worth, dignity, affiliation, and mutual support. Included in the delineation of that ethos, despite the historical context of slavery and oppression, were principles and practices such as self-determination and definition; the intergenerational continuity enhanced by and through the oral tradition; a strong religious faith, including participation in organized worship; immediate and extended family supports; language and expressive patterns; and personal expressions through music and the arts.

In further delineating the persistence of the African ethos into the life space of African-Americans, Parham (1993) has synthesized the work of Nobles (1972), White (1984), Myers (1988), and others through his comparisons of cultural worldviews. In contrasting the African-American and European-American worldview across selected primary dimensions, Parham suggests that the "designs for living" can be seen in the adherence to particular value systems by each cultural group. He first identifies eight variables that are then used to compare and contrast the two culturally different worldviews. The dimensions are listed as self, feelings, survival, language, time, universe, death, and worth. On one end of the spectrum is a Euro-American worldview; on the opposite end, the African-American.

Regarding the sense of *self,* Euro-Americans relate to a fragmented personality in which cognitive, affective, and behavioral dimensions are seen as separate and distinct. Regardless as to whether the psychological theories are classical (i.e., Freud's three structures of personality) or contemporary (i.e., Burne's transactional analysis), their analysis and application includes an imposition of a "difference equals deficiency" logic to particular segments of the personality structure. The African-American self begins with a holistic integration of its parts rather than fragmentation. At the core of the African self is an understanding of the fundamental nature of the self as spiritual, which permeates the cognitive, affective, and behavioral dimensions.

With regard to *feelings,* the Euro-American tradition values suppression of emotions in favor of rational imperatives. In the African-American tradition, emotions and feelings are intended to be expressed while serving as a check on expressions that are more rationally based.

The *survival* dimension in the Euro-American context embraces an individualistic and competitive relationship to people and the society at large. In contrast, the African worldview promotes a more collective orientation to people, family, and social interactions. This value of collective survival is reflected in the Asante proverb: "I am because we are; and because we are, therefore I am." In essence, this truth explains that an individual is only important to the degree that he or she contributes to the maintenance and the well-being of the tribe or the group.

Regarding *language,* the Euro-American culture gives credence to that which is written, that communicating with a style that appears to be formal and detached. In the African tradition, much more credence is given to the oral tradition with an emphasis on the interconnectedness between the speaker and the listener. With respect to *time and space,* Euro-Americans tend to be very future-oriented and perceive time as a commodity to be invested (i.e., "time is money"). African-Americans are more present-centered with a reference to the past. Time is also seen as something to be experienced in the moment, rather than invested with special emphasis or meaning given to circumstances surrounding an event.

In relationship to the *universe,* Euro-Americans relate to it with a desire and need for control and manipulation of things and people. In the African-American world view, the orientation is usually toward harmony and balance, as everything is seen as interrelated.

With regard to the concept of *death,* Euro-Americans see death of the body as the end. Therefore, there is an urgent, almost obsessive, desire to preserve life and avoid the realities of getting old. In the African-American worldview, death is seen as another transition from this life into the next. And because of the belief of spirit as the essence of the human being, one is able to better accept and embrace the spiritual transition of those who have joined the community of ancestors. Finally, *worth* in the Euro-American tradition is determined and measured by material attainment and possession. In the African tradition, one's worth was measured by contribution to community and collective uplifting. Parham's analysis, while allowing for individual variations, nonetheless recognizes how the African-American design for living and pattern for interpreting reality is reflected in the culture of the people.

With the persistence of the African ethos in the historical and contemporary life space of African-Americans, more recent scholars have utilized its principles as the foundation for this African-centered psychological perspective. Regardless as to whether the topic or analysis is African-American families in therapy (Boyd-Franklin, 1989), African-American male-female relationships (Powell-Hopson & Hopson, 1998), identity development (Cross, 1991), personal biographies (Gates, 1994), or the experiences of being a Black man in America (McCall, 1994), these themes discussed above continue to resonate with clarity and consistency.

THE DEVELOPMENT OF BLACK PSYCHOLOGY—THE MODERN ERA

In the opinion of the senior coauthor of this text, the modern era of Black psychology begins in 1968 with the formation of the Association of Black Psychologists (ABPsi). Graduate schools in psychology were still turning out a combined national total of only three or four Black

Ph.D.s in psychology per year. Some major departments of psychology at this late date had not produced a single Black Ph.D. psychologist. The grand total of psychologists among the more than ten thousand members of the American Psychological Association (APA), psychology's most prestigious organization, was less than one percent. At the annual convention of the APA in San Francisco in August/September of 1968, approximately fifty-eight Black psychologist delegates and their guests came together to give form and substance to the idea of a national organization of Black psychologists.

In the thirty years since its formal beginning in 1968, the modern era of Black psychology has established its presence across several areas of psychology. The impact of the efforts of Black psychologists have been felt in the community mental health, education, intelligence and ability testing, professional training, forensic psychology, and criminal justice. Black psychologists have presented their findings at professional conferences, legislative hearings, and social policy-making task forces. They have also served as expert witnesses in class action suits designed to make institutional policies more responsive to the needs of African people. In light of the social phenomena and institutional policies that continue to affect the mental health needs of the African-American community, we believe that ABPsi is a vital and necessary resource and will remain so for some time to come.

In order to better appreciate the ways in which ABPsi responds to more contemporary mental health needs of the African-American community, it is important to access the pulse of ABPsi's leadership. We have selected two past presidents of the association who served during the middle to late nineties and summarized their presidential messages to the association and the discipline of psychology. In their analyses is the best gauge of *why* an African-centered psychology is important; *what* are the central issues of our time; and *how* do we who commit ourselves to this struggle and extend it to the masses of African people.

We begin with Dr. Wade Nobles, an experimental/social psychologist out of Stanford University, who is recognized as one of the leading authorities of African psychology, philosophy, and culture. A distinguished psychologist, Dr. Nobles served ABPsi during the 1994/95 fiscal year and is currently a professor at San Francisco State University and director of the Institute for the Advanced Study of Black Family Life and Culture, Inc., in Oakland, CA.

Dr. Nobles began his tenure by introducing to the association his theme of the year entitled: "The MAAFA, the Media, and the Mind:

Keys to Illuminating the African Spirit." MAAFA is a term popularized by Marimba Ani (1994) and represents a great disaster of death and destruction that is beyond human comprehension and convention. By using that theme, Dr. Nobles believed that the ABPsi and Black psychologists should orchestrate a dialogue that was designed to understand and unravel the forces that have been so destructive to the psyche and the spirit of African people. During his term, a series of dialogues were held across this country that acquainted people with the constructs, analyzed their perceptions of the ways in which the MAAFA had impacted their lives, and catalogued suggestions for ways in which our communities could begin to initiate a process of healing. In seeking to extend his message to the larger African-American community, Dr. Nobles was able to secure grant funding from the Centers for Disease Control in Atlanta to facilitate these dialogues.

Dr. Nobles was also committed to advancing an international agenda in extending ABPsi's reach beyond the borders of the United States. In that regard, he was very successful in establishing a series of dialogues with the federation of traditional healers in Ghana. This effort, which was led by Dr. Cheryl Grills, helped to gain access to traditional healing methods.

Like Fanon before him, Dr. Nobles was also clear that "every generation must fulfill its mission or betray it," and he believed that our mission was to reclaim the status of healer. In doing so, he believed that African-centered psychologists could forge a union between those dimensions of reality that are less understood, but absolutely essential for the survival and advancement of African people. Dr. Nobles's message recognized that the mystical and spiritual were not just dimensions of a political and behavioral reality; they were intricately related to it. He believed that we simply could not entertain or romanticize notions about the glory of Africa; he thought that Black psychologists should engage in political action that was designed to build nationhood.

Believing that the task of the healer was to render African traditions relevant to contemporary national needs, Dr. Nobles advanced the notion that psychologists should be the voices that engage in discourse to assist our communities, from the youngest baby to the eldest elder, to perceive us as a nation. Thus, we must begin to see ourselves as a nation and everything that we do should be in service to our nationhood.

A second theme of Dr. Nobles's tenure centered around the idea that the spirit of the community needed to be awakened. In teaching the association about the principle of *sankofa,* he reminded us that the *sankofa* bird has the head looking back with an egg in its mouth. The egg represents the sustenance and substance of life. And so, Nobles reminded us that through *sankofa* we are able to go back and get the African essence and go forward into the future. Through his message, he implored Black psychologists to understand that the role of healer was to go back and fetch the essence of African life and culture. That essence was represented by the divine nature of each human being, and that that spiritual energy represented a power, or phenomenon, of perpetual veneration. Clearly, Nobles believed that a healer's task included the necessity of understanding the notion of spirit, and the spiritness in each of us is a living power, or force, that animates our thoughts, feelings, and behaviors. It is our responsibility, then, as African psychologists and thinkers, to begin to talk about the spirit as a nonphysical manifestation where we recognize that having energy, force, and efficacy directs the will and intent to control and/or otherwise impact life's circumstances.

In addition to the organizational, administrative, and fiscal challenges of running a national organization, Dr. Nobles also reminded the association that it had a covenant with destiny. This covenant, he believed, was a chance to do what the ancestors had prepared us to do; that ABPsi must serve as a guide into and for the future growth and development of the humanity of African people.

We continue our analysis by examining the presidency of Dr. Thomas Parham, who followed Dr. Nobles. Dr. Parham received his Ph.D. in counseling psychology from Southern Illinois University at Carbondale. In addition to being the first author of this text, Dr. Parham is considered among the most prominent African-American psychologists in the country and was recently recognized as a "distinguished psychologist" by the ABPsi (their highest honor). Dr. Parham is currently Assistant Vice Chancellor for Counseling and Health Services, Director of the Counseling Center, and adjunct faculty member at the University of California, Irvine. Like his predecessors, Dr. Parham believed that his abilities to lead the association successfully would be contingent upon the support he received from and the work produced by the collective membership. In recognizing that ABPsi was an organization that was then 27 years old, the goals for his administration paralleled his perception of the developmental tasks that 27-year-olds needed to confront in order to continue their growth and development. These goals included: (1) establishing a greater congruence between their chronological age and mental maturity (making mature and responsible decisions about association business); (2) developing "life direction" by establishing a consistent theme from which to conduct our discussions and directives during that year. That theme was "Ori-Ire: The African Psychologists' Response to the MAAFA"; (3) developing mature relationships with other Black psychologists and reaching out for those who for whatever reason have been absent from the association; and (4) developing a greater level of autonomy and independence that should be reflected in the increased administrative efficiency and broader visibility that the ABPsi received on the national scene.

In reflecting back on ABPsi's growth and development, Parham believed that ABPsi needed to increase its visibility on the national scene. Through his efforts and with the help and support of the board of directors and other members, activities during his administration included participation in the Black Congress on Health, Law and Economics, participation in the African-American Leadership Summit, attending White House briefings, participation in the Clarksdale- Mississippi rites of passage project for young African-American males, providing testimony on Capitol Hill, and continuing to support and seal the relationship with the Ghanian Association of Psychics and Healers. Parham also provided a written endorsement for the Million Man March, corresponded with President Clinton about issues of concern to African people, and created the association's first website.

Like his predecessors, Parham needed to confront administrative and fiscal challenges of running a national organization. In attending to those details, however, Parham took considerable pride in recognizing that the ABPsi was and remains the only autonomous ethnic psychology association in the country with a separate national headquarters, a scholarly journal (the *Journal of Black Psychology*), an informative newsletter (the *Psych Discourse*), and the national convention experience that ranks second to none in intellectual stimulation and professional development.

Although Parham took considerable pride in maintaining the association's sense of self-determination, he was clear that the association faced several challenges that were broader than the maintenance of fiscal integrity. The first of these challenges included the management of the tension that existed regarding our interaction with other professional organizations.

During his tenure, Parham sought to remind the association of the wisdom of the elders, which taught that it is our legacy and our task to know and engage the larger world lest we relinquish our right to have a voice in how it is managed. As such, Parham believed that regardless of our relationship with other organizational entities (i.e., APA), there were prevalent issues confronting psychologists of African descent that demanded that our sphere of influence extend beyond the borders of ABPsi. He recognized that African-American clinicians all over the country were being locked out of preferred-provider panels and new managed care systems. He also understood the difficulty clinicians were experiencing in being able to articulate comprehensive plans for treatment interventions with African people, which made their way into the standards of practice that were approved for reimbursement by managed care agencies and insurance companies.

A second challenge for Parham involved helping the association achieve a greater level of congruence between aspiration and actualization. As such, he established for his term of office a theme entitled "*Ori-Ire:* The African Psychologist's Response to the MAAFA". *Ori-Ire* is a Yoruba term that means "one whose consciousness is aligned with one's destiny." In holding to the truth that it was the role of African psychologists and healers to render African constructs relevant to contemporary African-American needs, Parham believed that this concept could help us realize a greater awareness of our gifts as healers and the proper purpose for which our gifts were intended. Parham also believed that *Ori-Ire* or properly aligned consciousness could also facilitate the development of knowledge that was based on genuine education rather than mere training. Parham then implored the association to understand the need to develop and acquire information about African people that is free of the contamination that blinds many of us into believing that the condition of our people and our communities is so bleak that there is little hope for transformation. Clearly, we cannot be healers without a consciousness that believes in the possibility of African people's elevation to rightful places of rulership and mastery over their own circumstance.

A third challenge for Parham involved helping the association to recognize and recommit itself to the idea that attempts to heal the spiritual dimension of African people required interventions in the larger social arena. He believed that we could not simply use our therapeutic theories and techniques to help people adjust to their individual circumstance. Rather, he advanced the notion, as others had before him, that interpsychic struggles represented evidence of structural defects in the fabric of society as a whole. Thus, the role of African psychologists and healers required intervention in the larger society, including confrontation with social ills (racism, sexism, classism), advocacy for statewide and national policies that positively impacted the lives of African people (affirmative action, welfare reform), and intervention in social ills that threaten the survival and growth of the community at large (poverty, unemployment, gang violence, child abuse, violence against women).

A final challenge of Parham's administration involved questioning how to make freedom and liberation real and substantial for the masses of African people. Believing that the time for discarding the chains of psychological slavery is now, Parham invited his membership and national constituency to consider the idea that Black psychologists as healers could not simply talk about liberation, they had to become liberators. That activity required making personal connections with people in our communities who had no one of consequence in their lives to tell them the truth and teach them to believe in it. And so, he invited the association to explore ways to teach the people and children the way toward mental liberation, physical liberation, and spiritual liberation.

SUMMARY

In summary, African-centered psychology, and the psychology of Blackness, is an attempt to build conceptual models that organize, explain, and facilitate understanding of the psychosocial behavior of African-Americans. Without question, these models are based in the primary dimensions of an African-American/African worldview. Having analyzed the administrations of two of ABPsi's recent presidents, one should be able to see specific areas of emphasis, which although rooted in an African-centered worldview, provide congruence and continuity with the tenets on which the discipline was founded in 1968. The discipline of African-centered psychology continues to define the construct in meaningful ways, render African psychological principles relevant to the contemporary needs of the African-American community, achieve better integration of the concept of spirituality, and help to define and in some cases redefine the task of therapists and healers. In addition, the discipline continues to promote the need for social advocacy and to plan interventions in the larger social arenas where public policy impacts on the mental health of people in the African-American community. Each administration has also committed itself to nurturing ABPsi, an organization whose mission it is to advance the discipline as a whole. Thus, although the necessity for the development of an African-centered psychology goes almost without question, the recognition that general psychology had failed and continues to fail to provide African-Americans full and accurate understanding of an African reality and that applications of Eurocentric norms result in the dehumanization of African people, were and are major forces that stimulate the growth of the contemporary African psychology movement.

2

The African-American Family

In the second edition of this text, considerable attention was devoted to describing and understanding the structural composition of the Black family. So much had been written about the Black family that we found it necessary to cite that body of literature that best synthesized the historical themes and contemporary realities. Having successfully done that, though, it is also important to discuss the functional aspects of the family. For instance, what purpose does the family serve?; what are the core needs around which the functional nature of the family is centered?; and how does the family go about meeting those needs? These and other questions will be discussed in this chapter. To begin our discussion, it is necessary, however, to review the literature on historical themes and conceptual pitfalls followed by an analysis of the functional nature of contemporary families.

HISTORICAL VIEWS

The attempt to synthesize the enormous amount of research on Black families will be difficult at best. Doing so, however, requires that we review a framework for categorizing the research as well as some of the problems and difficulties that have plagued previous research efforts.

Myers (1982) suggests that the research and literature on the Black family can be understood in the context of several themes. He has identified five distinct emphases and related hypotheses that serve as underlying themes for different segments of research. The themes identified by Myers include:

- *Poverty-Acculturation*—where research suggests that Black families were more successful and healthy to the degree that they emulated and assimilated the norms and values of the White middle class.
- *Pathology*—which is built on the principles of the Black matriarchy, emphasizing the consequences of poverty. The research in this area provided supposed empirical evidence for the disorganized family, which contributed to the supposed personality, social, cognitive, and mental deficits in children.
- *Reactive-Apology*—studies that challenged pathology notions and suggested that the Black families under study were similar to those of Whites, except for the fact that they have been subjected to racism, discrimination, poverty, and oppression.
- *Black Nationalist*—research and literature that sought to emphasize the strengths and competencies of Black families rather than the deficiencies and pathology. These studies also sought to provide legitimacy and validation for the Black culture, which was said to be unique and distinct from the White European norm.
- *Proactive-Revisionist*—research that allowed the old questions regarding the Black family to be restated and reconceptualized. Research from this era not only presented a more positive portrayal of Black families, but it also provided a more complex and realistic picture of Black families that had grounding in empirical research.

CONCEPTUAL PITFALLS

The research efforts represented by several of these themes have also been plagued by several fundamental mistakes. The first mistake is represented by researchers in the poverty/acculturation, pathology, and reactive-apology themes who attempted to use Euro-American family norms as a standard of comparison for Black families. White (1972) has clearly articulated the inappropriateness of such comparisons by suggesting that it is difficult, if not impossible, to understand the life-styles of Black people using traditional theories developed by Whites to explain Whites. Nobles (1984) has also speculated about the motives for making such comparisons and arriving at such negative conclusions by suggesting that those who control the information, control. Nobles contends that the most efficient way to keep Black people oppressed and powerless is to provide society with ideas that justify and certify the inferior status and condition of Black people. Accordingly, the domination and exploitation of Black people are guaranteed by the production of information and ideas that justify and give legitimacy to Black oppression (Nobles, 1984).

For example, when the offspring of matriarchal families met in the next generation as adults, the pathology theme found it difficult to conceive how they could develop a mutually satisfying relationship. The research suggested that the Black male was confused, didn't know who he was, and lacked the emotional maturity required for an ongoing responsibility of family living. The Black female was also thought to have an exaggerated sense of her own worth, didn't have much confidence in the male's ability to meet his obligations over a prolonged period of time, and felt that he had very little preparation for the give-and-take of male-female relationships. It was further assumed by deficit-oriented researchers that putting two people like these who have been reared in matriarchal families together in a conjugal union or marriage of their own would seem to represent the beginnings of another vicious, destructive, deficit-deficiency cycle with the "web and tangle of pathology" re-creating itself.

The proponents of the pathology-oriented matriarchal family model did not consider the possibility that a single-parent Black mother could serve as an adequate role model for the children of both sexes. The notion that the mother could reflect a balance of the traditional male and female roles with respect to mental toughness and emotional tenderness, was largely ignored because of the rigid classification of psychosexual roles in American society. In the Black community, however, the categorization of social role behaviors based on gender is not as inflexible. It is conceivable that a Black mother could project a combination of assertive and nurturant behaviors in the process of rearing children of both sexes as nonsexist adults.

With the reality of accelerating divorce rates, in recent years the single-parent family headed by a woman has become a social reality in Euro-America. This reality has been accompanied by an attempt on the part of social scientists to legitimate family structures that represent alternatives to the nuclear family while reconceptualizing the social roles of males and females with less emphasis on exclusive behaviors. The concept of androgyny has been introduced to cover the vast pool of human personality traits that can be developed by either sex (Rogers, 1978). In contemporary times, a well-balanced person reflects a combination of both instrumental and expressive traits. The latter include feeling-oriented behaviors formerly considered feminine, such as tenderness, caring, and affection. The former includes those characteristics that help the family to survive and meet its basic needs for shelter, food, clothing, wellness, and safety, using economic resources. Thus, it is conceptually possible for a White, single, and androgynous female parent to rear psychologically healthy, emotionally integrated children. It is interesting how the sociology of the times makes available to White Americans psychological concepts designed to legitimize changes in the family, in child-rearing patterns, and in relationships between the sexes. Yet these same behaviors when first expressed by Afro-Americans were considered as pathological. For example, what White psychologists considered to be a "tangle and web of pathology" and a disorganized family system in Black female-headed households is now renamed "single-parent families" because such phenomena are now being observed in White families.

A second fundamental mistake is represented by selected researchers from every period who attempted to characterize the Black family as a single entity (nuclear versus extended) and inferred that all Black families should be viewed as such. Adherence to any one model as a norm for *all* Blacks may be inappropriate because it inevitably, albeit unintentionally, excludes smaller segments of the Black community. This notion of a dynamic, flexible, changing Black family is also amplified in the writings of Jewell (1988), who views the Black family as an entity that changes in order to meet its needs during a given life cycle. To support her assertion, Jewell cites examples of how during the last two-and-one-half decades, the number of Black families headed by husbands and wives in 1960 (74%) has decreased (55% in 1980), whereas the number of female-headed households in the 1960s (22%) has increased to 41% during this same period. Jewell also reminds us, as do Billingsley (1968) and Hill (1971), that changes in the structures of Black families are often precipitated by changing economic fortunes and/or circumstances.

Despite the fact that his writings are three decades old, Billingsley (1968) ably illustrated this point by proposing that during a particular life cycle, the Black family could take any one of three basic forms (nuclear [related family members only], extended [other relatives living with family], or augmented [nonrelated friends living with family]), using three different dimensions (incipient [no children], simple [children], attenuated [single parent]) to create twelve possible variations. These variations include:

- *Nuclear-Incipient*—includes husband and wife in the home, no children, no relatives or others.
- *Nuclear-Simple*—husband and wife in the home, children present, no relatives or others.
- *Nuclear-Attenuated*—Single parent, children present, no relatives or others.
- *Extended-Incipient*—Husband and wife, no children present, other relatives in the home.
- *Extended-Simple*—Husband and wife, children present, other relatives also present.
- *Extended-Attenuated*—Single parent, children present, other relatives also present.
- *Augmented-Incipient*—Husband and wife present, no children, nonrelatives in the home.
- *Augmented-Incipient-Extended*—Husband and wife present, relatives and nonrelatives in the home.
- *Augmented-Nuclear*—Husband and wife present, children present, nonrelatives also living in the home.
- *Augmented-Nuclear-Extended*—Husband and wife present, children present, relatives and nonrelatives living in the home.
- *Augmented-Attenuated*—Single parent, children present, nonrelatives living in the home.
- *Augmented-Attenuated-Extended*—Single parent, children present, relatives and nonrelatives living in the home.

For a more extensive discussion of family variations, readers should consult Billingsley's (1968) *Black Families in White America,* pages 15–21.

Although many writers have sought to describe and/or classify the African-American family (Billingsley, 1968; Staples, 1994; Hill, 1972), more recent trends have begun to detail the challenges that African-American families face in contemporary America. To those who wish to understand the functional efficacy of the family unit, nowhere is this any clearer than in how families deal with life circumstances. Davis (1994) details some of these life circumstances by reminding us that research on Black families in the nineties recounts a struggle with issues of:

Personal Development

Including:

- *adoption*—the placement of African-American children in African-American homes, although the number of placements falls short of the actual need.
- *homosexuality*—choices by both men and women to choose same-sex partners as relationship mates. There is considerable debate about whether this threatens the stability and future of the family.
- *aging*—the degree to which elderly members of the community are cared for in the home and larger community.

Social Ills

Including:

- *poverty*—although most adults in families work, too many of our families live in poverty.
- *alcoholism and drug abuse*—are increasing at an alarming rate and are believed to be instigated by life pressures.
- *welfare reform*—facing the prospect of reduced government assistance and higher work expectations without the availability of jobs and marketable skills.
- *violence*—gang violence, violence from crime, and domestic violence continue to plague our community.
- *racism*—remains a formidable obstacle in the lives of African-American people.

Health and Wellness

Including:

- *stress*—despite expressing high levels of satisfaction with their families, stress is a constant theme in family life, testing members' willingness to seek support outside of the family unit.
- *hypertension*—reported to be on the rise, not only in adults but also in the children of those who currently struggle with it.

- *HIV/AIDS*—the incidence of those infected with the HIV virus is on the rise, with concern being expressed over the high numbers of women and children in particular.
- *cancer*—cancer rates for African-American men and women are increasing at alarming rates, with breast cancer for women and prostrate cancer for men being of particular concern.

Education

Including:

- *academic achievement rates*—continue to be low for our youth.
- *affirmative action*—policies that target underrepresented people of color and women for opportunities in employment and education are under attack across this nation.
- *access to opportunities in higher education*—are diminishing with the advent of antiaffirmative action coupled with low student achievement rates.

Thus, irrespective of the structural composition of the family unit, each household will need to confront and successfully negotiate the circumstances and dilemmas life can bring.

THE EXTENDED FAMILY MODEL

The extended family, in contrast to the single-parent, subnuclear family, consists of a related and quasirelated group of adults, including aunts, uncles, parents, cousins, grandparents, boyfriends, and girlfriends linked together in a kinship or kinlike network. They form a cooperative interface with each other, confronting the concerns of living and rearing children. This model of family life, which seems able to capture not only strength, vitality, resilience, and continuity of the Black family, but also the essence of Black values, folkways, and lifestyles, begins with a different set of assumptions about the development and evolution of Black family life in America.

The Black extended family is seen as an outgrowth of African patterns of family and community life that survived in America. The Africans carried with them through the mid-Atlantic passage a well-developed pattern of kinship, exogenous mating, and communal values, emphasizing collective survival, mutual aid, cooperation, mutual solidarity, interdependence, and responsibility for others (Nobles, 1974; Blassingame, 1972). These values became the basis for the Black extended family in America. They were retained because they were familiar and they allowed the slaves to have some power over destiny by enabling them to develop their own styles for family interaction. A consciousness of closeness to others, belongingness, and togetherness protected the slaves from being psychologically destroyed by feelings of despair and alienation, and the extended family provided a vehicle to pass the heritage on to the children (Frederickson, 1976; Gutman, 1976).

The Black extended family, with its grandparents, biological parents, conjugal partners, and other relatives, is an intergenerational group. The members of this multigenerational family do not necessarily reside in the same household. Individual households are part of a social-familial network that functions like a minicommunity. The members band together to share information, resources, and communal concerns (Stack, 1974). There is no central authority, matriarchal or patriarchal. Decisions are made on an equalitarian model with input and outcomes determined by who is available at a given time, who has expertise with reference to a given problem, and one's prior experience and track record in decision making. This is likely to give some edge to family elders. They are looked up to within the extended family network as resource people and advisors because they have the life experience that is highly valued in the Black community. As in the past, the family has held together over time and geographical space by a shared experience frame and a common set of values.

ALTERNATE CONCEPTUALIZATIONS

Obviously, any attempt to conceptualize the "Black family" must consider these possible variations in family structure, as well as the influence other variables such as social class based on socioeconomic status have on the structure of Black families. Our reactions, as well as those of other Black researchers, to the negative descriptions of the Black family have been intended to object to the conclusions reached by Euro-American scholars regarding the supposed "pathology" in the Black family. Although our reactions have succeeded in serving as a critique of poor scholarship, by implication, some of our reactions have also clouded the fact that specific phenomena observed exist in reality. The result is that many of us in the Black community ignore social pathology in our families and communities, believing instead that "since White folks said it, it must not be true." Consequently, we exert little effort in trying to address those issues that need correcting.

In essence, we believe that the problem with much of the Black family research is not in the phenomenon being observed, but in the implications and conclusions drawn from the observations. Moynihan (1965), for example, attempted to describe the family as a "tangle and web of pathology." Despite the fact that Moyihan's conclusions, assumptions, and methodology were questionable, inaccurate, and in some cases inappropriate, the observations that too many single women are heading Black families, that some families lack male leadership and support, that some children lack sufficient role modeling, and some Black males and females are struggling to get along are issues in need of attention. Logically, then, the challenge presented to contemporary researchers interested in the Black family is to follow the lead of those researchers who represent the "proactive-revisionist" trend of Black family research (i.e., Wade Nobles, Harriett McAdoo), and continue to restate old questions and reconceptualize family dynamics in ways that are more consistent with an African-centered cultural heritage. Certainly Billingsley (1968), Staples (1994), and others have been successful at reconceptualizing and restating questions and issues on the Black family.

The importance of Black family models and conceptual paradigms (i.e., Billingsley) however, has little or nothing to do with developing a conceptual system merely for classification's sake. The real merit of any classification scheme on the Black family is in its utility for examining family dynamics, not just family composition. Essentially, the real question is how do instrumental and expressive roles manifest themselves within the different family variations when needs have to be met? Also, how do changes in family composition impact the family system's ability to meet those needs? Borrowing from the works of Billingsley (1968) and Mbiti (1970), Mitchell (1989), for example, has been developing a five-generational model for continuity and enhancement in the Black family. The five generations reflected in Mitchell's model include the unborn, children, adults, elders, and spirits. Mitchell also outlines the important roles played by each generation and he describes the needs that must be met by the family system. For example, the unborn are important in that they represent a reaffirmation of life, as well as some cultural continuity into the next generation. Their needs include care and protection related to prenatal care for mothers, as well as planning for meeting their instrumental and expressive needs in the future. Children are important in that they provide rewards of parenthood, are extensions of two adult's physical and emotional love, and through their presence, assure immortality of their parents. Their needs include care and protection (from the larger society, from others, and themselves), affective development (formal schooling, culture-specific education), and preparation for a dual existence (development of effective responses to realities in both an Afrocentric and Eurocentric environment). Mitchell concludes by arguing that each family unit must assess, plan for, and provide ways to meet the instrumental and expressive needs of its members, regardless of family variation.

Any attempt to understand today's Black family must also involve a recognition of the role of social forces and public policies. We believe that Black families are disproportionately affected by social policies made at every level of government. The situation for many families, particularly those of working or low socio-economic status (S.E.S.), is analogous to being caught between a rock and a hard place, in that policies and programs that are designed to assist with basic family needs are sometimes a hindrance and a barrier for other families who find them restrictive, misdirected, and just plain unresponsive. Moore (1981) helps to crystallize this picture in her discussion of Black families affected by social policies. Unemployment rates among Blacks (both adults and youth) are usually among the highest in the nation, and typically twice the average for Whites. Yet, many of the community-based job development programs have Blacks disproportionately represented in those courses geared toward low-wage, low-demand occupations, with little, if any, upward mobility.

When work can be found, many Blacks find themselves trapped in jobs where income and wages are too low to raise them out of poverty, and yet, these meager earnings are too high to qualify them for public assistance.

Rising costs and inflation rates often require both parents or all adult members of a household to be out of the house earning income to support the family. Such situations often leave children without daycare or adequate adult supervision for significant periods of time. When daycare facilities are found, they are often too costly and as such, unusable. Thus, adequate child care is restricted to economically advantaged families who can afford them, or extremely poor families who can receive federal, state, or municipal subsidies.

Many Blacks must also live in impoverished neighborhoods under the poorest of conditions (i.e., unsafe housing, malnutrition, poverty), which make them more susceptible to illnesses and diseases than other family groups. Black children in particular are affected by these conditions, because many will receive inadequate prenatal care prior to birth, are born into the world prematurely and with low birth weights, have high infant mortality rates, are affected by mental retardation, and suffer from malnutrition (National Center for Health Statistics, 1979). Too many children go for long periods of time (years in some cases) without any care or checkups by a physician, do not receive adequate inoculations against childhood diseases, have greater incidences of hypertension and cancer, and have low life expectancy when compared to any other ethnic group in the United States. Although programs to address the health concerns of Blacks have been created, they too are prone to restrictive eligibilities and misapplications that limit their effectiveness.

FAMILY VALUE SYSTEMS: AN AFRICAN-CENTERED PERSPECTIVE

Our observations of the Black family over several decades leads us to believe that families differ less in structure and more in context, functions, and processes involving the transmission of culture, goals, values, roles, and norms. Structurally, most families (Black, White, Hispanic, Asian) have parents and children who share a common living space. Some have relatives who live in the home, whereas others absorb nonrelated friends into the family system. The fact that some families consist of one or two parents and several or no children, often depends on factors that are unrelated to the cultural prerequisites for family. They are often influenced by more environmental conditions (i.e., economics) and one's ability to adapt to such. Because one observes that a certain percentage of Black families are headed by single parents does not mean that the single-parent family becomes a cultural norm.

Contextually, the fact that more Black (than White) families exist under conditions of poverty and oppression is a reality shared by many in the Black community. Black families must strive to accomplish tasks of child rearing, schooling, providing for basic necessities, and maintaining one's spirituality with fewer resources than other family groups have. Yet, despite the fact that most are successful at negotiating their way through the obstacles of oppression and discrimination, one should be careful about viewing the impoverished

Black family as a cultural norm. On the contrary, one must look beyond the surface structure (family composition) to identify the underlying cultural imperatives.

Understanding these cultural imperatives is essential if we are to gain more insights into the functioning of the family. The first of these is the notion of *spiritness*. We believe that the essence of family is the spirit of our people. The energy or life force of African people inspires adherence to goals of mutual support and collective survival. These values are not only necessary for the perpetuation of individual family units, but help to connect families to one another across space and time. Thus, family systems have a power or an energy force that radiates, among other things, with the power of affirmation, nurturance, understanding, shelter and protection, the power of wisdom and enlightenment, and even the power of individual and collective self-healing.

A second cultural imperative relates to the notion of children. Children are the essence of family life and represent the possibility of the family to regenerate itself. Through child-rearing and socializing practices, families are able to direct the intellectual, emotional, behavioral, and spiritual paths that become individual and collective life pursuits. These life pursuits represent the transformative process of the human spirit because they symbolize the notions of "beingness" and "becoming." In essence, we would argue that the legacy (and the future) of a people is reflected in the faces of the children whose lives are nurtured in family systems.

In an attempt to illustrate the notion of cultural continuity, Sudarkasa (1981) helps us to examine the underlying propositions in identifying the African heritage in African-American families. The author correctly points out that the family kinship was composed of groups of related family members, both those in the bloodline (consanguineal) as well as those who joined the family by marriage (conjugal). In essence, "the family" can consist of a single household where members of two, three, and sometimes four generations occupy a common space; or the family can consist of many individual conjugal units who reside in separate dwellings where each is tied to the larger family unit through direct blood relations by one of its members. The latter point is an important one in that rather than being viewed as distinct nuclear family units (a practice endorsed by many Eurocentric researchers), all are considered as part of one family system.

McAdoo (1981) is also clear in her assertions that although there may be few direct one-to-one carryovers from Africa, the common patterns in family practices between traditional African and contemporary African-American families make it impossible to dismiss the cultural continuity. Given this emphasis on family, the values of innerconnectedness, mutual aid, responsibility, and cooperation can be seen in the daily operations of African-American families in the United States. For example, decision making in many family systems still centers in the consanguineal core group, particularly as decisions affect the entire family. Authority resides in the elders of the group, usually the oldest male, where brothers, uncles, and other males of that generation serve as an extension of the tribal elders found in African society, in forming a decision-making body (Sudarkasa, 1981). In absence of that male figure, the eldest female usually holds that position in recognition that age rather than gender is the prerequisite for wisdom. Child rearing and socialization was a practice shared by the extended family, even though each conjugal family maintained individual responsibility. This practice is readily seen in Black families where extended relatives and other significant others provide learning, support, encouragement, and even discipline to young children. For example, if caught doing something wrong, a child could expect to be reprimanded by his or her parents, as well as aunts, uncles, grandparents, and other family friends who recognize inappropriate behavior as a violation of family expectations for proper conduct.

Another important point made by Sudarkasa (1981) is the recognition that in Africa, the stability of the extended family was not dependent on the survival of conjugal unions, since the consanguineal ties were the most salient and influential. This point should be emphasized as African-Americans try to interpret the consequences of rising divorce rates and out-of-wedlock childbearing on the viability of contemporary Black families. There is little doubt that these phenomena seriously impact the individual family units; however, since many traditions, values, support systems, and cultural imperatives are tied to consanguineal connections, the functioning efficiency of the family as a whole may not be impacted as seriously.

Perhaps no challenge is more important in the 21st century than that of building strong, healthy families. Yet, there is a need to remind ourselves that building is a process that occurs over time; it is not a quick fix that can be assembled like a model kit or a powder that can be instantly transformed into a favorite drink.

Unlike family structures of the historical past whose composition was solidified by the coming together of individuals to form family units, modern day families cannot begin with decisions of marriage and/or living together. Our family dynamics may be too contaminated with residual baggage of distrust, distorted gender images, and faulty expectations to accomplish that. Building healthy families must begin with our youth and the socialization/child-rearing process. Among those lessons that must be taught are helping our children learn to love themselves with a specific focus on understanding and appreciating their divine nature and interrelationship to the Creator. This lesson is paramount. Another lesson centers around the need to develop an identity and vision of manhood and womanhood that is culturally congruent and is centered in the affirmation of humanity of both males and females. A third lesson relates to teaching our youth to recognize and emulate healthy, functional models of family development. Too often our youth are exposed to dysfunctional images that cloud their vision of what is healthy in relationships.

Assuming that the primary caregivers can teach them (youth) to love themselves, develop and crystallize their identities, and expose them to healthy functional models of parenting and family life, the next step in building healthy families is to teach them to successfully navigate the dynamics of male-female relationships. In this regard, there are several challenges that must be worked through. The first of these is learning to relate to potential partners out of a sense of respect, genuine caring, friendship, love, and true intimacy. Too often, young men and women seek to meet their own personal needs by manipulating others. This style of relating to others becomes so habitual that it becomes difficult to access and utilize more genuine styles of relating.

The second challenge involves learning to sustain relationships through tough times. When relationships with others are surrounded by a climate where everything is going well, it is easy to focus on the pleasantries of socializing. However, when the frustration and anxiety of negative circumstances exert an influence on the attitude of either person in a relationship, it becomes difficult to muster the level of understanding and tolerance necessary to endure through the unpleasant event or circumstance.

A third challenge requires that each person be taught to develop greater levels of personal insight and awareness into themselves and their background experiences. Generally, events from our past color and shape the way we respond to present circumstances. In a similar way, males and females must come to understand how their past experiences with pleasure and with pain exert an influence upon the contemporary realities of their relationships.

SUMMARY

Where many researchers on Black families have been successful is in showing how Black families have persevered and triumphed through years of oppression and adversity. Undoubtedly, the characteristics which have helped them to survive are those related to the African ethos. Therefore, we believe that the contemporary Black family in America, despite its variations, is an extension of many African traditions.

Fundamentally, the *family* rather than the *individual* is at the center of one's universe, and the point around which all else revolves. The African ethos of a holistic self in which one's individual self is perceived only in relation to the tribe or group is paramount. The family is held together by a set of common values involving interdependence, mutual aid, resilience, communalism, and collective responsibilities (Nobles, 1978); thus, the individual is connected to other persons in the extended family network. These values transcend gender roles and allow both men and women to participate in and contribute to the management of economic resources, child rearing, community activism, and other issues of family life without being categorically restricted on the basis of gender. The fluid distinction between social sex roles offers both men and women in the Black family network the opportunity to emerge as decision makers, influence molders, and household managers.

It could be argued that the Black extended family exists and persists primarily because Black people faced the common fate of oppressive economic and social conditions, and that it exists out of necessity as a way of surviving an oppressive class system. It would follow from this argument that the Black extended family would disappear as Black people moved up the socioeconomic ladder. Yet the extended family does not seem to be disappearing with rising economic fortunes. McAdoo's (1979) work with upwardly mobile and upper-middle-class Black families suggests that not only does the extended family model persist when Blacks move up the socioeconomic ladder, but the Afro-American values of mutual aid, interdependence, and interconnectedness also remain as the guiding ethos of family existence.

Ultimately, we believe the measure of a family's stability is its resourcefulness, its ability to adapt to environmental realities and challenges in ways that help the family unit meet its needs. Our belief is consistent with the position taken by Hill (1971) and Boyd-Franklin

(1989) who suggested that Black families utilize specific strengths in attempting to meet the needs of its members. Among other African-American researchers of the Black family, there is virtually unanimous agreement that the characteristics that help Black families to develop, survive, and enhance are consistent with Hill's (1971) analysis of Black family strengths. These include strong kinship bonds, strong work orientation, strong achievement orientation, adaptability of family roles, and a strong religious orientation.

Despite our belief in the continuity of African-centered traditions, an objective appraisal of Black family life in contemporary America reveals some inconsistency between core values of African-American families and modern practices. Staples (1994) echoes this point by suggesting that structural conditions help to create extreme dissonance between African-American family ideology and actual family arrangements. Thus, how a family wishes to function versus how it actually functions is oftentimes incongruent.

In an effort to suggest how families might achieve a greater level of congruence between ideology and common practices, we close this chapter with some perspective from Wade Nobles (1998). First, Nobles suggests that families must understand their common historical experience (i.e., racial oppression) and their common cultural ancestry (African spiritual essence). Doing so, then, allows the family, regardless of composition, to focus on specific tasks or performance expectations in understanding its mission and purpose. African-American families consist of several individual households with the family definition and lines of authority transcending any one household unit. Although role definitions are flexible and interchangeable, families exist to provide support, nurturance, guidance, protection, and security. Although child rearing is a primary function in most families, more common tasks involve the legitimation of beingness (one's humanity), establishing codes of conduct, delineating boundaries, establishing provisions for the acquisition of knowledge and the exchange of information, and mediating concrete conditions.

3

The Struggle for Identity Congruence In African-Americans

Questions about the identity development of African-Americans has been raised with renewed interest since the early 70s. This renewed interest in the topic introduced different perspectives on the identity development question (i.e., nigrescence, African self-consciousness, etc.), which became the focus of this chapter during the second edition.

During the last decade in particular, there has been a virtual explosion of studies and presentations that sought to extend the identity construct in theory, research, and clinical/counseling applications (Cross, 1991; Helms, 1990; Parham, 1993; Myers & Haggins, 1998; Carter & Boyd-Jackson, 1998; Stevenson, 1998). Although these models of identity development serve as important conceptual anchors in understanding the process dynamics associated with personality transformation, they are nonetheless considered less than comprehensive because they center identity development in the context of social oppression and avoid discussions of how identity develops in a more nurturing and supportive environment.

IDENTITY AS AN AFRICAN-AMERICAN

By some accounts, identity is defined as one component of an individual's overall self-concept. It involves the adoption of certain personal attitudes, feelings, characteristics, and behaviors (personal identity) and the identification with a larger group of people who share those characteristics (reference group orientation). Cross, Parham, and Helms (1998) further delineate the identity concept by asserting that for African-Americans, identity serves three functions: (1) it provides a social anchor and meaning to one's existence; (2) it serves as a connection to the broader African community across the globe; and (3) it serves as a protection or buffer against the social forces that continually bombard the psyche with nonaffirming and, in some cases, dehumanizing messages.

In recognizing America's racist social order, some researchers of the past depicted the African-American's personality and identity as reflecting a pathological adaptation to White American society's racism, resulting in a low self-esteem and a heightened sense of self-hatred (Kardiner & Ovessy, 1951; Karon, 1975). Another body of research has suggested that in the context of considerable social oppression, the African-American personality and consciousness evolve through a transformative process in which Black's struggle to move away from "oppressor identification" and move toward ethnic pride and internalization of positive racial attitudes (Cross, 1971; Thomas, 1971; Jackson, 1976). Still another group of researchers rejecting the previous thesis and hypotheses state that Black personality is in fact, Africentrically based (Nobles, 1976, 1980, 1986; Williams, 1981; Akbar, 1981) with an "African self-consciousness" (Baldwin, 1981) serving as the core for the personality system.

For the record, we continue to hold to our emphatic rejection of the Black self-hatred thesis that dominated the psychological literature from the early 1940s through the 1950s (Clark & Clark, 1947; Kardiner & Ovessy, 1951). Clearly, the authors of these research articles and manuscripts may have been perceptive in their analysis that White America provided no positive images through which African-Americans could see themselves reflected in a positive way. However, the inaccuracy and arrogance of their analysis lies in assuming that Black people look to Whites, and White America, as their only source of validation and emulation. Such a perspective completely ignores the necessity (and indeed the cultural imperative) of African-American people to use themselves, their culture, and their history as a primary referent.

We believe, however, that the latter two bodies of research may have some merit in explaining identity development.

CRITICAL QUESTIONS OF IDENTITY

In an attempt to better crystallize the identity question, we believe that the real challenge that individuals must confront is how to operationalize one's identity into everyday life. This process of discovery is initiated by asking several fundamental questions. Although human beings find it necessary to locate themselves in time, in place (geography), and in space (Hilliard, 1997), the self-discovery process must also answer questions of how to describe personal character and qualities, how to achieve congruence with one's self-description, and whether there is sufficient room for growth and actualizing of one's potential.

In support of these fundamental precepts, the work of Fanon (1967) is particularly relevant in delineating three essential questions that each African-American should both consider and be able to answer. The issues involve each person understanding: (1) Who am I?; (2) Am I who I say I am?; and (3) Am I all I ought to be?. "Who am I?" is the question of identity, where it is important to understand the nature of one's humanness. "Am I who I say I am?" is a question of achieving congruence in assessing how our spiritual, cognitive, affective, and behavioral dimensions align with our self-definition. "Am I all I ought to be?" is a question of self-actualization where one seeks to achieve the fullest expression of all one is supposed to become.

It is our belief that the personality, consciousness, and the core identity of Black people is African in nature. Whether conscious or unconscious, the personality manifests itself in the attitudes, feelings, behaviors, and spiritual essence of African-Americans. Baldwin (1985) provides a clear articulation of the African-American personality in his theory of "African self-consciousness." He writes, "The core component of the Black personality represents the conscious level expression of the 'oneness of being' communal phenomenology which characterizes the fundamental self-extension orientation of African people." According to Baldwin, although the African self-consciousness system is partly biogenetically determined, it is also subject to social and environmental influences. When this core system of the Black personality is nurtured developmentally as well as situationally through indigenous personal and institutional support systems, it achieves vigorous and full expression in terms of a congruent pattern of basic traits (beliefs, attitudes, and behaviors) that affirm African-American life in the authenticity of its African cultural heritage (Baldwin, 1985).

Despite Baldwin's assertion that normal Black behavior and consciousness is not merely a reaction to adverse environmental elements, his theory clearly recognizes the interaction between individual personality characteristics and social and environmental influences that help to form and shape the individual personality. Assuming that an African-American male or female is surrounded by positive (Black-oriented) institutional and social support systems throughout his or her formative years, then the expected consequence would be the development of a normal, healthy Black personality. Such would be characterized by a strong awareness of and identification with African cultural heritage, strong sense of motivation directed at ensuring collective survival of African people and related institutions, and the active resistance of any force (i.e., racism) that threatens the survival and maintenance of one's people and oneself.

Nobles (1986) has also outlined the prerequisites for normal human functioning based on a culturally centered identity. The parameters include

1. A sense of self that is collective or extended.
2. An attitude wherein one understands and respects the sameness in oneself and others.
3. A clear sense of one's spiritual connection to the universe.
4. A sense of mutual responsibility (for other African people).
5. A conscious understanding that human abnormality or deviance is any act that is in opposition to oneself (p. 96).

Other writers of the Black experience are quick to remind us, however, that African-American people are not always afforded the luxury of totally surrounding themselves with social and institutional support systems that enhance, promote, and affirm our humanity as African-Americans.

In fact, James Baldwin (1963), a noted Black author, writes that "to be Black and relatively conscious is to be in a constant state of rage almost all the time." His writings imply that Black people face constant exposure to racist and oppressive conditions in America from a society that neither validates nor cultivates our existence. If Baldwin's analysis is correct (and we suspect it is), then it is entirely likely that the forces that influence the identity development of many African-Americans are mitigated by oppression and racism.

COPING WITH OPPRESSION (NEED FOR LIBERATION)

With the dawn of the 21st century, individuals and groups alike are pondering the notion of how to secure their futures in the best possible way. Clearly, African-American people are similarly questioning what their futures will bring and what the critical issues of that time will be. Although it is tempting to project our focus into the future, African-American folks cannot lose sight of our historical past, for doing so leaves us potentially vulnerable.

In acknowledging that there are social forces and environmental circumstances (i.e., White supremacy, racism, sexism, discrimination, poverty, unemployment, violence, and drugs) that jeopardize and threaten our futures in significant ways, many of our communities have used, exhausted, and will continue to marshal resources to address these social ills. Yet, to confine our focus as well as our intervention strategies to external and systemic forces alone implies that we as African people in America have no part to play in our rehabilitation and recovery. Clearly, the principle of self-determination advocated by many of our historical and contemporary leaders demands that we take a critical look at self and explore ways in which internally oriented examination and intervention strategies might prove more beneficial.

OUR CONDITION

The myriad of social ills are formidable obstacles that haunt our contemporary reality. But I would argue, as others have before me (Akbar, 1984; Hilliard, 1997), that our biggest challenge is not racism or other social ills. Rather, I believe that our most daunting challenge as African-Americans is the need for mental liberation. Carter G. Woodson (1939) was prophetic indeed when he asserted that yielding control of your (our) mind to alien sources will have you seeking inferior status even before you can be assigned one. And yet it is difficult to argue against this characterization of our condition when one examines how we as African-American people respond to our contemporary reality. Whether the yardstick is economic empowerment, political power, health-related concerns, educational achievement, violence in our streets and families, crime, etc., we are substantial contributors to our plight.

Although the notion of mental enslavement is not a new concept, it is nonetheless one that the masses of our people have not yet embraced. We simply are not receptive enough to any construct or principle that forces us to take a critical look at self. But self-exploration is precisely where we must go, and the so-called educated and socially conscious among us must be charged with that task of helping to liberate the minds, bodies, and spirits of people of African descent. This is the critical work that must be done in our struggles to understand identity.

Within the context of self-discovery, it is essential, I believe, that we understand just how deep-seated our problems are. Thus, I would argue that the pathology of our people's condition is not simply in the chaining/shackling process that incarcerates our minds. A deeper problem is how we construct distorted mental representations of our chains such that they have now come to symbolize what we believe are basic life necessities or core needs. In essence, I am suggesting that we create dysfunctional associations in establishing cause-effect relationships among variables that shape our lives. As a consequence, instead of associating pain with enslavement, we now link pain with freedom, self-determination, and liberation. Our task, it seems to me, is to design processes and intervention strategies to correct these mental misrepresentations our people are so prone to make.

The challenge before us, then, as I have argued before, in operationalizing identity is how to make freedom and liberation real and substantial for the masses of people of African descent. The promising news, of course, is that there are remedies available that can assist in this process, and generally these models and programs are available in a myriad of texts, periodicals, and monographs that many of us have produced. The problem is that beyond the halls of academe, beyond our conventions and conferences, many of our people do not take the time to read, and many more do not immerse themselves in learning opportunities available in communities across this country. And so, the educational mission we seek to support cannot be restricted to those who currently occupy academic institutions. Rather, we must be aggressive in our attempts to support the development of partnerships and collaborations with other community interests such that the masses of our people begin to gain access to the knowledge that will assist them in achieving the mental, physical, and spiritual liberation they so desperately seek.

The key, however, is to help our people understand the difference between education and training. Malcolm X was clear in asserting that "Education is the passport to the future, for tomorrow belongs to those who prepare for it today." However, if our African-American professional organizations sit by while our people's minds are trained to develop skills in support of other people's communities and their livelihood, then we have not done our jobs well. Indeed, the role we must play as African-American psychologists and professionals requires that we help our people become educated such that their knowledge is used to crystallize their identities and enhance the survival and collective well-being of themselves and others in their own communities.

And so, we must teach the people and show them the way to mental liberation by teaching them to believe in the real value of themselves and their divine nature. If they understand that all persons are created in the image and likeness of the Creator, and there is an interrelationship among all living things on the planet, then no one group or people can be considered less than any other. Everyone is worthy of respect, praise, love, and honor. Consequently, we must tell them so and teach the people to stop looking to Eurocentric sources of validation as the only measure of worth and legitimacy.

We must teach the people and show them the way to physical liberation. We must care enough to instruct them that their intellectual genius is a gift from God and does not require any affirmative action programs in order to be revealed; it just takes work on our part. We must teach them that although welfare reform efforts are aggressive attempts to impact our families negatively, government programs cannot be viewed as our only source of sustenance and survival. We must teach them that although physical emancipation is well over 130 years old, it is past time for us and them to stop relating to society with plantation-style mentalities.

We must teach the people and show them the way to spiritual liberation. We must care enough to teach them that the peace and refuge they seek to cope with life's disappointments and frustrations cannot be found in external stimuli like drugs, alcohol, and/or material possessions. We must help them understand that that comfort can only be found through spiritual peace that derives from a relationship with the divine Creator. Clearly, the time for mental, physical, and spiritual liberation is now, and the synergy created by our collaborative efforts can and must be that beacon of light that helps to connect our communities with the knowledge that they require and the wisdom that they so desperately need.

THE PSYCHOLOGY OF NIGRESCENCE

If one can assume that the development of identity is a dynamic process, then movement from one set of attitudes or beliefs to another would be an expected outcome. In fact, a cursory look at the history of African-Americans in this country clearly illustrates this phenomenon. Cross, Parham, and Helms (1998), in their comprehensive review of the Black identity development process, remind us that in light of the obsessive attempts at deracination (attempt to erase Black consciousness) by White people and White America, it comes as no surprise that within African-American history are accounts of Blacks who, having first been deculturalized, experience revitalization through a process of *nigrescence*. Nigrescence is derived from the French, and means "to become Black." Nigresence models speculate that the identity development process is characterized by movement between various identity states and/or stages (Cross, 1971; Thomas, 1971; Helms, 1984; Parham, 1989). Cross (1971) introduced the description of the "Negro-to-Black" conversion experience by suggesting that the development of a Black person's racial identity is often characterized by his or her movement through five distinct psychological stages: Pre-encounter, Encounter, Immersion-Emersion, Internalization, and Internalization Commitment.

Pre-encounter: In this stage, the traditional description characterizes the individual who is prone to view the world from a White frame of reference. He or she thinks, acts, and behaves in ways that devalue and/or deny his or her Blackness. The person has accepted a deracinated frame of reference, and because that reference point is usually a White normative standard, he or she develops attitudes that are very pro-White and anti-Black. Cross (1998) refers to this stage as one where the conditions for transformation and change are ripe. He suggests that at the center of the Pre-Encounter mentality is both an assimilation-integration philosophy that is linked to an attempt to secure a place in the socioeconomic mainstream, but motivated by a desperate attempt to insulate themselves from the implications of being Black.

Encounter: This stage is characterized by an individual experiencing one or many significant (shocking) personal and social events that are inconsistent with his or her frame of reference. For example, a Black person who views his or her race as not important and wishes to be viewed and accepted simply as a "human being" is denied access to living in an exclusive neighborhood because of skin color.

These encounters successfully shake a person's self-image of non-Black or "be like White" and make them vulnerable to a new interpretation of self in relation to the world. The Encounter stage appears to involve two phases. The first is a realization phase where an individual recognizes that his or her old frame of reference or worldview is inappropriate, and he or she begins to explore aspects of the new identity. The second phase (decision) occurs when the person, first cautiously, then defiantly decides to develop a Black identity. During this second stage, it is difficult to predict which specific encounter or how many encounters will be sufficient to instigate the psychic disruption that encounters bring. Parham (1993) has argued that the vulnerability to examine one's attitudes and beliefs about race will be influenced by the degree of psychological defensiveness present at the time of each encounter. If the degree of defensiveness is low, then the probability of change is increased. If, however, the degree of defensiveness is high, then many more encounter experiences may be necessary in order for a person to challenge his or her Eurocentric beliefs and attitudes.

Immersion-Emersion: This stage represents a turning point in the conversion from the old to the new frame of reference. The period of transition is characterized by a struggle to repress or destroy all vestiges of the Pre-encounter orientation while simultaneously becoming intensely concerned with personal implications of the newfound Black identity (Cross, 1978). The person begins to immerse himself or herself into total Blackness, clinging to various elements of the Black culture while simultaneously withdrawing from interactions from other ethnic groups. Although the degree of overt manifestations of Blackness are high (i.e., Black clothes and hairstyles, attendance at all-Black functions, and linguistic style). The degree of internalized security about one's Blackness is minimal. At this stage, everything of value in life must be Black or relevant to Blackness. This stage is also characterized by a tendency to denigrate White people while simultaneously glorifying Black people (pro-Black/anti-White attitudes). Cross (1991, 1998) agrees that this stage represents the most sensational aspects of the identity development process, as it is the most disruptive of the stages. The emotional intensity required to both shake the vestiges of the old identity as well as that required to embrace the new identity is quite pronounced. Despite this emotional lability, through time and self-exploration, the individual is able to reconcile the various aspects of this transformative process and move toward a more crystallized picture of one's identity.

Internalization: This stage is characterized by the individual achieving a sense of inner security and self-confidence with his or her Blackness. The resolution of conflicts between the old and new world-views becomes evident as tension, emotionality, and defensiveness are replaced by a calm, secure demeanor (Cross, 1978). This stage is also characterized by psychological openness, ideological flexibility, and a general decline in strong anti-White feelings. Although still using Black as a primary reference group, this person moves toward a more pluralistic, nonracist perspective (Cross, 1978). Having viewed the transformative process of nigrescence through a linear lens, it is tempting to believe that those who arrive at this stage have similar attitudes and beliefs. However, it is important to recognize that although internalized attitudes may correlate with a high salience to issues of race, not everyone who emerges with these attitudes will have the same salience for their Blackness. Some may express attitudes of Black nationalism, whereas others may see and relate to life in more multicultural terms.

CONTEMPORARY VIEWS

Although the nigrescence models by Cross (1971, 1978) and others (Thomas, 1971; Jackson, 1975; Williams, 1975) are helpful in illustrating both changes in attitude over time, and the within-group variability reflected in the consciousness of African-Americans, they are also prone to limitations. Specifically, these models imply that although they are process in nature, their "development over time" focus is usually restricted to the late adolescence and early adulthood period in the life cycle.

Consequently, although the stages articulated by Cross document how a person's racial identity can change from one stage to another (i.e., Pre-encounter to Internalization) during the later adolescent–early adulthood periods, they fail to detail how various stages of racial identity will be accentuated at later stages of life. In an article entitled "Cycles of Psychological Nigrescence," Parham (1989) presents a life-cycle nigrescence model based on a modification of the Cross stages. The first object of Parham's concern is pinpointing the earliest phase of life at which one is capable of experiencing psychological nigrescence (the process of developing a Black identity). He presupposes that the manifestations of identity during childhood are "more the reflection of parental attitudes or societal stereotypes which a youngster has incorporated," than the integrated, cognitively complex, identity structures found in adults. Consequently, Parham hypothesizes that it is during late adolescence and early adulthood that one might first experience nigrescence, and thereafter the potential is present for the remainder of one's life. Parham also notes in his writings that there is a qualitative difference between the nigrescence experience at adolescence or early adulthood, than, say, the nigrescence experience at middle or late adulthood, because an African-American person's concept of Blackness will be influenced by the distinctive developmental task associated with each phase of adult life. Perhaps the most profound issue Parham raises is not so much that aspects of the initial nigrescence episode vary with age, but having completed nigrescence, he sees the demand characteristics of each phase of adult development making more likely a person's recycling through the stages. From Parham's perspective, recycling does not mean the person reverts back to the old (Pre-encounter) identity and then traverses all the stages. Rather, he is inclined to believe that the challenge or trauma acts as a new encounter episode that exposes small or giant gaps in a person's thinking about Blackness, and the person recycles in order to fill such gaps. Thus depending on the nature of the challenge or the new encounter, recycling may mean anything from a mild refocusing experience, to one involving a full-fledged Immersion-Emersion episode.

Another important advancement in Parham's (1989) writings is his recognition that a person's initial identity state is not restricted to Pre-encounter attitudes. This assertion represents a significant departure from the traditional nigrescence models presented by Cross, Jackson, and Thomas, which implicitly or explicitly suggest that one's racial identity development begins with a pro-White/anti-Black frame of reference or worldview. Parham speculates, for example, that if a young adolescent is exposed to and indoctrinated with parental and societal messages that are very pro-Black in orientation, the personal identity and reference group orientation initially developed by that youngster might be pro-Black as well. Contrary to the assumptions implicit in the original nigrescence models, we concur with Akbar (1989), who suggests that the process of identity formation that results from the positive encounters and affirmations of one's racial identity, rather than that which results from the negative encounter situations experienced in life, are a different and much healthier form of identity development. In fact, Parham (1989) is also clear in his assertion that African-American cultural identity is an entity independent of socially oppressive phenomena. This independent identity notion provides a critical extension of the original nigrescence theories that initially conceptualized Black identity and the affirmation of oneself as an African-American as only a reaction to the oppressive conditions of White American racism.

A third point of interest in Parham's model is his articulation that identity resolution can occur in at least three ways: stagnation (failure to move beyond one's initial identity state), stagewise linear progression (movement from one identity state to another in a sequential, linear fashion), and recycling (movement back through the stages once a cycle has already been completed). The Cross (1971), Jackson (1976), and Thomas (1971) models imply that nigrescence occurs in a linear fashion, with no other alternatives being proposed. More recent advancements in the nigrescence theory and research have both added to the expansion of specific stages as well as opened the model up to renewed criticisms. Cross (1991, 1998) has recognized that the original definitions of the Pre-encounter and Internalization stages may have been limited by their focus on single dimensions in each stage. In the case of the Pre-encounter stage, he now posits a continuum of racial attitudes that extend from low salience, to race neutral, to anti-Black. Thus, a person with Pre-encounter attitudes may acknowledge his or her Blackness while believing that it has little importance or meaning in their life (low salience); or he or she may express strong anti-Black sentiments as a way of denigrating the culture and distancing themselves from other African-Americans who are perceived to be "too Black" for their personal comfort.

With regard to the Internalization stage, Cross now takes the position that an individual's resolution of internalized attitudes will also vary, for example, from a monocultural focus (nationalistic) to one that is more multicultural in orientation. In either case, as with the Pre-encounter stage, it is important to remember that the nigrescence process does not evolve into a single ideological stance. Rather, there are a multitude of ways in which one's cultural pride and internalized identity may be expressed.

The most recent additions in the nigrescence area are being promoted by Cross and Phegan-Smith (1996). In consolidating the nigrescence work of writers like Spencer, Stevenson, and Parham with other developmental theorists, they have advanced a model depicting the relationship between ego identity development and nigrescence. The model is based on the establishment of six sectors or periods that describe a life-span scenario potentially influencing the evolution of one's ethnic identity. In each of the six life-span intervals, Cross and Phegan-Smith detail how African-Americans embrace various aspects of their culture in reconciling the degree of salience ethnicity holds in their life.

Although work continues on advancing the nigrescence construct, it is also important to mention that the theory is not without its critics and detractors (Azibo, 1998; Stokes, Murray, Peacock, & Chaney, 1998). Some of the critique emerges from the orthodox African-centered school (i.e., Azibo) that apparently believes that the nigrescence construct lacks sufficient grounding in the cosmology of African-centeredness to be relevant. Additional criticism suggests that the theory is anchored in the reality of African ethnic groups' experience with an oppressive French government (nigrescence is derived from the French language), thereby rendering it irrelevant to African-descent people in America. Unfortunately, Azibo (1998) fails to recognize that the oppression of African people is a global phenomenon related to the advancement of White supremacy. Therefore, whether you are in Europe, South Africa, the Caribbean, or America, the dynamics are similar.

Interestingly, the opinions advanced by Azibo and others do provide much needed exchanges on the discourse of identity and personality development for African people. After all, no theory or the theorists who advance them can afford to insulate themselves from feedback, legitimate or otherwise. Furthermore, it seems nonsensical to react to the hostile language and analyses contained in some writings with more of the same. Suffice it to say that well-intentioned critique should always be welcomed as long as it refrains from personal attack and resist the tendency to engage in a process of denigrating others in order to affirm itself. Such is not only inappropriate but contrary to an African-centered worldview of interpersonal relations.

SUMMARY

Achieving identity congruence in the face of racist and oppressive elements represents a significant challenge for most African-Americans. Undoubtedly, the achievement of congruence will be facilitated by several important propositions being promoted by contemporary Black psychologists. The first is borrowed from the ancient Africans and simply says, "know thyself." Fundamentally, to know oneself (or one's nature) means to recognize, understand, respect, appreciate, and love those characteristics and/or attributes that make us uniquely African-Americans. In addition, self-knowledge helps to dictate behaviors that ultimately support, sustain, and enhance our individual and collective beings as African-Americans. Nobles (1986) asserts that in knowing one's nature, one is less likely to allow social and environmental conditions to become internalized, and in so doing, become the instruments of psychological maladaptation and dysfunction.

The second proposition is borrowed from Baldwin (1986) and Akbar (1981), who suggest that a healthy African self-consciousness is probable if one's personality is nurtured in an environment of supportive personal and institutional systems. In their analysis, a healthy Black psyche is a prescription and a challenge. A prescription is a written (in this case) rule or law that outlines the necessary conditions to achieve a purpose or goal (identity congruence). Their prescription suggests the imperative to identify and utilize resources, networks, and institutions within the Black community that affirm and reaffirm our humanity as African-Americans. Our families, schools, churches, social clubs and organizations, and other personal acquaintances must become the instruments by which we maintain congruence in African values and beliefs, and our primary sources of validation. The challenge is to recognize our collective responsibility to provide support and nurturance to persons and institutions within the Black community. Recognition of the sameness in ourselves and other African-Americans and self-affirmation are natural outcomes when we extend ourselves to provide support, nurturance, and validation to others. Those who seek validation outside of their "community" will undoubtedly find identity congruence an unachieved goal.

Lastly, Nobles (1986) also reminds us that ideas are the substance of behavior. Consequently, if our consciousness is culturally congruent, then our behavior should be focused on responding to our environmental realities in ways that help to enhance, maintain, and actualize our individual and collective beings as African-Americans. In the African context of "being," the self is extended and collective, implying one's connections to others in the community, those yet unborn, and those belonging to the community of ancestors. It is critical to note, however, as Myers (1985) reminds us, that one's "being" did not automatically make one a part of the community, nor admit one to the position of ancestor at a later date (p. 35). Both roles required that each adopt a "proper" belief structure as evidenced through attitudes and behaviors.

4

PSYCHOLOGICAL ISSUES IN THE EDUCATION OF AFRICAN-AMERICAN PEOPLE

Perhaps no other endeavor is more important to a people or a society than the education of its youth. After all, our youth represent our individual and collective hope for the future. Historically, the success and continued vitality of any society has been predicated upon its ability to prepare future generations for varied life challenges. Consequently, education has been the primary method employed by societies in orchestrating the successful development of future generations for their societal roles and responsibilities. It is our belief that the foundation for the educational success of our youth has been predicated upon a collaborative relationship between the home, the school, and the community.

Unfortunately, this collaboration is nonexistent in many communities across this nation and consequently, our children suffer because of it. One has only to examine the academic profile of African-American youth to realize this truth.

ACADEMIC PROFILE

In the first and second editions of *Psychology of Blacks,* White (1984) and White and Parham (1990) painted a dismal picture of the educational system, and the progress, or lack of, African-American youngsters were making in it. Their collective statements of the problem generally suggested that the longer Black children remain on the educational conveyor belt, the farther behind they fall. A contemporary update of the academic progress and achievement of African-American youngsters reveals some slight change from the dismal reports of the 1960s through the 1980s.

A series of reports on the American educational system appeared in the early 1980s (National Commission on Excellence In Education, 1983; Goodlad, 1983; Task Force on Education and Economic Growth, 1983), and all commented on the overall failure of the educational system in preparing America's youth. To quote from *A Nation at Risk,* the most heralded report at the time:

> We report to the American people that while we can take justifiable pride in what our schools and colleges have historically accomplished and contributed to the United States and the well being of its people, the educational foundations of our society are presently being eroded by a rising tide of mediocrity that threatens our very future as a nation and a people.

To support this claim, the report sited, among other data, that 23 million adults were functionally illiterate, that there had been a decline over 17 years in SAT scores (a 50-point average decline for verbal scores, a 40-point average decline for mathematics) and that according to standardized tests, high school students were achieving at lower rates than they were some 26 years prior when Sputnik was launched.

The academic profile of minority youth, particularly African-Americans, was especially disturbing. Nearly 60% of African-Americans have completed high school, whereas only 12% were reported to have completed four more years of college. The reports further indicated that African-American youngsters typically lagged behind their Anglo mates on almost every objective index of academic achievement. Most reports concluded that on standardized tests, average achievement scores of African-American youngsters in all subject areas are generally one standard deviation below their Anglo age-mates.

In addition, the National Assessment of Education Progress (NEAP) measured achievement of youngsters at ages 9, 13, and 17, in seven content areas including reading-literature-comprehension, music, art, citizenship, social studies, science, and mathematics. In tests administered from 1975 through 1982, African-American youngsters, in each age category, scored several points below the mean in each of seven content areas (NAEP, 1983).

Data from the NAEP's 1996 report reveals that the gaps between African-American students and their White counterparts may be narrowing. Specific progress was noted in the areas of science, mathematics, and reading. However, the trend in writing continues unchanged (NAEP, 1996). Although the progress in certain areas is noteworthy, the factors that contribute to these trends are worth mentioning as well. National Center for Educational Statistics (NCES) data indicate that many African-American parents are involved in their children's education and actively participate by attending school events and helping their children with homework assignments. For example, 1996 data indicate that 86% of African-American students reported having parents who attended scheduled meetings with their teachers, whereas almost half reported having parents who assisted with homework assignments at least three times per week.

It is also clear from the data that African-American children seem to start their educational lives with cognitive, sensory, and motor skills equal to their Anglo age-mates, yet academic achievement levels for them seem to decrease with the length of time they stay in school. One of the culprits seems to be a family's socioeconomic status. It would not be uncommon to find, for example, that African-American children have fallen from one to three grade levels behind their White peers by the time they are in high school. African-American youngsters also seem three times more likely to be labeled as educable mentally retarded and to be enrolled in remedial educational programs. They are also half as likely to be enrolled in programs for gifted students when compared with their White counterparts.

The illiteracy rate for African-Americans (44%) is more than two and one-half times that of Whites. Their high school dropout rates also continue to be high. Entrance rates into college for African-Americans also decreased over the last several years. In the late 70s, slightly over 50% of African-American high school graduates entered college. By the early 80s, the proportion of African-Americans entering college had dropped to 36%. In California, for example, less than 4.5% of Black high school graduates were eligible for admission to a University of California school, and less than 11% were eligible for admission to one of the nineteen California State University campuses California Post-Secondary Education Commission (CPEC), 1988. The trend for African-Americans finishing high school and entering college in the 90s seems to be on the increase. NCES data indicate that as of 1996, 87% completed high school, whereas 56% of those African-American students completing high school enrolled in college by October of that same year. Data also indicate that the percentages of 25- to 29-year olds finishing four or more years of college has risen to 16% in 1997.

In the earlier editions of this text, it was also pointed out that many African American youngsters attended schools which were "in crisis." Several reports documented a growing number of cases of violence (e.g., student-student, student-teacher) and vandalism. Many of these same schools also had fewer experienced teachers and less-than-adequate teaching equipment and facilities. More recent data seem to suggest that similar factors continue to hinder educational achievement in the 90s, but that school location may have an impact as well. The vast majority of African-Americans attending schools are located in the urban centers of this country. Teachers at schools in urban areas appear more likely to report the following: student apathy, drug use and abuse by students and some parents, student pregnancy, classroom discipline problems, weapons possession, and absenteeism (U.S. Bureau of the Census, 1995, 1997).

The educational attainment profile of African-American youngsters just presented is slightly better than in previous decades, but still somewhat distressing. The continued travesty of this situation is all too apparent and the prospects of any positive, substantive change occurring in the very near future is a bit more promising. Yet taken collectively, these are the precise social and educational conditions under which the majority of African-American children live and are educated.

Most profiles of the kind reported herein, however, need to be viewed with some caution. These kinds of statistical summaries, although useful, often fail to provide a balanced picture. The academic achievement profile of African-American youngsters just presented, for example, says little about those youngsters who are in fact succeeding academically. Many of these youngsters are reared in the same environment within which many of their African-American peers are failing, yet some are succeeding at rates equal to, if not in excess of, their White peers. What factors contribute to the differential academic success rate of African-American youngsters given that all of them are essentially products of the same environment? Perhaps an understanding of the correlates of achievement might provide us with an answer of these questions. Parham and Parham (1989) have identified four correlates of achievement that they feel are key to the academic survival of African-American youth. We, in turn, have added two others.

CORRELATES OF ACHIEVEMENT

Identifying the correlates of positive and negative achievement for the African-American youngster has been the focus of several investigations. The list of factors that potentially correlate with (either positive or negative) academic achievement is almost endless. Yet several factors are more consistently identified as contributing to or inhibiting academic achievement in Black youngsters. Parham and Parham (1989) and White and Parham (1990) have suggested that these factors include self-concept, value orientation, teacher expectation, and family composition. This third edition adds to that list: poverty and parent educational attainment.

Poverty

Among the variables that significantly impact our children and their educational achievement is the issue of poverty. Recent data now available indicate that nearly one in four children (23%) under the age of 6 lived in poverty during 1996 (NCCP, 1998). Research also indicates that poverty rates disproportionately impact African-Americans with 44% of children under 6 affected. This figure is more than three times the rate for White children (13%) nationwide. When accounting for children up to the age of 18, 34% of African-American youth were classified as poor.

The recitation of these statistics is distressing when one considers how far-reaching the impact of poverty can be. The Children's Defense Fund (CDF) (1994) found that children living in poverty were more likely to be classified as learning disabled and to experience educational failure when compared to more socially advantaged, nonpoor children. It is also important to note that according to research data, nearly one in five of these poor children will experience homelessness during their lifetime, putting them at further risk for educational failure and dropout (CDF, 1996).

These data continue to support the analyses provided by entities such as Education Week's Quality Counts, who also assert that achievement scores nationally show a strong correlation between low achievement and higher concentrations of poverty, particularly in urban areas (Education Week, 1998).

Self-Concept

Another variable that undoubtedly influences the achievement aspirations of Black youngsters is self-concept. Yet, exactly how self-concept impacts achievement aspirations yields debatable answers. Psychologists and sociologists have argued that the self is found to be in direct relation to how a person thinks others perceive him or her (Mead, 1934; Rogers, 1961). Thus, a person in our society validates his or her identity through the evaluations of significant others. If the notion of necessary external validation is accurate, it seems reasonable to assume the achievement aspirations of Black youngsters would be influenced by evaluations by significant others in the child's life.

Although such an assertion might be reasonable, researchers have had difficulty agreeing on from where the child's source of validation is derived. Some research suggests that validation and approval are derived from the Black community (Banks, 1972; Barnes, 1972; Norton, 1983). Unfortunately, the larger body of research suggests that approval is sought from the dominant White culture (Kardiner & Ovessey, 1951, 1968), and because of the negative attitudes perpetuated by the larger White society, positive achievement by Blacks was not an unexpected outcome.

Investigations of the Black self-concept and self-esteem have generally assumed that every aspect of Black life is a reflection of the group's castelike position in the dominant society, and that Black Americans are incapable of rejecting the negativistic images of themselves perpetuated by the dominant White society. The prototype for these studies was presented by Clark and Clark (1947) in an investigation in which they found that Black children preferred White dolls to Black dolls. They concluded that the children's White doll choice was a reflection of their group self-hatred. Other studies followed (Goodman, 1952; Morland, 1958) that similarly pointed out the tendency for Black children to identify with and/or prefer White skin, White dolls, and White friends. These identity problems, the literature suggested, were linked to problems of self-evaluation. In addition, the literature further pointed out that Black people's assignment to second-class status, together with White racists' insistence on Black people's innate inferiority, no doubt was instrumental in creating doubts in Black people concerning their own worth (Arnaz, 1972).

Several authors have sought to explain this self-hate phenomenon by hypothesizing that Black people's hostility toward the oppressor was so threatening that repression of hostile feelings was the only means by which they could deal with their feelings (Kardiner & Ovessey, 1968). In turn, the repressed hostility was redirected internally, and thus stimulated self-hatred. Other attempts were made to explain Black self-hatred by pointing out Black people's simultaneous feelings of hatred of the oppressor and desires to imitate him or her, thus resulting in feelings of self-hate, confused identity, and the like (Kardiner & Ovessey, 1951). It was, in fact, Kardiner and Ovessey (1951) who clearly exemplified this negative analysis of Black subgroup status when they asserted,

> The Negro has no possible basis for a healthy self-esteem and every incentive for self-hatred. The basic fact is that the Negro's aspiration level, good conscience, and even good performance are irrelevant in face of the glaring fact that the Negro gets a poor reflection of himself in the behavior of Whites, no matter what he does, or what his merits are. The chief distinguishing factor in the Negro is that he must identify himself with the Negro, but this initiates the compensatory identification with the White (person) who is also hated. (p. 297)

Dansby (1972) suggested that an example of this "identification with the aggressor" or imitation of Whites could be seen in Black people's use of cosmetic products to make themselves appear White (i.e., straightening hair or lightening skin tones). In addition to these behavioral examples, the literature was replete with studies describing this identification with the oppressor phenomenon. Bayton et al. (1956) described minority group persons as tending to idealize the majority group, thus contributing to their own self-rejection. Also, Pettigrew (1974) cited a large body of psychological literature that demonstrated the power of role playing on conceptions of self. He postulated that Blacks had played the role of "stupid," "slow," and "inferior" to appease the White power structure to the detriment of their own self-esteem and integrity.

Wyne (1974) has also addressed the consequences of this role-playing behavior. He asserted that when the minority tends to use the majority as an emulative reference group, as Blacks have done, the result is usually that the minority tends to adopt those behaviors and beliefs about the self that they feel the majority holds to be desirable.

Wyne concluded that the effect becomes a self-fulfilling prophecy, reinforcing the prejudiced feelings and beliefs of the majority.

What might be added to the observations by Pettigrew (1964) and Wyne (1974), however, is the possibility that such role playing may also hinder attempts by researchers to perceive, understand, and/or interpret the nature of Black self-concept. Both authors seem to suggest that Black people have often felt it necessary to conceal their true selves in order to survive in a racist social order. Ames (1950) speaks to this phenomenon of "role playing" or "mask wearing" as he states, ". . . got one mind for White folks to see; another for what I know is me." Although explanations and observations of this tendency to disguise oneself appear less frequently in the literature, they do provide additional data through which to evaluate studies on the Black self.

As the above studies indicate, it was common for White and Black social scientists to write and reiterate that Black people, in general, have had a negative self-concept. Furthermore, these tendencies toward negative self-conceptions have been linked to phenomena such as identification with the aggressor, overassimilation, and low achievement.

In contrast to the low self-concept/low achievement oriented studies of the past, more contemporary research cites evidence that, indeed, African-American children do have positive racial self-concepts (Powell & Fuller, 1970; Soares & Soares, 1969). In fact, Powell (1983) concludes that the concept of low self-esteem in Black children should be disregarded in light of several extensive literature reviews (Wylie, 1978; Rosenberg, 1979; Weinberg, 1977) that revealed (1) little or no differences in self concept between Black and White children, and (2) higher self-esteem scores in Black children.

The low self-concept conclusion of the past has also been questioned by challenging the notion that Black children agree with and internalize the negative evaluations of them promoted by the larger society. On the contrary, several studies have indicated that African American children do not believe or agree with negative stereotypes about themselves or that they are inferior (Brigham, 1974; Campbell, 1976; Rosenberg, 1979). According to Gurin and Epps (1975), what has been overlooked is the minimization of the role of the oppressor (in influencing self-images), and more specifically, the adaptive strengths of the African-American (child). Consequently, social scientists, teachers, and students themselves must come to grips with the fact that positive academic achievement among Black children is not only a possibility, but a realistic expectation.

Although the debate over the disposition of the Black child's self-concept may be temporarily suspended, the notion that a child's sense of self influences his or her academic achievement appears to be unanimous. If such is the case, how can the community contribute to the development of a healthy self-image? We believe that parents and immediate family must provide reinforcement for a child's self-image by instilling a sense of pride, and by acting as a filter for the negative images a child is exposed to. Parents and schools must play a role in communicating both expectations and encouragement for achievement, and constant praise and reinforcement for a child's mastery of various developmental and educational tasks. Children must also be assisted in identifying and participating in positive peer relationships and group activities that reinforce a positive sense of self. Each of these influences, together with other community resources (churches, parks and recreation, business leaders) must collaborate to reinforce for the African-American child principles of self-affirmation and self-determination. Other suggestions for enhancing self-concept were provided by Powell (1982) in her study on the effects of school desegregation on the self-concepts of Black children. Her investigation concluded that in order for self-concept of children in various schools to develop in a normal pattern, several criteria seem to be necessary. Those factors included: (1) maximum participation by parents and teachers, (2) mores and values of the home reinforced in the immediate community and school, (3) Black culture and lifestyles reflected in the educational curriculum, and (4) academic achievement being encouraged regardless of social class.

Value Orientation as a Correlate

Thomas (1967) defines values as a normative, conceptual standard of desired behavior that influences individuals in choosing among personally perceived alternatives of behavior. Values are believed to influence ways in which people think, feel, and behave (Kluckjohn & Strodtbeck, 1961). As such, values may also influence academic achievement of Black youngsters. Much of what a Black youngster comes to value positively and negatively in the world is influenced by what significant others in his or her life value as well. Typically, values of specific ethnic groups are transmitted from generation to generation in ways that allow cultural traditions to continue and self-actualizing behavior to flourish. Occasionally, however, perceptions that culture-specific values are less functional than values of other cultures force many Black youngsters to abandon traditional African-American values in favor of Eurocentric ones. One consequence of this phenomenon is the adoption of many behaviors that are perceived as functional but ultimately prove to be self-destructive to the individual and the community. Nobles (1980, 1986) helps to clarify the relationships between personal values and academic achievement by suggesting that ideas are the substance of behavior. Essentially, Nobles implies that the development of a strong desire to achieve academically, and behavior directed toward that goal attainment are facilitated by a conceptual grounding in the philosophies of African culture.

The notion that education is a necessity for survival and advancement of one's people and oneself is a value that must be promoted by significant others in the child's life. We believe that academic achievement in Black youngsters occurs when achievement is encouraged and supported by the community at large. Families, schools, churches, community organizations, and peer groups must come together in a collective voice and support efforts toward excellence.

In absence of a unanimous consent for this idea, there must be enough support from particular significant others in the child's life, in order for that value to be internalized and practiced by the youngster.

The present authors would also argue that academic achievement is stifled when motivation to achieve is nonexistent and the desire to achieve is challenged by environmental obstacles that prevent goal attainment. If the Black community is to be the reference point around which Black youngsters seek validation and support, then the community must also accept the challenge of eliminating those barriers that prevent Black youth from achieving academically. Ironically, the very institutions that are supposed to encourage achievement are the ones that hinder it. Nowhere is this example clearer than in some of our schools.

Primary and secondary educational institutions have become havens for drug abuse, gang violence, extortion, and misconduct. Many youngsters are more concerned with mastering the intricacies of selling drugs for profit than they are about learning the intricacies of reading, writing, and counting. The idea of making large sums of money without much work proves to be a powerful distracter to many youth. Clearly, there is a deterioration of African values when the attainment of wealth and material possessions at any cost are valued over the uplifting of one's people.

However, there are many youngsters who emerge from what is perceived to be negative environments with the determination to succeed in life's endeavors. We believe that youngsters who make it, and who are successful in achieving academically, manage to remain focused on an ideal of self-determination. They develop the will and intent to succeed in spite of negative elements and seemingly insurmountable obstacles in the environment. Indeed, it is the child himself or herself who must choose a commitment to excellence over destructive distractions. Having said this, however, we do recognize that individual choices are influenced by elements in the environment that shape the way our children process information and make sense out of their world.

Kunjufu (1986) suggests that values are the foundation for motivation, which in turn influences one's behavior. He further asserts that values are developed and nurtured through exposure to information. If Kunjufu's assertion is at all correct (and we suspect it is), then some analysis of the types of information our children are receiving (or not receiving) is in order, and may help to crystallize how incorporation of values influence achievement of Black youngsters.

Exposure to massive amounts of television on a daily basis has been identified as one of the prime socializers of African-American youngsters. In subtle and some not-so-subtle ways, our children's value systems are being influenced and shaped by what they visually and auditorily absorb from that medium (Berry, 1982). This realization is compounded by the notion that Black children devote a disproportionately high amount of time to television viewing (as high as 6 hours per day), and like other children are likely to believe that television accurately reflects life as it really is or should be (Greenberg & Dervin, 1970). Berry (1982) helps to further clarify the question of television's influence on the development of values and the desire to achieve by asking two questions. First,

> Television depicts levels of academic and occupational attainment. To what extent does television convey to African American children the concept that they can be successful only in a (Black) environment, and to what extent must aspiration for broader occupational and academic positions in a multicultural world be limited?

Second,

> Television occupies a prestigious position in our society and for some young people, it tends to validate and add glamour to the roles being played. To what extent are children patterning their behavior and establishing personal attitudes (and values) from television characters who may not be wholesome role models?

Children are being exposed to images and role models that depict the Black community in very negative ways. Images of street-smart children and adults who will do whatever it takes to "get over" (lie, cheat, steal, murder, sell narcotics) are very inappropriate. Images of Blacks being confined to low-status jobs and being prevented from exploring a wider variety of career options are also inappropriate, and may be especially damaging to a child's achievement aspirations. Scenarios that promote money, status, material possessions, and sexual exploits as measures of manhood and womanhood are extremely destructive.

In many cases, the Black community has reacted strongly to these negative portrayals of Blacks on television by calling for a change of venue. Yet, the very community that demands that television images change, fails to realize that the validation for our children adopting these negative stereotypes and portrayals is being provided in and by the community itself.

Street corners are filled with dozens of individuals who have simply given up on life and feel helpless to change their condition. Parents also fail to support their children in their educational pursuits in a number of ways.

If exposure to information is to remain as a prominent influence on values, and values in turn influence behavior, then manipulating the type, amount, and quality of information our children receive will help them to develop a value system that is more consistent with their African culture. Such values might include, for example, the principles of *Nguzo Saba* (Karenga, 1976), which are part of the yearly Kwanzaa celebrations. These include

Umoja—Unity
Kujichagulia—Self-determination
Ujima—Collective work and responsibility
Ujamaa—Cooperative economics
Nia—Purpose
Kuumba—Creativity
Imani—Faith

Presentation of, and teaching about, Africentric value systems may be an important strategy in helping our children to develop the will and intent to achieve.

Teacher Expectations as a Correlate

Teacher expectations is yet another correlate of academic achievement that spawned wide scale interest among researchers. The bulk of the studies suggesting that teacher attitudes and expectations affect a child's school performance began to appear in the late 1960s and early 1970s, when Rosenthal and Jacobson published their now classic study, *Pygmalion in the Classroom,* (1968).

At the heart of the Rosenthal and Jacobson experiment was a belief that teacher's expectations would significantly affect the learning of a group of socially and racially mixed elementary school children whose teachers were told possessed special intellectual talents. The teachers were also told that these "talented" children would show marked intellectual improvement by the end of the first few months of the experiment. The results confirmed the experimenter's prediction in that these intellectually talented students scored significantly higher than the control group on measures of IQ.

In explaining their results, Rosenthal and Jacobson speculated that teachers are especially attentive to students who are expected to show intellectual promise. These students are often treated in a more encouraging manner, and teachers tend to show increased tolerance and patience with the child's learning process. The converse is true for students perceived to be less intellectually gifted. When students are not expected to make significant educational gains, then less attention and encouragement is given to them.

Several other studies (Beez, 1968; Goodacre, 1968; Palardy, 1969; Pidgeon, 1970; Rothbart, Dalfen & Barrett, 1971; Rubovitz & Maehr, 1973) documenting the teacher expectancy effect came on the heels of the heralded "Pygmalion" experiment. In a study conducted by Beez (1968), for example, faked psychological dossiers that described "high-ability" preschool students in favorable terms and "lower-ability" preschool students in less favorable terms were given to teachers who worked with these high- and low-ability preschoolers on simple word learning tasks. As predicted, high-ability preschool students learned more words than their low-ability peers. This differential in performance among the preschool students, according to Beez, was attributable to, at least in part, the expectations of the students held by teachers of both groups.

Palardy's (1969) study examined the differential perceptions of teachers and wondered what effect these perceptions would have on boys and girls learning to read. Despite every child receiving above-average reading pretest scores, boys taught by teachers who perceived their ability to learn to be as good as girls, learned as well as girls. Boys taught by teachers who perceived their ability to learn to be lower than girls, were outperformed by girls.

The Rubovitz and Maehr (1973) investigation took a slightly different slant in that differential teacher expectations with respect to student's race and learning ability were of interest. A group of four mixed-ability eighth-grade students (two African-Americans and two Anglos) were assigned to 1 of 66 women teachers (creating 66 teacher-student groupings), and two of the four students in each group (one African-American and one Anglo) were randomly given high IQ scores. The experimenters found differential teacher expectancy effects in predicted and unpredicted directions, and the student's race proved to be a very salient factor. African-Americans, both gifted and nongifted, received less favorable treatment than gifted and nongifted Anglos. In rank order, increased attention and encouragement were given to gifted Anglos, nongifted Anglos, nongifted African-Americans, and gifted African-Americans. In essence, African-American giftedness was penalized with less attention and praise, whereas Anglo giftedness was rewarded. By way of balance, it should be pointed out, however, that not all teacher expectancy studies resulted in a finding consistent with the investigations just cited. The Claiborn (1969) and Fleming and Anttonen (1971) studies are cases in point. Both involved the usual teacher-student grouping, and expectations of students intellectual talent (or lack thereof) were shaped using fake data. Posttest results in both studies failed to show greater relative gains in learning between experimental and control groups.

PARENT EDUCATION ATTAINMENT

The relationship between a child's educational achievement and poverty is even more pronounced when one considers the effects of a parent's educational background. The high poverty rate of children in families in which the parent has less than a high school degree results in part from lower wages paid to those without college degrees (NCES, 1997). The disproportionate impact on African-American families can be seen in rates nearly four times higher when compared to White families. The NCES estimates that in 1995, 16% of African-American parents had not completed high school compared to just 4% for White parents.

Family Background as a Correlate

Historically, many social scientists have attempted to answer the question of academic achievement in Black youngsters by assuming that the environment negatively impacted the child. That is, it was assumed that low achievement was related to an absence of supportive attributes external to the child himself or herself. The chief scapegoat in these studies appears to have been the family.

As early as the 1930s, research sought to document the consequences of poverty on the perceived instability, weakness, and disintegration of the family (Frazier, 1939). Not surprisingly, much of the research that followed attempted to validate these prior assumptions about the pathological Black family (Moynihan, 1965; Rainwater, 1966). Moynihan (1965), for example, characterizes the family as "tangled and a web of pathology."

Similarly, Rainwater (1966) suggested that the functional autonomy of the Black family reflected destructive features that expressed themselves in violent, repressive, and depraved life-styles. These studies went on to further suggest that this disorganized family contributed to personality, social, cognitive, and mental deficits in Black children.

By and large, the family variables that were identified as culprits included low socioeconomic status, a matriarchal family structure, and a lack of educational resources (Clark, 1983). Assuming these factors are absolutely essential in promoting academic achievement in some youngsters, perceived low achievement by Blacks came as no surprise.

Explaining positive achievement of Black youth who are nurtured in a supportive environment has been a recent, albeit infrequent, focus in the literature. For one thing, crediting the Black family (supportive or not) with helping to develop and promote achievement ideals occurs on too few fronts.

Images of the pathological and disorganized family have begun to change over the past decade, however. In some respects the formation of positive family images has been assisted by researchers who understood that previous characterizations of the unhealthy Black family were in part influenced by biased assumptions and conclusions of the previous researchers themselves. Not surprisingly, then, these latest studies (Billingsley, 1968; Hill, 1971; Ladner, 1975; Stack, 1973) have served as a reaction to previous Black family research by criticizing previous research efforts, and by attempting to explain family dynamics and composition in a way that highlights strengths of the family. For example, Billingsley (1968) cautions researchers against classifying the "Black family" as a single entity, rather than recognizing that, indeed, there is not "one" description that accurately characterizes the Black family of today. Similarly, Hill (1971) presented strengths or factors that have helped Black families to sustain themselves under less than ideal circumstances. These include strong orientations to work, religion, and achievement; strong kinship bonds; and role flexibility by family members.

Recent studies on the Black family have continued to substantiate the work by Billingsley, Hill, and Ladner by isolating those factors that help modern-day Black family members in meeting their needs (McAdoo, 1986; Nobles, 1986). Although these studies have been successful in characterizing the Black family as a vehicle that presumably helps to foster academic achievement in Black youth, they (studies) have been limited in their ability to explain exactly how achievement is supported and encouraged. One of the most important studies to emerge in the literature over the past 20 years that attempts to explain this phenomenon was conducted by Clark (1983). Clark attempted to answer the question of why poor Black children succeed or fail in his book on *Family Life and School Achievement.* Essentially, he compares and contrasts five high-achieving with five low-achieving students, and identifies parenting and child development strategies used by each family. He concludes that parent's dispositions and interpersonal relationships with the child are the main contributors to a child's success in school. Perhaps the most profound statement made in Clark's research effort is that communication and quality of interaction are more important than sociodemographic variables (i.e., family composition, income status) in predicting high achievement in Black youngsters. It is our contention, however, that although quality of interaction between parent and child is an important component in school achievement, we cannot overlook a youngster's willingness and motivation to respond to supportive environmental cues. Indeed, motivation is a characteristic that emerges from within the child himself or herself.

EDUCATIONAL CHALLENGES FOR THE NEW MILLENNIUM

One of the most important challenges facing African-Americans in the new millennium is to reexamine the purpose of education. In many corners of our communities throughout this nation, education has been linked to one's career aspirations. Thus, the purpose of education in the minds of too many young people and their parents is to secure the best possible job or career position with the ultimate intent of securing greater access to wealth and possessions. Too many of our families have joined the race for higher scholastic achievement (i.e., SAT and ACT) scores and admission to prestigious colleges and universities at the expense of some equally important ideals. Be clear that we do not argue against preparing ourselves to compete with society's standards of excellence. However, if our purpose for education is relegated to these academic pursuits alone, then we miss something very valuable about education in an African-centered context.

Hilliard (1997), in his text entitled *SBA: The Reawakening of the African Mind,* reminds us that in ancient, historical, and contemporary African societies, education emphasized the process of socialization. Thus, the education a student received was intrinsically linked to one's personal development and transformation. This transformation not only led to a more enlightened self, but helped each student explore a deeper relationship with the Divine, commit to a set of cultural values (i.e., MAAT, which is defined as a code of conduct and standard of aspiration for the Ancient African Egyptians.) that were life-affirming principles, and explore ways of achieving maximum congruence between thought and behavior.

In a similar way, our educational practices need to reengage the process of socialization such that we prepare current and future generations of students and teachers to have more enlightened minds, more spiritually principled values, and more culturally congruent behaviors that contribute to the individual and collective uplifting of African people. Although we also recognize that African-descent people control few, if any, educational institutions (particularly at primary and secondary levels), our task is to convert those institutions that do exist in our communities into centers for the socialization and transformation of our people. In that way, our communities and our families help facilitate the transmission of culture and guide the transition from personhood to peoplehood.

We have attempted to point out in this chapter that the academic achievement of African-American youngsters, generally speaking, continues to be less than satisfactory. If one looks at the data presented and concludes that educational and academic achievement is a hopeless enterprise, then the future of African-American educational achievement is bleak indeed. If, however, one views the data with concern and uses them as an opportunity to make a difference, then there are some additional challenges that face school systems, the African-American community, and indeed the students themselves as we move into the next millennium.

There also is the question of role definition, which requires all of us to ask ourselves whether or not we define our roles as educators in terms of function, or in terms of needs of our students. Defining our roles in terms of function relegates us to certain activities (lecture, answering questions, office hours, grading tests). Defining your role in terms of needs of students requires that educators become a barometer of student needs such that one learns to translate student needs into social change.

Educators may also have to assist parents and provide them with some feedback on how best to support the intellectual growth and development of their children. In our experience, we have found that parents make several critical errors when it comes to educational achievement in their children. Included among these are

1. Failure to review lessons with children who are completing homework assignments.
2. Failure to insist that homework be completed before engaging in any extracurricular activities (including television).
3. Failure to articulate parental expectations regarding their child's academic performance to the teacher, and insisting on periodic review.
4. Failure to provide guidance when viewing television programming with their children.

Educators must also help parents to understand, as Reginald Clark (1983) points out in his book entitled *Family Life and School Achievement,* that there is a strong correlation between family expectations for youngsters and those youngsters being high achievers. The four parental dispositions observed by Clark include

1. Parents' willingness to put their children's growth and development above their own.
2. Parents who believe that schools cannot do and teach everything to their children; consequently, parents take personal responsibility for assisting their children in developing skills needed for success in the classroom.
3. Parents who believe that children are personally responsible for pursuing knowledge and consequently expect regular classroom attendance and active participation in classroom activities. Such a practice also provides parents with a daily monitor of a child's academic progress.
4. Parents who routinely emphasize that their children should exceed their own goal attainment, and even consider pursuing secondary training beyond what they personally received. Active involvement by parents is

not only beneficial to a child's cognitive growth, involvement also helps to strengthen the emotional bond between parent and child.

Another challenge before us is how to extend opportunities for learning and cultural socialization beyond the halls of academia. The problem is that beyond this realm, many people in the African-American community do not take advantage of the learning opportunities available, nor do they occupy institutions of higher education in large numbers. As such, any educational mission involving the resocialization of our people cannot be restricted to those who occupy academic institutions. Rather, we who are in education must be aggressive in our attempts to support the development of partnerships and collaborations with other community interests such that the masses of African-descent people begin to gain access to the knowledge that will assist them in achieving the liberation they so desperately seek. The key, however, is to help people understand the difference between education and training, for if African-descent people's minds are only trained to develop skills in support of other people's communities and livelihood, then we have not done our jobs well. Indeed, the role of African-American psychologists and educators is to help our people become more enlightened such that their knowledge is used to enhance the survival and collective well-being of themselves and others in their communities.

Another challenge facing African-American people and youth in particular is the need to more critically examine and hold accountable the institutions that educate our children. If we listen to our youth and family constituents, it is clear to us that many of the difficulties and challenges that our young people face on a daily basis have less to do with individual obstacles and barriers and more to do with systemic/institutional ones. As a consequence, we have little hope of affecting the educational endeavors of our young people if we cannot in turn impact the educational institutions that we trust with the intellectual growth and development of our children. Thus, we would like to propose that each community across this country develop a regional report card that would be issued jointly by a coalition of community interests as we analyze the degree to which school systems throughout the country are effectively meeting the needs of our children. This "report card" might take the form of a regional survey that would be administered to various school districts throughout a particular locale as a way of measuring those variables that both impede and/or facilitate the educational success of African-American children.

Obviously, the development of a report card instrument will require extensive time, professional expertise, and unique sensitivity to the issues impacting our youth in school systems throughout this nation. However, we believe that a team of individuals could be persuaded to pull their collective expertise in developing such an instrument. For example, we might propose that a regional report card would evaluate school districts on seven content areas. Those areas would include the following:

1. Faculty/staff composition
   - percentage of teachers who are African-American
   - teachers certified to teach particular subject matter
   - teachers trained to work with African-American children via multicultural education
   - the extent to which professional development opportunities are available in that particular school system
2. Curriculum
   - availability of African-American history
   - the degree to which the school district integrates African-American content into the curriculum
   - the degree to which the district sponsors schoolwide programs designed to foster a sense of cultural pride and affirmation
   - cultural celebrations that are designed to highlight and identify the unique aspects of African-American culture and traditions
3. Methodology
   - instructional method (active versus passive learning)
   - technology
4. Special education
   - What are the criteria for placement?
   - What is the percentage of African-American children enrolled?
   - How does the individual education plan (IEP) benefit learning?
   - What is the congruence between traditional educational curriculum and the special education curriculum?
   - What services are offered for those persons classified as needing special education?
5. Gifted education
   - What are the criteria for placement?
   - What is the percentage of African-American children enrolled?
   - How does the IEP benefit learning?
   - What services are currently offered for gifted students?
6. Administration
   - To what degree do the policies and practices of this institution positively impact African-American children and families?

- To what degree is the leadership sensitive to the needs of the African-American community?
- To what degree is the administration knowledgeable about the educational needs of African-American children?
- What are the graduation rates from each category of instruction?
- What are the dropout rates from each category of instruction?
- What are the discipline rates?
- What percentage of students obtain college admissions?

7. Parental involvement
   - What is the percentage of African-American parents attending back-to-school nights?
   - To what degree does this school system develop and utilize parental advisory boards?
   - To what degree does this school system outreach to parent groups?

The development of a regional or local report card might accomplish several things in the desire for better educational practices:

1. It would assist in the development of collaborative partnerships between home, school, and communities.
2. It would help concerned community interests call attention to the educational needs of our youth.
3. It would help to standardize the way in which communities across the country assess the quality of the educational experience that African-American youth receive.
4. It provides a measure of accountability for school systems around the country and serves as a barometer for progress on issues identified as paramount in a particular year.

PROMISING PRACTICES

Holding schools more accountable for how they educate our children is certainly an important goal. However, the responsibility for properly educating our children must be shared by our families and communities as well. Educational success in the new millennium will depend on how effective African-Americans are at developing collaborative relationships and community partnerships.

An example of such a collaboration exists in the southern California region of the country where the first author of this text, through his membership in the 100 Black Men of America's Orange County

Chapter, has helped to develop a promising program. Parham (1994) believes that student success depends on a cooperative relationship between the home, school, and community. In attempting to reconnect this "triangle for success," Parham and his colleagues developed the *Passport to the Future Program.* The Passport program is a four-year sequential experience where each year, ninth-grade high school students and their parents are invited to participate in the educational support initiative. Invitations to participate are extended through the high school principal, who gives his or her endorsement of the program and the 100 Black Men to the parents.

Students who are accepted in the program are exposed to curricular and experiential activities which include:

- a Rites of Passage program in the ninth grade
- a Mentoring program in the tenth grade
- a Personal and Leadership Development Program in the eleventh grade
- an Apprenticeship/College Preparation Program in the twelfth grade

Through Parham's instruction, students are reminded that in a society that awards privileges based on chronological age, criteria for manhood and womanhood cannot be restricted to such simplistic attributes. It is true that youth can obtain a work permit at 14 years of age, a driving permit at 16 years of age, can vote at 18, and consume alcohol and gamble at age 21. But does that make them men and women?

The *Passport to the Future Program* supports a more African-centered perspective by suggesting that manhood (and by extension womanhood) are status earned by mastering several fundamental areas of skill, knowledge, and experience. Parham has recommended that these areas include self-awareness, history, relationships, skill development (career development, conflict resolution and anger management, and economic empowerment), leadership, and community service. Although this list is far from exhaustive, it will provide you with an example of criteria more relevant than age.

Having reviewed the six areas of mastery and the four levels of intervention (ninth through twelfth grades), you can see how this six (areas of mastery) times four (levels) matrix can be used to construct a model of educational intervention and resocialization of African youth.

Table 4–1 provides a more detailed diagram of the program.

TABLE 4–1 100 Black Men of Orange County, Passport to the Future Program (Parham, 1994; 1998)

Yr & Trg. Orientation	Self Awareness	History	Relationship	Skill Development	Leadership	Community Service	Validation Marker
Rites of Passage	Personality vs Principle Principle of Maat 3 critical questions African-centered values 7 cardinal virtues 5 dimensions of character	Ancient Kemetic Historical Africa African-American Heroes and sheroes History of White supremacy	Relationship definition Types of relationships Male/female relation issues	Career development (intro) Conflict resolution (intro) Economic empowerment (intro)	Definition Qualities of effective leaders	5 hours/week Each individual Sites vary by personal choice with approval	Rites of Passage Mastery of six areas of content knowledge
Academic							
Mentoring **100 Black Men and Community Members**	Introduction of mentor/mentee Asessment: talents/skills of the mentee Integrating spirituality	Teacher Ancient Kemetic African-American Heroes and Sheroes Examples of mentoring relationships Elijah Mohamed ↓ ↓ Malcolm X Mary McCloud Bethune ↓ Dorothy Height	Advising Exploration of the dream/passion Exploration of family relationships (how they got to where they are)	Coaching Exploring conflict/tension within Developing a model of personal finance Careers—intro to transferable assets	Guidance How to identify leadership opportunities How to plan and conduct a meeting Understanding vulnerability to manipulation	Volunteering 5 hours/week Mentoring a younger child	Presentation by mentor—gift Mastery of six areas of content and experience Mastery of mentoring obligation

Academic							
Personal/ Leadership Development	Exploring self as a leader	Understanding geo-political issues with African-Americans	Intimacy in relationships	Résumé preparation preparation	Leadership project	Applying for a part-time job	Presentation of placements by corporate employers
	Understanding and resisting manipulation	Study influential African-American leaders (Ron Brown, Randall Robinson, college presidents, CEOs)	Sexual responsibility and abstinence	Job interview techniques	Ethics of leadership	Developing a commitment to serve in a leader capacity	
	Health and wellness		HIV and teen pregnancy	Time management	Teamwork		
			Masculine/feminine equals	Financial investments (intro)			
Apprenticeship Opps. 10 hrs/wk	Managing anxieties of new job	Employment trends for African-Americans: historical→contemporary	How careers impact personal relationships and vice versa	Handling conflict in the workplace	Roles and responsibilities of leaders in the workplace	Explore community in context of corporation	Graduation Passport presentation
College Applications Readiness	Understanding "what my workplace behavior says about me and my future"	Understanding obstacles to advancement	Developing relations on the job with the boss, supervisor, and coworkers	Understanding workplace budgets		Understand what foundations support with their grants	
				Future career visions			

TABLE 4–1 ***Continued***

Yr & Trg. Orientation	Self Awareness	History	Relationship	Skill Development	Leadership	Community Service	Validation Marker
Academic							
Learning Resources: Books/ Readings/ Video	Akbar (1994) *Visions for Black Men* Du Bois (1903) *Souls of Black Folks* Van Zant (1998) *One Day My Soul Just Opened UP*	Bennett (1962) *Before the Mayflower* Van Sertima (1976) *They Came Before Columbus* Diop (1974) *African Origins of Civilization* Clegg (1991) *When Black Men Ruled the World* (video) Hilliard (1990) *Master Keys* (video)	White & Parham (1990) *Psychology of Blacks* Oba T'Shaka (1994) *Return to the African Mother Principle of Masculine/Feminine Equivalence* Powell-Hopson, Hopson (1994) *Friends, Lovers, Soul Mates*	Bolles (1990) *What Color Is Your Parachute?* Kilman (1990) *Conflict Resolution Styles Scale*	Madhibuti (1990) *Black Men: Obsolete, Single, Dangerous* Clegg & Watson *Black Life in Corporate America* Landrum (1998) *Profiles of Black Success*	To be determined	

Classes are held every other week in the local school site during the school year. By combining the talents and expertise of the community (100 Black Men), together with support from the home and the school, initiatives like these provide an important supplement to the education our youth typically receive. The Passport program promotes the idea that African-American students learn best and contribute more in an active, participatory, instructional environment where African-centered values, history and heritage, and collective responsibility are emphasized. By combining the psychological expertise and youth development interests of the community with the dream and aspirations of the home and school, this community is taking an active role in preparing African-American youth for the future.

5

Contemporary Approaches to Developmental Psychology—African-American Perspectives

Our purpose in this chapter is to provide the reader with a cursory overview of the history of developmental psychology, its theoretical range, possibilities, and contemporary contributions, while highlighting the emerging African-American perspectives that have influenced and continue to shape the prevailing thinking in developmental psychology today.

The reader encountering developmental psychology for the first time is likely to view the field with both a sense of awe and trepidation. In awe of the vast array of theories and methods that seek to address the questions surrounding human development, while experiencing some trepidation around the range of opportunities and complexities that each theory presents. Given the wide array of theories, methods, and issues, if uncritical, one may mistake the theoretical range, complexity, and diversity for disciplinary chaos and confusion. However, upon closer scrutiny one is likely to find that these differing theoretical approaches often share motifs, foci, and more importantly, historical roots. Miller (1993) suggests that behind the apparent diversity and complexity in developmental psychology a unity of purpose exists and that from its inception developmental psychology has concerned itself with four salient issues:

1. What is the basic nature of humans?
2. Is development qualitative or quantitative?
3. How do nature and nurture contribute to development?
4. What is it that develops?

The historical quest to address these four central issues has resulted not only in the diversity present in the field but has also provided much of the conceptual impetus and insight for contemporary thinking in the field.

HISTORICAL OVERVIEW

The history of developmental psychology is best understood in terms of two dominant trends that can be distinguished through an overview of the field's history. First, there has been a shift in focus from description to an emphasis on explanatory frameworks. Hence, as Baldwin (1980) and Lerner (1986) suggest, developmental psychologists are now more concerned with the explanation of developmental change than just the description of development. Second, developmentalists have of late begun to utilize some of the more viable theories or methods of analysis. As a result of this shift in emphasis, a great deal of the contemporary developmental research is directed at theory testing rather than just the construction of developmental benchmarks.

The major contemporary theoretical systems in developmental psychology can be traced historically to two common intellectual inspirations: the European Enlightenment of the seventeenth and eighteenth centuries (i.e., Francis Bacon, Rene Descartes) and the historical and evolutionary theories of Charles Darwin and others in the intellectual context of the nineteenth century. Thus one can make a good argument that the presence of theoretical diversity is a by-product of the distinct ways that different developmentalists produced their theories of development by focusing on different aspects of Enlightenment thinking and Darwin's evolutionary theory (Lerner & Dixon, 1994). Although Brofenbrener (1963) suggests that from the 1930s to the early 1960s there was a continuing transition toward research that was centered on abstract processes and constructs from research efforts that solely embraced the gathering and description of data.

The trend toward attending to both the description and explanation of developmental processes has been gaining momentum since the 1970s in a number of ways. For example, increasingly, a number of developmentalists have begun to realize that there are a variety of equally valuable ways in which to theorize about the range and scope of human development. This pluralistic viewpoint further implies that theoretical concerns may guide the research enterprise and that theory, data collection, and interpretation should be assessed in terms of each other (Looft, 1972; Brofenbrener, 1963; Lerner & Dixon, 1994).

The other important and ongoing debate in developmental psychology is the nature/nurture debate. This debate speaks directly to Miller's four central questions we presented earlier:

1. What is the basic nature of humans?
2. Is development qualitative or quantitative?
3. How do nature and nurture contribute to development?
4. What is it that develops?

It is in response to these four basic questions that the field of developmental psychology arose. We now direct attention to a brief discussion of some of the major theoretical orientations in developmental psychology.

TRADITIONAL THEORETICAL APPROACHES: A SUMMARY

Dixon and Lerner (1994) have suggested that the nature versus nurture debate and the various attempts to theorize about the nature of human development can be best understood in terms of five clusters or theoretical orientations and the thinkers that brought these theories to prominence. These theoretical orientations are discussed in the following paragraphs:

Organismic

In this model developmental change is characterized as qualitative rather than quantitative and development is viewed as unidirectional and irreversible. This model was developed from the early efforts of thinkers like Arnold Gesell, G. Stanley Hall, James Mark Baldwin, and later in the seminal work of Jean Piaget.

Psychoanalytic

Developmental change in this theoretical approach is viewed as qualitative and stagelike, proceeding through conflict resolution from one stage to the next. Its direction is generally viewed as linear, although regression is possible. Within this tradition the influence of ideas of Sigmund Freud, Erik Erikson, and Carl Jung figure most prominently.

Mechanistic

This model views the human being as machinelike, composed of disparate yet interrelated parts. Behavioral functioning is viewed as a result of environmental forces rather than of intrapsychic causes. Thus, development depends on the history of the organism, level of environmental stimulation, and the kind of environmental stimulation. The organism is seen as passive in an active environment. Thus developmental change is more quantitative and cumulative. This theoretical orientation derives from the intellectual impetus of early psychological thinkers like Sir Francis Galton, Wilhelm Preyer, and later in the work of John B. Watson.

Contextual

The individual and the social environment are viewed as mutually effectual, acting upon one another in symbiotic interaction. In this model the basic impetus is social-cultural or the historic event. Contextualism is informed by the pragmatic philosophic tradition as professed in the writings of William James, John Dewey, George H. Mead, and Charles Sanders Pierce.

Dialectical

For research guided by this orientation, the basic motif is contradiction or conflict. Development is seen as the result of a continuous process of thesis, antithesis, and synthesis. The activities of the individual are viewed in a dynamic interaction with a particular context. This perspective emphasizes the continuing nature of change, as well as the fact that change occurs on multiple levels. The work of Karl Marx and George W. F. Hegel provided the theoretical foundation for this approach, whereas it was the work of the Russian Lev Vygotsky that ushered it to prominence in psychology.

As we have seen, contemporary developmental psychology is marked by a great deal of theoretical diversity that is nonetheless linked by a common heritage. And although developmental psychology appears to embrace a more pluralistic perspective, this is, as we shall soon see, not to suggest that developmental psychology is without some serious limitations and conceptual pitfalls with regards to its application with African-American populations.

LIMITATIONS AND CONCEPTUAL PITFALLS

The research drawn from some of the aforementioned theoretical approaches have been hindered by at least three fundamental conceptual flaws with regard to their use with African-Americans. The first fundamental conceptual flaw has to do with the first three theoretical orientations' unwillingness to acknowledge the centrality and salience of culture in the study of human development. As is well known, psychologists often carry their own cultural orientations and biases with them when researching and theorizing about other cultures. As a result, these theories are often the initial sources of biases to be confronted and reduced. Moreover, many psychologists have tenaciously disputed the view that cultural factors play a role in the psychological process and have proceeded to gather and present culture-bound findings as universally valid. As a result of this line of thinking, psychology in general and the organismic, mechanistic, and psychoanalytic schools of thought in particular have paid little attention to culturally sensitive methods that place an emphasis on more innovative and qualitative techniques. Instead, Western quantitative and reductionist methods that obscure the centrality of culture on human development and behavior are stressed (Hughes, Seidman & Williams 1993). The unwillingness to acknowledge culture as central to the analysis and understanding of human development creates an atmosphere wherein the culture of the theorist becomes the lens through which the culture under study is viewed. In the case of European-American psychology, this allows for European-American culture to set the standard by which all elements of human development are to be measured.

A great many researchers (Akbar, 1991; Nobles, 1986; Cole, 1995; Greenfield, 1995; Ajamu, 1998; Hughes, Seidman & Williams 1993) have noted that theories are often tied to the theorist's perspective on human nature. As a result, theories are intimately connected to the theorist's worldview or his or her beliefs of how the world operates. When the theorizing is done about a cultural group other than the one to which the theorist belongs, the result is often the imposition of some form of cultural bias. In the case of Western psychology, this cultural bias takes the form of a priori Eurocentic cultural universality.

The second flaw shared by the first three approaches is their assumed cultural universality, which has often resulted in the use of European-American developmental norms as the standard of measurement for African-American development. Because universality is assumed in advance when dealing with other cultural groups, the cultural strengths of other cultural groups are often either overlooked or deemed irrelevant and the European-American perspective becomes not simply one perspective among many but the only perspective. For example, McLoyd (1991) notes the way this false universality is implied and maintained through the insistence by a great many psychological journals on the use of a European comparison group when doing research with African-American populations, in effect positioning the European-American comparison group as the standard of measurement.

The result, as we (White & Parham, 1990) and others (Guthrie, 1998; Akbar, 1990; Nobles, 1986; Ani, 1994) have noted, is often inferiority-based and deficit- and deficiency-oriented conclusions about the nature of African-American psychological functioning in general and human development in particular. Thus under the assumption of universality, Western psychology often overlooks the cultural biases of its theories in ways that negate the validity of other cultural norms and perspectives as salient and meaningful, while giving Western psychology the appearance of consensus (Nobles, 1985). This allows for Eurocentric psychological theories about African-Americans to stand as the only theories worthy of consideration, discussion, and debate. This helps to explain why African-American psychology has been regarded with a high degree of skepticism and indifference by mainstream psychology and psychologist (Banks, 1982, 1992).

The third conceptual flaw has to do with the treatment of culture as a variable. The majority of approaches in psychology when studying culture tend to view culture as just another variable (e.g., socioeconomic status or gender) among many to be controlled and manipulated. Here the result is the same as with the previous two conceptual flaws: the use of European-American norms as the standard of appraisal. It should be noted that recently a number of psychologists have begun to call for the inclusion of culturally centered as well cross-cultural approaches to Western psychology (Cole, 1995; Rogoff & Chavajay, 1995; Segall, Lonner & Berry, 1998). Furthermore, there have been a number of articles noting the centrality race, culture, ethnicity, and importance of studying culture by psychological researchers (Betacourt & Lopez, 1993; Cole, 1984). Nevertheless, Western psychology, in general, has continued to ignore culture as a source of influence on human behavior and still lightly regards theories or data derived from other than European-American cultures.

AFRICAN-AMERICAN PERSPECTIVES: THE IMPORTANCE OF CULTURE IN UNDERSTANDING AFRICAN-AMERICAN PSYCHOSOCIAL DEVELOPMENT

Although Western psychology has only recently begun to address the question of culture seriously, a close examination of the history of the contemporary Black psychology movement reveals that from its inception over two decades ago, Black psychology has addressed the question of culture. White (1970) suggested that a Black psychology be derived from the cultural experiences of Blacks in America. Nobles (1972), on the other hand, argued that Black psychology should be rooted in the traditional African cultural experience. This was due in part to the fact that the utilization of Western theories often resulted in the diminishment, devaluation, and sometimes dehumanization of African-Americans (Guthrie, 1998), and in part by a need to articulate the strength and value of the African-American experience on its own terms, in its own words. Since that time there have been an abundance of theories that have sought to highlight and give meaning to the African-American psychological experience (Akbar, 1984; Cross, 1971; White & Parham, 1990; Nobles, 1986; Boykin, 1994). However, only recently have African-American psychologists begun to address explicitly the question of African-American culture in the form of rigorous research programs designed to illuminate the salience of African–African-American culture in the psychosocial development of African-Americans. In this regard, a number of psychologists have begun to address the question of culture within the confines of developmental psychology.

The examination of African-American culture in developmental psychology has generated a variety of diverse and creative theories about culture and its impact on psychological functioning that crosses disciplines and international boundaries, from Patricia Greenfield's (1994) research on (re)conceptualizations of culture and history as paramount in developing a universal theory of development through an understanding of cultural diversity to Pachter and Harwood's (1996) study of cross-cultural methodological issues and the relationship between cultural beliefs, values, practices, behavior, and their impact on psychosocial development. Michael Cole (1995), working from the dialectical approach, seeks to explore and evaluate the importance of a psychology that places culture, context, and biology in the forefront of analysis of psychological phenomena. Anthropologist John Ogbu (1990) researches the areas of the American racial caste system and its impact on educational achievement with minority students, while anthropologist Lisa Delpit (1995) examines the linkage between cultural hegemony, power, knowledge, and cultural context. Bame Nsamenang's (1995) research explores the effects of differing cultural contexts on the socialization of African children. Barbara Shade's (1991) groundbreaking research on African-American social cognition argues empirically that cognitive style, in which people organize and understand their world, is culturally induced, further arguing that African-Americans have a distinctive cognitive style that should be embraced, understood, and appreciated. The earlier works of Margaret Beale-Spencer (1987) explore the factors such as psychological risks, adaptational processes, and psychological health that adversely impact Black children's school achievement. Beale-Spencer's (1997) contemporary efforts seek to integrate Brofenbrener's ecological approach with an emphasis on the phenomenological features that characterize her earlier research efforts. These research efforts represent a small sample of the amount of research with African-American populations employing an emphasis on culture.

One of the most provocative new theories on the contemporary landscape in developmental psychology is A. Wade Boykin's Afrocultural theory (1994a,b; 1996). Boykin's research seeks to integrate an African philosophic approach with a Western empirical methodology into a rigorous research program. Philosophically, Afrocultural theory shares with other Africentric conceptions (Nobles, 1972, 1986, 1997; Asante, 1980; Ani, 1989; Forde, 1964; Holloway, 1990; Herskovits, 1958; Akoto, 1992; Kambon, 1992; Diop, 1959; Wobogo, 1976) the view that there is a core African philosophy that undergirds African-American culture, and that this deep structure of culture is informed by a worldview that asserts that there is a cultural unity among all African peoples. For Boykin (1983) this cultural unity expresses itself in the form of nine distinct but interrelated dimensions of African-American culture: (1) spirituality, an approach to life as being essentially vitalistic rather than mechanistic, with the conviction that nonmaterial forces influence peoples' everyday lives; (2) harmony, the notion that one's fate is interrelated with other elements in the scheme of things, so that humankind and nature are harmonically joined; (3) movement, an emphasis on the interweaving of movement, rhythm, percussiveness, music, and dance, which are taken as central to psychological health; (4) verve, a propensity for relatively high levels of stimulation, to action that is energetic and lively; (5) affect, an emphasis on emotions and feelings, together with a special sensitivity to emotional cues and a tendency to be emotionally expressive; (6) communalism, a commitment to social connectedness that includes an awareness that bonds and responsibilities transcend individual privileges; (7) expressive individualism, the cultivation of a distinctive personality and a proclivity for spontaneous, genuine personal expression; (8) oral tradition, a preference for oral/aural modes of communication in which both speaking and listening are treated as performances and in which oral virtuosity—the ability to use alliterative, metaphorically colorful, graphic forms of spoken language—is emphasized and cultivated; and (9) social time perspective, an orientation in which time is treated as passing through a social space rather than a material one, in which time can be recurring, personal, and phenomenological.

Methodologically, the Afrocultural theory attempts to employ a contextualist approach to the study of culture as implicated in William Macguire's contextualist theory of knowledge (1985). Contextualism asserts that what determines the strength and validity of any theory is the context or situation to which the theorist applies the theory. In effect, it posits that all theories are both true and false depending on the context. As a theory of knowledge production it shares with logical empiricism the basic assumption about hypothesis generating and hypothesis testing (i.e., deductivism and empirical confrontation), as vital to developing significant and sound scientific hypotheses, while repudiating the logical empiricist belief in right and wrong theories. He further suggests that empirical confrontation is a discovery process by which the theorist is able to ascertain which contexts are most appropriate for a given theory. This, then, has the effect of revealing hidden assumptions and specifying in which contexts its misrepresentations are tolerable and in which seriously misleading. The theory of contextualism place a priority on the importance of the hypothesis-generating phase of research, viewing this as paramount to developing theories that are able to cover multiple contexts and thus strengthen the overall efficacy of the theory.

Another central aspect of Boykin's Afrocultural contextualist orientation is his Triple Quandary Theory (1983). Building on an earlier theoretical articulation by Cole (1970), he posits that African-American students must successfully navigate three distinct but interrelated realms of experience: (1) the mainstream experience—as typified by the European-American cultural experience as normative; (2) the minority experience, as typified by the African-Americans' marginalized status in American society; and (3) the Afrocultural orientations, as typified by the previously aforementioned nine Afrocultural dimensions. Boykin (1995) further suggests that the key to educational success for many African-American children is predicated on their ability to negotiate successfully these distinct realms of experience. He further notes that optimal education achievement occurs when educators and schools begin to build on the cultural strengths that African-American students bring with them to the classroom.

A. Wade Boykin and his associates (Allen & Boykin, 1991; Cunningham, 1997; Dill, 1996; Marryshow, 1996; Martin, 1997; Miller, 1997) at the Center for Research on Students Placed At Risk (C.R.E.S.P.A.R.) have begun to utilize his Afrocultural theory in the area of education with African-American students with encouraging results. For example, the work of Allen and Boykin (1991) explores the role of music and movement expressive modalities in the educational achievement with African-American students. The research of Sean Martin (1997) examines students' attitudes toward Afrocultural learning orientations versus Eurocultural learning orientations, and Oronde Miller's (1997) work looks at the effects of European cultural hegemony on African-American children's classroom perceptions. The work of Ebony Dill (1996) explores the optimality of communal learning contexts for African-American children. Building on Boykin's notion of psychological integrity, this area of research has promising implications not only for education of African-American children but for the ways in which we view and define ourselves as cultured beings.

With regard to the body of research now being done by African-American developmentalists, it is clear that culture has now become an important topic of discourse as well as a salient aspect of the research process in developmental psychology. In this regard there are a number of issues that African-American developmentalists will need to attend themselves if they are to assist in improving the quality of life for African-Americans. These include, but are not limited to, (1) exploring the necessity for an African-American developmental theory that is rooted in the African cultural experience; (2) defining and delineating the tasks associated with this new African-American developmental theory (i.e., the points of convergence and divergence) with the current paradigms, as well as examining the ways in which these new theories accurately capture or miss the mark when describing African-Americans; and (3) learning the implications of an African-American developmental theory for child rearing, identity development, parenting styles, and life-span perspectives.

With regard to these issues, a number of psychologists have begun to articulate a variety of theories that seek to address the integrity of the African-American psychocultural experience (Boykin, 1994a; Nobles; 1997; Wilson, 1978). And although there is no comprehensive theory of African-American development, the late Amos N. Wilson, in his seminal work, *The Developmental Psychology of The Black Child,* attempted to lay out a comprehensive theory of Black child development. Although he raised a number of important questions with regard to the misapplication of European developmental norms to African-American children and attempted to theorize about the nature of an African-centered approach to understanding human development, the major limitation with his body of work to date has been the lack of empirical validation.

Additionally, McLoyd (1991) notes that African-American researchers must continue to be vigorous in their efforts to defend the integrity of scholarly representation. She writes that the insistence on comparative research utilizing European-Americans as a comparison group further reinforces the Eurocultural reality as normative, while simultaneously discouraging the kinds of within-group research that serves to illuminate the contours and complexities of African-American life and culture. Moreover, any theory of development must consider the impact of globalization and lack of socio-economic prosperity of African-Americans and the ways that adaptive realities inform and transform notions of development in post modern, post industrial America (see Vonnie McLoyd, 1998).

SANKOFA: SOME PRELIMINARY THOUGHTS FOR THE NEXT GENERATION

Sankofa is a Twi term derived from the Akan people of Ghana, West Africa, which means "to go back and fetch what has been lost or stolen." As a symbol it is represented iconographically in the form of a bird looking back with an egg in its mouth. Nobles (1986) has noted that one of the keys to understanding African culture lies in our ability to understand the role of symbol in African and African-American culture. In that regard, it is important for our purposes to examine more closely the *sankofa* symbol. In the African worldview the bird is sometimes seen as representative of ascendancy, whereas looking back represents the process of reflection and remembering; and the egg represents the source or origin of one's beginning. Thus when expressed as a cultural axiom, *sankofa* is understood to mean that as one reflects on or returns to his or her source or origin, one ascends.

In that regard, the discussion of human development is indissociable from the discussion of human origins. It is now indisputable that human beingness began in Africa (Leakey, 1994; Diop, 1981), and as such our discussions of human development ought begin by studying the first humans to develop. Moreover, half of human history had transpired before Europe was born; in this regard, it would appear self-evident that the first forays into the understanding of human development could not have begun anywhere other than Africa. In fact, rather than focusing our thinking on the cultural artifacts of Africa (i.e., the pyramids or *Hor em aket* [the sphinx]) perhaps our efforts would be greatly enriched by understanding the Kemetic culture that gave rise to over three thousands years of uninterrupted cultural growth and development. What can we learn from those primordial and traditional African cultures about human beingness and human development? We should ask ourselves: How might our discourse on human development be enriched by an understanding of the Bantu belief that human beings are "a power, a phenomenon of perpetual veneration" with the capacity for self-healing? (Fu-Kiau, 1991). Or how might we approach the question of prenatal care if we saw a pregnant woman as "a carrier of a new and holy package full of power and energy"? How might our current conceptualizations of child development be enhanced if we saw each newborn child as an old spirit reborn with an important destiny to fulfill (Erny, 1968) or a newborn child as the rising of a living sun in the community (Fu-Kiau, 1991). What kind of paradigms and concomitant theoretical formulations might we derive from the African concepts of personhood rather than the current Western paradigms of individuation? For example, in many African societies the notion of an individual is deferent to the concept of personhood. The Akan, among others (i.e., Yoruba, Wolof, Zulu) have identified seven constituent elements of personhood: (1) the Okra—the soul given by *Nyame* (God); (2) *Kradin*—name given to the day representing your birthday; (3) *Nkrabea*—your destiny; (4) *Sumsum*—accounts for ones personality, character, and intelligence; (5) *Ntoro*—life force transmitted through the father's sperm; it is believed to spiritually bond the child to the father; (6) *Mogya*—represents the bloodline through the mother, it is believed that the physical body comes through the mother; and (7) *Suban*—which is one's character. Although it is beyond the scope of this chapter to explore fully the implications of this body of knowledge for human development, it may be worthwhile to ask ourselves: How might these notions of personhood inform development from a lifespan perspective? What we have attempted to provide is a rationale for the exploration and excavation of African culture and deep thought (philosophy) as a salient point of departure for the discussion of an authentic African-American theory of human development rooted in the image and interest of African peoples. Human development, like reading a good book or telling an important story, is best understood when we start at the beginning. *Sankofa!*

SUMMARY

In this chapter we briefly reviewed the history of developmental psychology, its theoretical range, and possibilities, while highlighting the emerging African-American perspectives that have influenced and continue to shape the prevailing thinking in developmental psychology today. The failure of mainstream psychology to acknowledge the role and value of African-American culture has been a source of discussion, controversy, and debate in developmental psychology circles for some time now. This is due in part to the fact that those theorists who refuse to acknowledge the salience of culture in psychology may indeed be viewing the same phenomena through a very different analytical lens. In order to bridge this gap in perception between many African-American and European-American theorists, it is essential that mainstream psychology begin to expand its strictures to include the cultural insights of other groups as meaningful in the expansion of understanding of human possibilities and potentialities. Additionally, we have posited an African foundation for the study of human development in general and for African-Americans in particular. We believe that the African-American psychological contributions in developmental psychology represent a positive step in the right direction. *Sankofa!*

6

Mental Health Issues Impacting African-Americans

Throughout the discipline of psychology, there is a restless tension as professionals struggle with the notions of cultural competence and how a clinician can prepare herself or himself to intervene effectively with culturally different populations. Clearly, the discipline of African-centered psychology has been a primary instigator in these debates through its writings (White, 1984; Myers, 1988; Akbar, 1994), advocacy (i.e., the Association of Black Psychologists), and training. Beyond the perspective that traditional psychology is sometimes inadequate when applied to African-Americans, there is a challenge to more clearly delineate an authentic, workable theory of mental health for people of African descent.

In discussions, lectures, and training workshops throughout the country, Parham (1997) has argued for more cultural specificity in psychological theories and constructs, as well as treatment methods regarding African-Americans. His assertions are grounded in the assumption that as "mental health" professionals, it is difficult to facilitate psychological health if one has no idea of what constitutes being mentally healthy for African-descent people. Certainly, the definitions advanced by traditional psychology are inadequate to describe the life space and life experiences of African-Americans. Given this predicament, it seems reasonable to articulate a definition of African-American mental health. This chapter seeks to do that, while also exploring methods of mental health intervention.

Our discussion will begin with an exploration of the questions "What is mental health?" and "How is mental health operationalized in the Black community?" The chapter will continue with discussions about therapeutic prognosis, help-seeking behaviors in African-Americans, and the discussion of the dynamics and therapy involved in working with an African-American client. This chapter will conclude with a brief discussion of training issues as they relate to mental health professionals delivering service to African-American clients.

MENTAL HEALTH OR MENTAL ILLNESS: A QUESTION OF PERSPECTIVE

Despite considerable disagreement regarding what constitutes mental health and/or mental illness, most mental health professionals generally assume that a state of mental health exists when individuals are mentally free of the psychological ailments and/or distortions that negatively affect cognitive, emotional, and behavioral abilities, or in some way impede an individual's growth and ability to reach his or her full potential; and when one feels his or her life has moved, is moving, or has the potential to move in a meaningful direction.

In the first and second editions of *The Psychology of Blacks,* White (1984) and White and Parham (1990) discussed the notion of mental health for Black people. Among other things, they concluded that a psychologically healthy Black person is one who interprets the African-American ethos into his or her own life space. As Ani (1994) explains, that ethos refers to the emotional tone of a group of people. It represents an emotional bond created by shared cultural heritage and life experiences. A healthy person is also psychologically open to self and able to relate to others, is resourceful, inventive, imaginative, and enterprising in his or her approach to life. White and Parham also contend that mental health for Blacks requires that a person be centered in, grounded in, or otherwise in touch with one's African-American makeup.

The importance of their assertion is underscored by the assumption that what constitutes mental health for Blacks needs to be understood in the context of one's own culture. Traditionally, Eurocentric standards of what constitutes mental health are often inappropriate for

Blacks because they are based on the philosophies, values, and mores of Euro-American culture, and they use these variables to develop normative standards of mental health based only on Euro-American culture. Thus, what constitutes sane or insane behavior, mental health or mental illness, or normal or abnormal behavior is always in relation to a White normative standard.

In the second edition of this text, White and Parham (1990) reviewed some of the work of African-American scholars who began to articulate their own definitions of what constitutes mental health and self-actualizing behavior for African-American people (Akbar, 1981; Parham & Helms, 1985; Ani, 1995). Those models were based more on culturally specific views of mental health and mental illness and are seen as more accurate indicators of normal and/or abnormal behavior in Black people.

In this third edition, there is a need to delve more fully into the concept of mental health and illness because our thinking and study has yielded new insights. In defining African-centered psychology, Parham (1995) has asserted that it examines processes that allow for the illumination and liberation of the *spirit*. Relying on the principle of harmony within the universe as the natural order of human existence, African-centered psychology recognizes: *the spiritness* that permeates everything that is; the notion that everything in *the universe is interconnected;* the value that *the collective* is the most salient element of existence; and the idea that *self-knowledge* is the key to mental health. As we then review the construct of *Ore-Ire* or properly aligned consciousness (introduced earlier in the text), one might conclude that mental health is aligning one's life space with these values and assumptions. Being in touch with one's spiritual essence, having knowledge of oneself as a cultural being, and accessing the "collective" for one's source of sustenance and support would then define a sense of order and normality.

In other corners of the African-American community, definitions of equal interest have also emerged. Farrakhan (1996), for example, has suggested that mental health is tantamount to functioning in accord with the nature, aim, and purpose of one's creation. That purpose, according to some texts, is to cultivate the god within each of us, such that we use the gifts we are blessed with to master our life circumstances. Fu-Kiau (1991), on the other hand, has suggested that to be healthy, one must be in balance or harmony with oneself, one's environment, and the universe. He contends that each of us is endowed with a power or energy (life force) and that power represents a self-healing potential. When a person acts in opposition to one's nature, he or she loses (moves further away from) his or her self-essence, as well as balance.

What implications, then, do these definitions and descriptions have for psychologists and therapists who work with African-American clients in therapy? Personality theory of African-Americans, especially those articulated by Nobles (1986); Akbar (1981); Myers (1988); Baldwin (1984); and Parham and Helms (1985), stress the necessity of achieving congruence between the "self" one wishes to become, and one's true African-American makeup if one is to be a fully functioning and well-adjusted individual. If there is an aspect or factor of personality that does not fit well with, function well with, or contribute constructively to the overall personality organization, then the efficient functioning of the personality is decreased, or perhaps even seriously disrupted. Thus, attitudes and behaviors that devalue one's Africanness, overassimilate White cultural values, and the like, can be seen as representing degrees incongruent between an African-American's real self and idealized self because they violate the natural order of that person's African makeup.

If one assumes that disordered behavior is related to an absence of spiritual enlightenment, an overreliance on the material versus the spiritual elements of the universe, or an inability to access that deepest core of our self that illuminates our humanity, then it is likely that therapists and psychologists will see different degrees of psychological maladjustment in the clients that they treat. As such, service providers may need to assist clients with achieving some sense of personal transformation, recognizing who and where they are in time and space while helping them move toward a greater manifestation of what they have the capacity to become. In doing so, therapists will need to deal with the client's past experiences and the stress surrounding such experiences, which have shaped his or her perceptions in a disordered fashion. Service providers may also need to assist clients in analyzing their behaviors that hinder, threaten, or impede their growth as human organisms. Service providers may also want to assist clients in becoming more comfortable with themselves as African-American persons, while helping them to identify their resistance to more positive Black perspectives. Such efforts might include a thorough examination of clients' self-esteem or self-worth.

What we are suggesting here is that therapy can and should be a process of human transformation. As such, spirit, thinking, feelings, and behaviors can each be transformed from their present state to one that is more healthy and culturally self-actualizing. But what is the goal? If our desire to facilitate transformation in clients is genuine, then therapists themselves must understand the fundamental nature of the African humanity.

One of the models of human transformation is reflected in the principle of *Ma'at*. *Ma'at* was not simply a principle; it can be more fully understood as a code of conduct and a standard of aspiration. *Ma'at,* for the ancient Africans and for those who embrace its principles today, is characterized by seven cardinal virtues:

- Truth—sincerity in speech, behavior, and character that is in accord with fact.
- Justice—principle of just dealing and right action where fairness and equity reign.
- Righteousness/Propriety—acting in accord with divine or moral law such that one is free from guilt or sin.
- Harmony—proper arrangement or alignment of things such that they function together.
- Order—the natural and harmonious arrangement of things that helps to define one's purpose.
- Balance—stability produced by an even distribution of elements.
- Reciprocity—giving of oneself in ways that honor the ways that we have been blessed in our lives.

Ma'at also defines the five dimensions of the African character (Karenga, 1990). Character in this regard speaks to the notable or distinguishable traits that emerge as one responds to life circumstance. In our opinion, they help to define the elements of a healthy personality where spiritual enlightenment and African self-consciousness are present. The dimensions include:

- Divinity—the interrelationship between each individual and the divine force (Creator) in the universe.
- Teachability—the capacity to know, understand, and share knowledge and wisdom.
- Perfectibility—the transformative process of the human spirit that is always in a state of becoming better.
- Free Will—the capacity to make conscious, deliberate choices to respond to one's reality in ways each of us chooses.

- Moral and Social Responsibility—the mandate to have morally and ethically grounded relations with others.

If therapists desire to facilitate healing and restore wholeness to clients who are in distress, models like these will help to outline more clearly the personality and character dynamics they seek to understand and treat.

THERAPEUTIC PROGNOSIS: CONTRADICTORY FINDINGS

If one attempts to gain an historical overview of mental illness as it relates to African-American populations, an examination of that literature will readily reveal that African-Americans were perceived to be more prone to psychological disorders than Whites and characterized as having higher rates of mental diseases. However, a closer look at the research reveals that although extensive in scope, the literature was often contradictory in its findings. Furthermore, it was clear that many investigations made gross generalizations from their data and/or biased their data with *a priori* assumptions (Thomas & Sillen, 1972). Although the scope of this chapter and this edition limits the time that we can devote to this particular topic, mention should be made of the revised work of Robert Guthrie's *Even the Rat Was White* (1998) and an excellent review article (Fisher, 1969) that, although over 30 years old, has much contemporary relevance.

Fisher reviews the literature on mental illness in Blacks and cites several problems with the research. The first has to do with the conceptualization of the problem, and the fact that service providers employ a different frame of reference than their clients. Ultimately, what emerges as mentally ill or not depends upon how one defines mental illness and his or her frame of reference. More recent reviews continue to show that Blacks are often stereotyped in the psychiatric literature as not being psychologically minded, and lacking the psychological sophistication and motivation necessary for successful psychotherapy, thus having a primitive character structure, and as being too jovial to be depressed and too impoverished to experience objective loss (Adebimpe, 1981). This tendency to misdiagnose and overdiagnose severe psychopathology has persisted despite the awareness of social-cultural differences between Blacks and Whites brought about by the Black

Revolution (King, 1978). Even in contemporary service delivery, Adebimpe (1981) was quick to recognize that Black patients run a higher risk of being misdiagnosed as schizophrenics, whereas White patients showing identical behaviors are more likely to receive diagnoses as depressed.

A second issue discussed by Fisher (1969) has to do with the fact that statistically, mental illness is sometimes defined as persons who are admitted to treatment. Fisher then cites research that suggests that in some cases, Blacks are admitted to hospitals faster than Whites. The third issue he addresses is the fact that most research on race or mental illness historically use state facilities for subject pools. Therefore, one would expect an uneven distribution of Black and other low socioeconomic status S.E.S. populations in state versus private facilities. The fourth issue has to do with the fact that assessment of illness rates is also measured by incidence (number of new cases) and prevalence (total number of cases present in a population at a given time). Therefore, since there are significantly higher numbers of Blacks in state hospitals, and research samples were taken from state hospitals, obvious biases result when incidence and prevalence data from those institutions were used for assessing mental illness. These biased samples then were used to make generalizations about Black people as a whole.

The contemporary literature appears to be a little more sensitive to race and ethnicity and less biased in the assumptions and conclusions. In fact, although the literature on rates of mental illness is infiltrated with demographic indicators, one is now hard-pressed to find the blatantly biased studies of previous decades where African-descent people were characterized as a more mentally disordered population.

According to the *Archives of General Psychiatry* (1994), 24% of all 18- to 24-year-olds will experience some form of mental illness during their lifetime. Slightly less than 3% (2.6%) will be afflicted with a severe mental disorder. Although people experience different types of mental illnesses, depression continues to be the most frequently occurring mental disorder in the country, followed by alcoholism and phobias (irrational fears and anxiety). Demographic trends seem to suggest that among children, rates of mental illness appear to be the same until late adolescence. Then, girls tend to experience and manifest more distress. Among the elderly, rates are increasing with incidence of dementia (impaired intellectual functioning) and Alzheimer's disease on the rise. Mental illness continues to be associated with low socioeconomic status, as data indicate that individuals and families with incomes below $19,000 a year are twice as likely to develop a mental disorder as those earning $70,000 or more.

What data are available on African-Americans and mental disorders are interesting and somewhat contradictory. Fabrega, Ulrich, and Mezzich (1993) compared the profiles and charts of 613 African-American adolescents to 1,577 of their White counterparts who were treated in a university-based facility. Although Caucasians showed greater clinical morbidity with a higher number of Axis I symptoms (i.e., eating disorders), African-Americans showed higher levels of symptoms such as social aggression and conduct disorders. Interestingly, the authors speculated about possible referral bias, because Blacks were referred to psychiatric facilities with lower levels of diagnosed clinical psychopathology, but higher levels of social oppositional behavior.

The trend toward African-Americans having fewer clinical symptoms when referred was also echoed by Kendall, Sherman, and Bigelow (1995). In their study of 69 Black and 25 White polysubstance abusers seeking outpatient detoxification, they found White subjects reporting significantly more psychiatric symptoms as rated by the Symptom 90 Checklist (SCL-90). These data, however, were contrasted by the study of Munley, Vacha-Haase, and Busby (1998), who reported a somewhat different outcome. Their sample of 65 Black and 164 White psychiatric inpatients who were administered the Millon Clinical Multiaxial Inventory-II (MCMI-II) showed scale elevations for Black patients on Histrionic, Narcissistic, Paranoid, Drug Dependent, and Delusional Disorder. However, a second analysis (MANOVA) with match samples for primary diagnosis revealed no significant differences.

In elderly populations, Hargrove, Stoeklin, Haan, and Reed (1998) compared 207 Black and 1,818 White patients with Alzheimer's disease. They reported that African-Americans had: (1) less education and higher rates of hypertension, (2) shorter durations of illness at the time of initial diagnosis of dementia, and (3) more frequently reported insomnia and less frequently reported anxiety.

These data provide examples of more recent studies that report incidence and prevalence of mental disorders in African-American and other populations. Although the reports do show varying rates of clinical symptomatology, it would be inaccurate to assume that any one segment of the population is more prone to mental illness than another. In fact, Adebimpe (1994), in his article entitled "Race, Racism, and Epidemiological Surveys," describes some of the factors that may lead researchers to find higher prevalence rates of mental disorders in particular populations (i.e., Black). They include racial differences in help-seeking behavior, likelihood of involuntary commitment (based on race), representation of research samples, presentation of psychiatric symptoms and resulting diagnosis, accuracy (validity) of psychological tests, and disparities in treatment.

Regardless of the rates of mental disorders in African-Americans, there is some evidence to suggest that African-Americans cope with the burden of caring for a psychologically impaired loved one. Pickett, Vraniak, Cook, and Cohler (1993) compared Black and White parents on coping mastery ability and self-esteem scores and found Black parents to have higher self-esteem scores and lower levels of depression.

HISTORICAL TRENDS

Another interesting analysis related to African-American people in the process of therapy was written by Block (1980), and questions arise as to whether her analysis is still relevant as we move to the new millennium. Block suggested that the status of Black people in psychotherapy could be understood via several trends. The first trend, which spanned the first half of this century, indicated that Blacks were depicted as persons limited in cognitive, emotional, and social abilities who were, or should be, content with their low status because of their relative immaturity compared to the dominate White culture (Thomas & Sillen, 1972). This emphasis on immaturity and innate limited abilities led White clinicians and other researchers to diagnose higher rates of hysteria and impulse character disorders among Blacks. The second trend discussed by Block began to take shape around the end of World War II when there were large numbers of Black servicemen being treated by White psychiatrists. The psychological literature then began to focus on Blacks' suspicion, hostility, and distrust of White therapists and their preoccupation with discussing racial issues during therapy sessions. These characteristics, according to Block, were interpreted either as resistance or as manifestations of early psychotic processes with diagnosis such as incipient paranoia, uncontrolled aggressive reactions, and chronic schizophrenia being assigned to those Black patients. The third trend began to take shape during and after the Civil Rights/Black Power era when the psychological literature on Blacks shifted to an acceptance of the need for Blacks to develop different defensive coping styles to handle their environmental realities.

Racial consciousness, anger, and distrust could now be viewed as appropriate, adaptive behavior (Grier & Cobbs, 1968), particularly since such characteristics were being proposed and validated by Black and other minority psychologists. Regardless of whether or not these characteristics were seen as normal or abnormal, the assignment of these particular descriptors to Black patients made them poor candidates for psychotherapy in the eyes of many White clinicians.

From time to time, we continue to ask our students to detail for us what characteristics they would like to find in their "ideal" patient whom they might see in therapy. Whether we sample graduate or undergraduate students, or even some professionals, we continue to see a familiar pattern. The characteristics most highly valued in clients continue to be:

1. Intelligent
2. Motivated
3. Verbal
4. Attractive
5. Ability to pay
6. Articulate person
7. Personable
8. Trusting
9. Disclosive

Once this list has been generated, students and other people sampled readily agree that these are the characteristics of their "ideal" client. We then asked our respondents to examine the psychological literature as well as generic societal stereotypes in an attempt to ascertain the degree of congruence (correlation) between characteristics most highly valued in typical clients and those stereotypically associated with persons from different ethnic groups. Figure 6–1 represents an illustration of how closely Black clients are perceived to mirror those qualities most highly valued in ideal clients, particularly when compared to their White counterparts. The figure accurately illustrates how closely therapeutic stereotypes of typical White clients match those characteristics most highly valued in ideal client populations. Conversely, the figure is equally clear in illustrating how stereotypic attitudes of Black clients conflict with those characteristics most highly valued in ideal clients. Based on these generalizations and the charac-

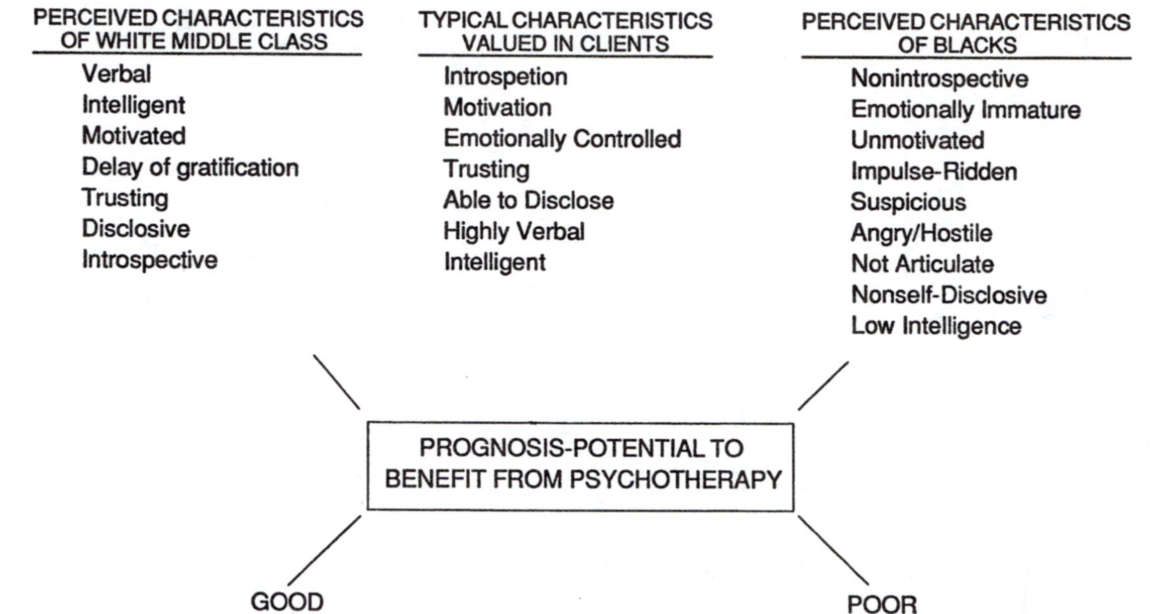

FIGURE 6–1 Characteristics Valued in Black and White Clients

teristic portrayals of Blacks, many Black patients were assumed to be poor candidates for psychotherapy. Stereotypic presentations of Black clients set the tone for stereotypic treatment of Blacks. If Black patients continue to be characterized as being less verbal, impulse ridden, more concrete than abstract in thought, and having difficulty dealing with intrapsychic material, it was thought that therapists might be encouraged to adopt more action-oriented versus insight-oriented therapeutic strategies when working with Black patients (Kincaid, 1969; Smith, 1977).

The explosion of the multicultural counseling literature and those articles concerned with treating African-Americans in therapy have helped to challenge some of the stereotypes about appropriate treatment options (Sue & Sue, 1990; Carter, 1995; Parham & Helms, 1981, 1985; Ponterotto et al., 1995). African-Americans are exposed to insight-oriented therapies (i.e., psychodynamic, Gestalt), are assessed with supposedly more culturally relevant assessment instruments (i.e., MMPI-II) and diagnostic nosologies (DSM-IV), and are treated by clinicians in public and private treatment facilities. Although these advancements have been applauded by many people, it may be overstating the case to assume that African-American clients in therapy are receiving the best treatment.

One of the challenges for this new millennium is to ascertain just how committed the disciplines of counseling and psychology are to effectively treating African-American clients and patients. If the commitment is superficial, then "dressing up" or otherwise disguising traditional approaches to treatment with a few layers of cultural relevance will be the outcome. If, however, the commitment is genuine, then much more work must be done on presenting new conceptual paradigms, developing culturally grounded assessment instruments, and utilizing therapeutic approaches that are anchored in an African-centered framework or worldview.

African-American psychologists and those who are serious about treating African-descent people cannot fall victim to the former. The spirit of self-determination and the cries of our people demand that we embrace the latter.

HELP-SEEKING BEHAVIORS IN AFRICAN-AMERICANS

Contemporary service delivery models in some respect represent a shift away from hospitalization and institutionalization to more outpatient and community mental health center facilities. Unfortunately, even those facilities are in danger of folding, and many have closed under a climate of state and federal government cutbacks and managed care. Despite this shift, African-American patients and clients are still underrepresented and underserved. This suggests that the majority of African-American persons needing some type of psychological care are not receiving such. Historically, of those who began treatment, better than 50% of them discontinue treatment after the initial session (Sue, 1977). Although several factors were cited for this alarming statistic, diagnosis and treatment by non-Black therapists was often implicated. Other factors included differential expectations between clients and therapists and service by paraprofessional versus professional workers. Unfortunately, reports from the nineties yield similar conclusions.

Examination of literature suggested by and large that therapy or counseling have not been adequately utilized by African-American people to deal with their problems. In fact, African-descent people are more likely to rely on traditional support networks (relatives, grandmothers, ministers) during times of stress, anxiety, and tension. The conclusions from the contemporary literature are not much different from those of the past. There is, however, more specificity to the analysis, which provides a greater insight into the conditions and circumstances that motivate a person to seek any type of assistance. Neighbors (1991), in his *National Survey of Black Americans,* reports that decisions to seek help were related to problem severity and type of problem. When the client's presenting problem was rated high on severity, there was a greater likelihood of seeking help for a physical ailment. For other types of personal problems, less than half of the more than 1,300 respondents sought assistance from traditional sources (physicians, human services, etc.). Neighbor's data also revealed that women are more likely than men, and younger African-Americans (18–24 years) are less likely than older groups, to seek help.

If, however, a Black person makes a decision to utilize psychotherapeutic services, it is likely that several factors are involved. Block (1980) discussed these issues sufficiently. The first is an extreme willingness on the part of African-American people to take a risk with the mental health system despite a negative past and recent history of Blacks with respect to the delivery of psychological services. It is also probable that since African-Americans may initially utilize traditional support networks in times of stress, that these traditional support systems are not functioning effectively for that individual, either because of unavailability or because the person chooses not to use them. Consequently, service providers may see clients who are more debilitated since the amount of time between the presenting problem and therapeutic intervention is apt to be longer.

There is also the possibility that a Black client may display a greater sense of fear and suspiciousness. These feelings are not only stimulated by the prospect of therapy itself, but also by the possibility and probability of working with a non-Black professional, and having to entrust one's life stories and pain to a non-Black person. This sentiment is borne out in studies like Nickerson, Helms, and Terrell (1994). Their data support the hypothesis that higher levels of cultural mistrust negatively predict help seeking attitudes in African-American students. In fact, greater mistrust of Whites was associated with more negative general attitudes about help seeking from clinics staffed primarily by Whites and with the expectation that services rendered by White counselors would be less satisfactory. It is also likely that persons seeking therapeutic services may be partially to well-educated since these individuals tend to have a better understanding for and trust in more traditional psychological services. It is also probable that children and adolescents seen in mental health clinics in community facilities may be referrals from two primary sources. Those include the courts and schools. If such is the case, a clinician can expect to encounter a heightened sense of resistance, suspiciousness, and even hostility from the patient related to what may possibly be a mandated participation in therapy.

RECOMMENDATIONS FOR SERVICE DELIVERY

White (1984) and White and Parham (1990) suggested that in order to increase effectiveness with African-American clients, both African-descent and non-African-descent therapists need to be cognizant of four major issues: (1) the impact of oppression on the lives of Blacks; (2) African-American psychological perspectives as a source of strength; (3) African-American language styles (to facilitate communication); and (4) identity concerns that arise as a result of an admixture of African-American and Euro-American influences. Therapists who plan to work with African-American clients would do well to familiarize themselves with these issues.

Cultural confirmation for White's (1984) suggestions can be found in the writings of other Black psychologists. Block (1980), for example, also talks about therapist errors and cautions service providers about being influenced by and promoting the illusion of color blindness (e.g., "I don't view you as an African-American client, I see you as a human being."). Although the intention of this statement may be admirable, such attitudes implicitly deny the authenticity of one's African makeup, and work against the client's moving toward rediscovering and maintaining Afrocentric values into his or her own life space.

Our observations of Black people lead us to believe that throughout their lives, African-American people will be confronted again and again with the developmental issues of becoming comfortable with one's identity, physical makeup, and ego ideal. These phenomena (issues) are similar to those articulated by Peck (1955) in his discussion of developmental crises of the late adulthood era. His research suggests that individuals in this society must successfully work through issues of identity, body image, and ego in order to gain a sense of self-satisfaction about their lives.

Counselors and other psychological service providers need to recognize that as long as Black people are subjected to racist and oppressive conditions in this society, and are confronted with the question of how much to compromise one's "Blackness" in order to successfully assimilate, they (Blacks) will continue to need therapeutic assistance in struggling with issues of:

1. *Self-differentiation versus preoccupation with assimilation*—where an individual strives to become comfortable with the recognition that he or she is a worthwhile human being regardless of valuation and validation from Whites.
2. *Body transcendence versus preoccupations with body image*—where an individual strives to become comfortable with one's physical self, which may be characterized by a continuum of possibilities ranging from African to Afro-European characteristics (i.e., very dark vs. very light skin, very coarse vs. very straight hair, very thick vs. very thin lips).
3. *Ego-transcendence versus self-absorption*—where a person strives to become secure enough in oneself that they are able to develop personal ego strength by contributing to the uplifting of one's people, rather than oneself exclusively. Such efforts are consistent with the African worldview of "*I* am because *we* are, and because *we* are, therefore, *I* am" (Nobles, 1972; Mbiti, 1970).

In addition to the need for a culturally specific therapeutic knowledge base, psychological service providers in particular, and service delivery agencies in general, need to struggle with the question of how to assist African-American clients in developing a commitment to remain in therapy until their presenting problems are resolved. Earlier in this chapter, we reported that better than 50% of ethnic clients terminate therapy after the initial session (Heitler, 1976; Sue, 1978), yet few service providers have a clue about how to eradicate this dilemma. Unlike their practicing colleagues, however, Fiester and Rudestam (1975) have recognized that lower socioeconomic class patients contributed disproportionately to the dropout rate, with unmet expectations most often being reported as reasons for their dissatisfaction. Differential expectations of clients toward therapists lead clients to expect direct authoritative opinions from therapists while they (clients) sit passively waiting to be cured. Therapists, on the other hand, often expect their clients to be more active and disclosive, and assume a greater sense of responsibility for their concerns, while they practiced a nondirective approach to assessing clients problems. When the expectations of both therapy participants are not met, clients discontinue treatment believing the therapist himself or herself, or the process of therapy, to be ineffective and irrelevant, whereas the therapist is left with images of an uncommitted or even resistant client.

We believe that one approach that continues to have merit and that might assist service providers in facilitating client commitment to treatment is pretherapy education. This procedure involves giving the client an orientation to therapy prior to his or her initial session. Although various mediums (audiotape, printed handouts, etc.) have been used, the strongest research support has been demonstrated using videotape film (Dyke, 1983). Surprisingly, many mental health service delivery units have not adopted pretherapy education in any form; however, we believe that this approach has merit and deserves to be tested further to empirically assess its utility.

The third recommendation centers around the recognition that therapeutic strategies that promote African-centered values are more likely to be effective with an African-American client who also subscribes to that value system. For example, group rather than individual psychotherapy, in some cases, may be a preferred or even more effective mode of treatment for Black clients (Shipp, 1983). Although the notion of using groups is not a new idea (Brayboy, 1971; Yalom, 1975), Shipp contends that clinicians fail to recognize how and why group approaches may be effective with their Black clients. Group approaches help to promote the Afrocentric notion of collective survival, commonality among individuals, mutual cooperation, and shared responsibility, which are traditional values in the Black community. Group approaches also encourage sharing among individual members and facilitate the development of group cohesiveness. Shipp (1983) believes that studies that imply that the cohesiveness that results from sharing experiences and backgrounds has therapeutic value often overlook the relationship that exists between group work and the client's cultural dispositions. Family systems approaches may also be effective modes of treatment because of the reliance on the group. Hines and Boyd-Franklin (1982), for example, document how the utilization of family kinship networks and bonds during the course of therapy with an African-American client provides an important source of support. McAdoo (1981) also suggests that reliance on natural support systems (extended family) rather than institutional supports may reduce feelings of guilt, defeat, humiliation, and powerlessness some clients feel. A further recommendation for service providers seriously interested in effectively treating Black clients is to familiarize themselves with a broad-based curriculum of Afro-American and African psychological principles. Nobles (1986) contends that much of what is meaningful in African psychology has gone unnoticed or unrecognized because of psychologists' and other service providers' inability to understand basic African psychological principles that were revealed to humanity by the ancient Africans through the use of symbolism. If Nobles' contention is accurate (and we suspect it is), it seems possible that suggestions for useful treatment strategies with African-American clients may also become more crystallized if practitioners attempt to understand the symbolism of ancient African teachings.

Nobles (1986) teaches us that in ancient Africa, for example, the symbol of an animal was worshipped as an act of consecration to the vital functions that characterized the animal. "So-called primitive animal worship is not in reality the worship of animals, but a method used to identify and clarify the essential function or law of nature embodied in the particular animal" (p. 34). The jackal, for example, in ancient African thought, was the symbol of judgment and represented the law of digestion. Digestion, in turn, should be viewed as a precise act of innate discrimination and analysis, wherein things ingested into the body, mind, and spirit are transformed into useful energy and separated from that which is to be discarded as waste. In essence, digestion is a destructive-productive process of transformation wherein that which contributes to the survival of the organism is stored by the body and used, and that which has no usefulness to the organism's survival is expelled.

Nobles' interpretation of that law of nature through his understanding of symbolism may have some contemporary relevance for clinicians who work with African-American clients. Oppression, discrimination, and racism are unnatural human phenomena. As such, these conditions are often internalized (ingested) and help to stimulate feelings of confusion, anxiety, anger, guilt, frustration, and self-doubt in Black and African-American people. Sometimes, these factors cause them to become disconnected from self as well as other African-Americans in spirit and in physical proximity. However, the traditional African-centered view of self is contingent upon the existence of an interconnectedness with other Black people. As such, therapists might need to assist clients in reconnecting themselves in body and spirit to other African-American people or at least help them to realize that their personal sense of discomfort (anxiety, guilt, confusion, etc.) may be related to being disconnected from those Black experiences.

It might even be necessary for therapists to assist Black and African-American clients in having a culturally corrected experience whereby the client is assisted in: (1) promoting thoughts, feelings, and behaviors that affirm his or her humanity as a Black person of African descent; and (2) purging from one's mind, body, and spirit those ideas, feelings, and behaviors that prove destructive to oneself as an organism and do nothing to affirm one's humanity as an African-American.

Assisting an African-American client with a culturally corrective experience may also force the therapist to question his or her role within the therapy process itself. Some theoretical orientations assume that the most important role of the clinician working with the client is to be an objective outsider who supports the client in working through his or her issues in ways only important to the client.

Counseling is assumed to be an interactive process in which the therapist attempts to facilitate the client's personal awareness and movement toward self-actualization. Seldom is a therapist expected to align himself or herself with the client or confront the client in ways that might violate the unwritten rule of remaining neutral, anonymous, objective, and a passive listener or observer. However, Basch (1980) reminds us that there is nothing wrong with influencing the client, and there is no ideal way for a therapist to behave. Certainly, nonpsychodynamically oriented theories practice alternate approaches.

Indeed, we would contend that a theoretical orientation that encourages a therapist to be a subjective companion rather than just an objective outsider may be an effective approach with African-American clients. Therapists adopting a subjective companion role attempt to become interpersonally connected to the client (development of a kinship bond), and may be guided by personal biases about what is ultimately best for the client's mental health. The therapist's attitudes are influenced by the recognition that confronting a client about his or her self-destructive attitudes and beliefs may be the catalyst that stimulates a client's movement toward becoming a self-actualizing Black or African-American. Therapists should be cautious, however, about interpreting the client's self-actualization efforts as a process of simply becoming a better individual for self's sake. In the African ethos (Nobles, 1972, 1980, 1986; Mbiti, 1970) the self one seeks to become is related to and influenced by a more collective consciousness defined by the community or group. Unlike Western philosophical systems, the African tradition does not place heavy emphasis on the individual; it is recognized that only in terms of other people does one become conscious of his or her own being. Only through others does one learn his or her responsibilities toward himself or herself and others (Nobles, 1980, p. 29).

THE INFLUENCE OF IDENTITY STATES ON THE THERAPEUTIC RELATIONSHIP

Regardless of which theoretical orientation a psychologist chooses to adopt, one factor seems to remain constant. That is, the *relationship* between the therapist and the client is a vital and necessary part of the therapeutic process (Highlen & Hill, 1984).

Parham (1981, 1989) has recommended that service providers look beyond the skin color of a client, or the clients' racial self-designation (i.e., Black, Negro, African-American) in trying to determine an appropriate therapeutic match. Furthermore, he asserts that recognizing the within-group variability that exists among African-American clients may assist a therapist in understanding how the racial identity attitudes of a client discussed in Chapter 3 may influence the ability to establish a qualitative (workable) relationship with that client (Parham, 1989). Figure 6–2 illustrates how racial identity attitudes impact the ability of the service provider to break down the social distance between himself or herself and the client.

For example, a Caucasian therapist who begins treatment with a Black person possessing pro-White/anti-Black attitudes will have little

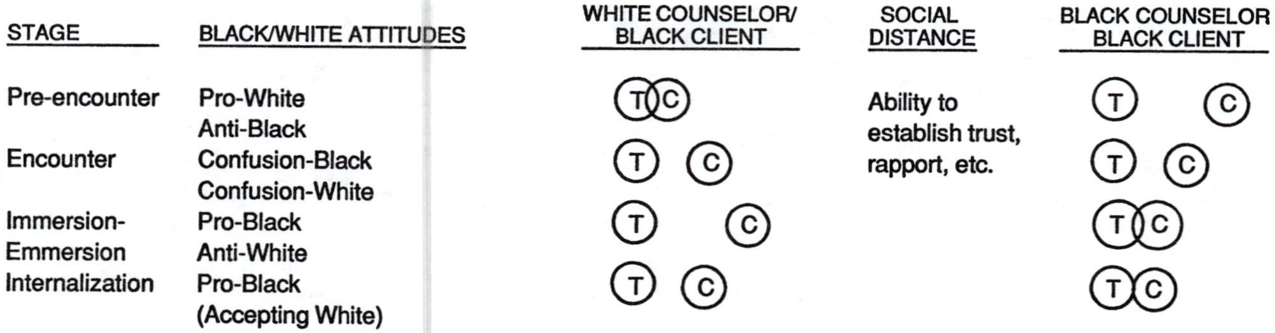

STAGE	BLACK/WHITE ATTITUDES	WHITE COUNSELOR/ BLACK CLIENT	SOCIAL DISTANCE	BLACK COUNSELOR BLACK CLIENT
Pre-encounter	Pro-White Anti-Black	(T)(C)	Ability to establish trust, rapport, etc.	(T) (C)
Encounter	Confusion-Black Confusion-White	(T) (C)		(T) (C)
Immersion-Emmersion	Pro-Black Anti-White	(T) (C)		(T)(C)
Internalization	Pro-Black (Accepting White)	(T) (C)		(T)(C)

Parham (1989).

FIGURE 6–2 Relationship Between Social Distance and Racial Identity Attitudes

difficulty breaking down the social distance between himself or herself and the client where ethnicity is concerned. However, one might expect ethnicity to be an obstacle if the client treated by the Caucasian therapist were more immersed in his or her racial identity.

Given this latter scenario, readers should be cautioned against inferring that a relationship between White therapists and Black clients with strong ethnic identification is impossible. Indeed, positive therapeutic work can occur if these issues of the client's perception of the therapist are worked through in the *initial* stages of therapy.

Service providers should also be cautious about assuming that an inability of the client to become "hooked" on the therapy process is indicative of client resistance, and/or factors beyond the therapist's control. Although this may be the case in some instances, it is also possible that the service provider has not spent sufficient time exploring trust issues related to cross-ethnic interactions and relationships.

Figure 6–2 also provides a prediction of the ability of a Black therapist to work with Black clients at various attitudinal stages. This issue is particularly important, since many service providers and even entire agencies assume that a Black staff member is a better therapeutic match for a Black client with strong pre-encounter attitudes. One consequence of such an interaction might be premature termination by the client who believes that the therapist is an "affirmative-action psychologist" who is less qualified than her or his White counterpart, and thus less capable of delivering effective treatment.

In the same context, it is also inappropriate to assume that ethnicity alone and not training is a necessary and sufficient criterion to work with a client. This assumption is also questionable, since most Black service providers receive similar training and degrees as their White counterparts, with little if any ethnic content as part of their core curriculum (Franklin, 1975). Arguably, similarity in ethnic background *may* provide one with a common life experience, but such is not always the case. Certainly, courses in African-American psychology are essential and are considered by us to be a minimum prerequisite for anyone working with Black clients.

TRAINING SERVICE PROVIDERS

Although the disciplines of psychology and counseling struggle with the desire to better serve African-American populations, perhaps no other issue is more important than the training of mental health professionals. After all, serving culturally different clients generally, and African-Americans in particular, does require some requisite knowledge in how to provide the most effective interventions.

In response to this demand for better training, and a recognition of the ethical responsibility to provide culturally sensitive services, training programs have begun to slowly address the issue (Rogers, Ponterotto, Conoley, & Yiese, 1992). We mention "slowly" since Rogers et al. (1992) report that although 90% of training directors in college and university psychology programs and counseling centers agree that multicultural training is essential, 40% of their programs incorporate little, if any, ethnic content into core courses of the curriculum. Despite this alarming trend, Rogers, Hoffman, and Wade (1998) provide other evidence that American Psychological Association (APA) approved counseling psychology programs may be faring somewhat better. In citing Hill and Stroyier's (1992) survey of faculty in such programs, 87% reported offering one multicultural issues course in their curriculum.

Although we applaud the strides that have been made in providing some training over the last decade, we are generally appalled at what passes as acceptable training. Furthermore, we are concerned that the "bar" (standard of excellence or acceptability) is so low that any addition to the curriculum or the faculty is seen as acceptable. In this regard, it is interesting to note that most psychology programs who train therapists/clinicians require an average of five years of study to achieve a doctorate degree and two years for a master's. Included in the standard training curriculum are courses (i.e., personality theory, testing and assessment, psychopathology, counseling/clinical interviewing skills), research training (statistics, measurement, research design, thesis, dissertation), and practicum (hundreds of hours of counseling/clinical training in mental health agencies), little, if any, of which is culturally specific. Yet, it is expected that trainees and professionals alike will develop genuine competence in working with African-Americans in one course on "multicultural counseling," where ethnicity is but one of several demographic dimensions (i.e., gender, sexual orientation) covered during a single semester. Is it any wonder that clinicians are ill-equipped to treat African-Americans effectively?

One of the more promising movements to emerge in the counseling field in particular is the focus on the development of competency in specific areas (Sue, Arredondo, & McDavis, 1992). In their presentation of cultural competence requirements, Sue, Arredondo, and Mc-

Davis (1992) suggested that the domains of competence should include awareness, knowledge, and skills. The promise of this effort lies in the ability to identify specific areas of expertise and training needed to consider one's self skilled enough to work with culturally different populations.

Despite this promising practice and the revisions it has undergone, a limitation of this approach is its reliance on generic principles of multicultural theory and practice to treat what may be very unique cultural groups. Certainly, similar critique was leveled at Sue, Ivey, and Pedersen (1997) by Parham (1997) as he evaluated the efficacy of their Multicultural Counseling and Therapy (MCT) model. Parham (1997) advocates for, and we support, the development of a more culturally specific set of competencies from which to train clinicians.

Although space and the focus of this text do not allow for a thorough and comprehensive detailing of the components of a counseling competency model for African-Americans, we do want to provide a framework for this. In doing so, we embrace the structure of the model provided by Sue, Arredondo, and McDavis (1997) in highlighting the awareness, knowledge, and skill dimensions of cultural competency for African-centered psychology and therapy. We believe these attributes are essential for anyone working with African-American populations.

AFRICAN-AMERICAN PSYCHOLOGY PROPOSED PRACTICE COMPETENCIES (PARHAM, 1999)

Awareness

- Therapists must be cognizant of his or her own personal biases and assumptions about African-descent people.
- Therapist must be aware of how they have been impacted by the MAAFA, a great disaster of death and destruction beyond human comprehension and convention. The chief feature is the denial of the humanity of African people (Ani, 1994) and how the residuals from those experiences impact their lives.
- Therapist must be aware of his or her own role as "healers."
- Therapist must have access to his or her own historical memories about the majesty of African life and culture as well as the pain and tragedy of historical and contemporary Black suffering.

- Therapist must be aware of how people and elements in the universe are interconnected.
- Therapist must have a sense of his or her own essence as spirit and be in touch with his or her own spirituality.
- Therapist must have a relationship with the divine force in the universe.
- Therapist must have strong knowledge of himself or herself and provide answers to the three critical questions: Who am I?; Am I who I say I am?; Am I all I ought to be? (Fanon, 1966).
- Therapist must have a sense of his or her own ethnic consciousness, which is not simply anchored in race (biology), but in the shared struggle and collective heritage of African people.
- Therapist must have a vision for African-descent people that embraces the transformative possibilities of the human spirit.
- Therapist must be aware of how to move from possessing intellect to dispensing wisdom.

Knowledge

- Knowledge of African psychology and history in ancient Kemetic, historical African, and contemporary African-American societies.
- Knowledge of the essential components of an African-centered worldview.
- Knowledge of the principle of *Ma'at.*
- Knowledge of the limitations of traditional Euro-American psychological perspectives when applied to African-descent people.
    - ◊ Knowledge of how science has been used as a tool of oppression.
    - ◊ Knowledge of the limitations of traditional approaches to therapy.
- Knowledge of the characteristics and dynamics of personality development.
    - ◊ Dimensions of the soul (Akbar, 1994; Nobles, 1986).
    - ◊ Dimensions of African character (i.e., Ma'at).
    - ◊ Models of nigrescence (i.e., Cross, Thomas, Parham & Helms).
    - ◊ Models of African self-consciousness (*Kambon,* 1995).
- Knowledge of assessment instruments appropriate for use with African-descent adults, youth, and children.
- Knowledge of the limitations of traditional assessment instruments when used with African-Americans.

- Knowledge of therapeutic rituals.
- Knowledge of the diagnostic nosologies used to classify disordered behaviors in African-Americans.
- Knowledge of the ethical principles germane to treating African-descent people.
- Knowledge of how traditional ethical standards of some psychological and counseling associations may be culturally inappropriate for African-descent people.
- Knowledge of a geopolitical view of African people and their condition in America and throughout the world.
- Knowledge of what racism and White supremacy are and how individual, institutional, and cultural racism impact the lives of African-descent people.
- Knowledge of traditional help-seeking behaviors in African-Americans.
- Knowledge of communities, institutions, and resources that provide both tangible and intangible support to the African-American community.
- Knowledge of the dynamics of family in the African-American community.

Skills

- Ability to maximize congruence between healing messages and proper conduct.
- Ability to connect with, bond with, or otherwise establish rapport with African-American clients.
- Ability to conduct and participate in rituals.
- Ability to hear both the surface structure and deep structure messages as client communicates.
- Ability to administer and interpret culturally appropriate assessment instruments.
- Ability to advocate on behalf of clients to social agencies and institutions.
- Ability to utilize theories and constructs in forming diagnostic impressions.

7

Praxis in African-American Psychology: Theoretical and Methodological Considerations

> In every discipline there are thinkers, visionaries; persons whose thinking and ideas are so advanced that they appear to be beyond the scope of reason. While most scholars simply seek answers, these visionaries seek to ask better and better questions; and as a result they often present us with answers long before we've had a chance to formulate the right questions. These thinkers tend to grapple with present day issues in ways that often illuminate the way to the future; in effect by dealing intelligently with the present they help the rest of us prepare for tomorrow. The late W. Curtis Banks was such a person, his genius and commitment to the psychological well-being of African Americans was unparalleled. This chapter is dedicated to the spirit of his genius and life work. (Ajamu, 1999)

THE VALUE OF PRAXIS IN AFRICAN-AMERICAN PSYCHOLOGY

From its inception African-American psychology has been concerned with three fundamental issues: (1) the need defend and protect African-Americans from the pernicious use of culturally biased psychological theories, methods, and paradigms; (2) the development of theories, methodologies, and paradigms that help to give meaning to the African-American cultural experience; and (3) the need to humanize Western psychology by making it more pluralistic and inclusive of the multiplicity of human expression. It is those three fundamental issues with which this chapter is principally concerned.

Praxis is the self-conscious attempt to insure that maximum congruence is achieved between thought and practice. In this regard, this chapter is meant to be an examination of the self conscious attempt by African-American psychology to insure that maximum congruence is achieved among the three aforementioned fundamental issues. Thus praxis as a conceptual tool allows both for reflection on the state of the field and representation in the form of future directions the field might pursue.

BLACK PSYCHOLOGY AS A DISCIPLINE: PARADIGMATIC CONCERNS, THEORETICAL AND METHODOLOGICAL CHALLENGES

Achieving the paradigmatic coherence, theoretical consistency, and methodological conciseness necessary to fashion a discipline can be an arduous and protracted process that often involves extended periods of discourse and debate before a tenuous agreement (i.e., consensus of compromise) can be made about the philosophic foundations upon which the discipline should be grounded. When this precarious agreement about the nature of reality (ontology), the relationship of that reality to the larger world (cosmology), the implications of that knowledge for human interactions (axiology), and the parameters of that knowledge (epistemology) are arrived at by critical mass of well-trained thinkers, then the conditions of possibility for the creation of a discipline can be said to exist.

However, in order for this tenuous agreement to be achieved and more importantly, maintained, most of the thinkers engaged in this process must share or at least agree upon the same set of deep structure cultural assumptions (i.e., ontology, cosmology, epistemology, etc.). The resultant worldview such that the paradigms, theories, and methodological conventions in turn generates, governs the pursuit of knowledge and gives rise to the subsequent epistemological assumptions (evidence), all of which defer to and are consistent with the worldview that brought the discipline into being in the first place. The results are paradigms upon which the construction of theories and methods that verify, validate, authenticate, and exclude particular types of knowledge production rest. This, then, renders these paradigms immune to critiques that operate under a different set of cultural assumptions by generating rules for refutation and critique that rely on the internal cultural logic that spawned the paradigms in the first place (Carruthers, 1972; Banks, 1992; Semaj, 1995). However, when that tenuous consensus about the dimensions and proportions of the field are in turmoil or nonexistent, then the state of the field is said to be preparadigmatic (Kuhn, 1970; Banks, 1992).

As is the case with any emerging discipline, the great difficulty in achieving paradigmatic coherence and methodological consistency speaks to, in no small measure, the lack of fragile consensus about the parameters of knowledge construction and the subsequent evaluation of various approaches to knowledge configuration. That is to say, there has yet to be a tenuous agreement by a critical mass of well-trained African/African-American psychologist about the philosophic foundations upon which the field of Black psychology should be grounded.

Although contemporary discourses in African/African-American psychology have increasingly focused on orienting the field toward an Africentric/African-centered worldview, efforts to create a general unified field of inquiry that explores, examines, creates, and critiques a culturally consistent paradigm and methodology while guiding praxis have been, at best, inconsistent. This is due in part to the lack of philosophic and conceptual clarity as to what constitutes an Africentric/African approach to knowledge construction, and in part to the relative lack of consensus about how best to utilize and incorporate the African/African-American cultural experience into a replicable research methodology that is consonant with the cultural assumptions of African peoples. To put it another way, African-American psychology, like African-Americans, has struggled and continues to struggle with how best to understand, study, and appreciate Africanness in an American context.

Although Black psychology has yet to achieve the paradigmatic coherence necessary for it to achieve disciplinary status, there are a number of areas in which its contribution to psychology has been invaluable. One such area is its critical examination and severe critique of psychology's use of culturally exclusive paradigms, theories, and methodologies as tools of oppression with culturally different groups.

Paradigmatic Challenges in Black Psychology

Numerous scholars have rightly noted that theory and methodology develop out of, in response to, and in defense of the demand functions of a particular worldview (Nobles, 1978; Asante, 1980; Banks, 1982; Boykin, 1991). Hence, there can only be worldview-specific theories and methodologies, which are themselves anchored in culturally derived epistemologies. Moreover, it should be clear that what is authenticated as truth in one culture may not be perceived as truth in another and therefore have little, if any, authenticity, relevance, and/or saliency when applied in a different cultural sphere, other than to perpetuate cultural domination. Therefore, the theoretical and methodological demands for authenticating truth should be developed within culture and be consistent with that culture's worldview orientation, if it is to reveal truths to and about that culture.

Moreover, it should come as no surprise that science (or scholarship) is ideology. Equally apparent is the inescapable reality that theory, method, and methodology do not evolve from an objective and valueless vacuum. Rather, theory and methodology and their resulting products (methods and concepts) evolve in the context of, and in response to, certain sociocultural realities. Within the domains of Western psychology, verificationist empiricism has been the barometer by which the value of modern and postmodern scholarship, inquiry and research have been judged as having value.

Toward that end, the most salient factor in scholarly inquiry and research has been the degree to which theories can be authenticated by data derived from the empirical method. The empirical method, in this regard, thus operates under the guise of objectivity and provides the paradigm within which truth is pursued and evidence of claims are verified. It is in this context that it has been advanced that the role of theory is to expose ideas optimally to falsification (Feyerabend, 1978).

However, upon closer scrutiny it appears that objectivity is an illusion maintained, in part, by conceding that although the projects (i.e., theories) and products (i.e., empirical evidence) may at times be fraught with cultural, social, political, economic, and psychological biases, the prevailing logic argues that the processes (i.e., methodologies) of Western research and inquiry are nonetheless objective—and thus universal. Hence, in psychology the prevailing logic posits that if a problem exists at all, it lies with construction of the theories and interpretation of the evidence and not with the methodological protocols that guide the modes of inquiry. Accordingly, it has been posited in various ways that the projects (i.e., theories) and processes (i.e., methodologies) of academia in the West are part and parcel of an "objective" endeavor to authenticate truths about temporal and spatial phenomena based on objective appeals to empirical evidence.

However, a closer look behind the veil of universality and the "illusion of objectivity" reveals the obverse. The methodological demands of scholarship in psychology have not given rise to objective efforts to reconcile theoretical postulates through an appeal to evidence but rather to protect them "subjectively" from it. As Professor Curtis Banks has rightly noted, "theory is bound by particular methodological protocols and by the worldview that governs the specific paradigm within which the scholarly community operates." Furthermore, it should be clear that theory and methodology are culture-bound, that is to say that they are derived from a people's worldview and concomitant assumptions about the nature of reality. In the West, scientific notions of what constitutes truth, and by extension evidence, are invariably connected to the Western epistemological assumption of "ontological corporeality" or the belief in material reality. Hence the paradigms, theories, and methodologies in Western psychology are all derived from and informed by the belief of material reality as the only reality.

To illustrate, in the areas of Western psychology and sociology, complex human behavior and its equally complex social order are methodologically reduced to statistical quantification's that then become the evidence upon which psychological and sociological theories are viewed and received as valid. Thus, the whole expanse of human interaction is reduced to what can be measured and quantified, i.e., the material.

With regard to theory, the function of theory in the West has not been to advance ideas but simply to justify them. Thus, in Western episteme, inconsistencies in the theory are rectified not by discounting the theory as invalid, but rather by simply finding the right method to explain away the inconsistencies in the theory. For example, one need only to trace the invidious Western theories regarding African intelligence from Francis Galton's theory of eugenics in 1869 (see *Hereditary Genius: Its Laws and Consequences*), to Arthur Jensen's theory of the heritability of intelligence and the concomitant intellectual inferiority of Africans in America (see *Educability and Group Difference*, 1973) to Murray and Hernsteins' *Bell Curve* (1995) to get a firm grasp of ways in which the "theory" of African intellectual inferiority has been protected despite its myriad "falsifications" (refutations). In this regard, it has been the theory of African intellectual inferiority that remained constant, whereas only the methodologies employed in pursuit of proving the theory correct have changed. Toward this end, it is apparent that the purpose of methodology in psychology has served to protect theory from refutation rather than expose it to refutation.

With regard to the science of Western psychology, the verificationist-empiricist orientation has been in operation and advanced as the objective (e.g., culturally neutral and thus universal) method. Hence, appeals to evidence are mediated and authenticated by the conventional framework of this verificationist-empiricist method. Thus, in Western psychology, material evidence, which is statistically quantifiable and therefore empirically verifiable (and thus consistent with the European worldview and epistemology) is thus believed, *prima facie,* to be the more "authentic" form of evidence. Although the belief in the centrality of spirit, which is consistent with the African worldview and its consonant epistemology, is dismissed as lacking "empirical" reliability and validity (i.e., authenticity). This allows for European-American psychological perspectives, which are rooted in the European cultural experience, to position themselves as the only psychological perspectives worthy of consideration, discourse, and debate. This, then, helps to explain in part, why the African-American psychology movement has been regarded with indifference and apprehension by mainstream psychology and psychologists.

It is in the context of understanding the culturally hegemonic relationship between worldview, paradigms, theory, and method in Western psychology that some African-American psychologists have regarded this approach to understanding African-Americans as useless (Clark, et al., 1975). Arguing this position from that standpoint, we suggest that it is the responsibility of the African-American scholars to reject any system of ideology, theory, and methodology that proves itself to be antithetical to the sociocultural interest of the African community (Clark, et al., 1975; Wilson, 1993).

With this in mind, some African-American psychologists are beginning to advance culturally centered paradigms that seek to articulate and advance the psychocultural integrity of African-Americans while paying attention to the protective demands of theory for an African-centered methodological framework (Akbar, 1991; Boykin, 1994; Myers, 1992; Banks, 1992; Nobles, 1998).

Scholarly and scientific inquiry become extensions of a people's worldview. A codified system of truth makes claims about reality that have cultural relevance, authenticity, and agency. Service and scholarship, then, are intimately connected to the people in whose culture they are anchored (Nobles, 1986; Carruthers, 1972). It is, therefore, the role of the African-American scholar to present the "truth" of one's people in a scientific manner. In effect, the goal of the scholar and scholarship is to help a people make sense of the world in which they live in order to comprehend their cultural reality.

This, then, suggests that when African-American scholars attempt to understand African-American reality by uncritically utilizing Eurocentric paradigms, theories, and methodological frameworks, the scholar may also inherit European-centered biases toward African-Americans and unwittingly produce Eurocentric truths about African-American realities while giving the appearance of producing knowledge about African-Americans. Wade Nobles (1985) has identified this phenomenon as transubstantiation, literally the transference of meaning from one cultural context to another incompatible context. The Black scholar becomes "incarcerated" by the European worldview.

In this vein, a number of African-centered scholars (Akbar, 1991; Ajamu, 1998; Ani, 1994; Nobles, 1998; Azibo, 1996; Wilson, 1978) have suggested that any attempts to uncover, recover, and restore truths about African-Americans must be authenticated by utilizing African-centered paradigm and theories and methodological frameworks rooted in an African worldview. Although African-American psychologists seek to establish a body of knowledge rooted in the best image and interest of African-Americans, they must also seize the ability to help define the African-American reality.

This position raises several questions relative to the establishment of the discipline called Black psychology: (1) Who will define African-American reality, African-Americans or European-Americans?; (2) Upon whose frame of reference, normative assumptions, and worldview will that reality be authenticated; and (3) Whose definitions, theories, and methodologies will attempt to define and explicate that reality? Furthermore, when one acknowledges and understands the axiom "power is the ability to define reality and have other people respond to your definition as if it were their own," the continued need for African-American psychology to assist in defining African-American reality becomes increasingly self-evident.

SEIZING THE POWER TO DEFINE: PRACTICAL APPLICATIONS AND CONSIDERATIONS IN RESEARCH WITH AFRICAN-AMERICANS

In advocating culturally centered modalities, a number of questions and concerns arise that have profound implications for research with culturally different populations: (1) Given the inherent biases in some Western models and methods, should we eschew the use of Western models, theories, and methods? (2) If we simply use African-centered methods, how are we to make sense of our Americanness? (3) What are some of the ways in which we can balance the use of Western and African-centered theories and methods to apprehend a fuller understanding of what it means to be African and American? (4) Can and should researchers from outside a particular culture do research in that culture, and what is lost and what is gained by such an endeavor? In our review of theories and methods thus far, we have discussed a few of the philosophical limitations with utilizing Western models and theories with culturally different populations.

The importance of raising these questions centers around the issue of power. For our purposes here, power is not necessarily military might, brute force, or other similarly material or physical capabilities. In our opinion, knowledge is power and is seen as the ability to define reality and to make other people respond to that definition as if it were their own (Nobles, 1978). Real power lies in the questions we raise, how we raise them, how we investigate them, and what conclusions emerge from our processes of discovery and confirmation, which, in turn, direct our thinking and behavior.

Having said that, let us now direct our attention to the three central aspects of research methods: (1) subjects/participants, (2) instruments, and (3) design and data analysis, as well as some of the limitations, practical applications, considerations, and challenges in attempting to eliminate biases in research methods.

Subjects

There are three areas of concern that need to be addressed regarding the selection of subjects if research with African-Americans and other culturally different groups are to be relevant and inclusive. The first relates to the need to develop samples that are representative of the population being researched. Although this precept is commonly understood, when this principle is applied incorrectly to culturally diverse populations, a number of distortions can occur. For example, the use of demographic indicators like race and socioeconomic status are often conflated with cultural affiliation. In this regard, it is often assumed that because African-Americans share demographic similarities, they also share the same types of attitudes and cultural affinities. This obscures the complexity of the African-American experience by presenting it as monolithic. Moreover, there is an tacit assumption that within-group comparisons involving African-Americans yield little in the way of generalizabilty to shared American cultural practices. In effect, this positions the African-American experience outside its American context and thereby reinforces assumptions about African-American marginalization.

The second limitation has to do with the inherent biases that are created and maintained by many psychological journals' insistence that European-American populations be included in studies involving African-American populations. This has the effect of positioning European-American cultural practices, attitudes, and behaviors as the normative standard by which African-Americans and other culturally diverse populations are to be judged and measured as having value and meaning. For example, Vonnie McLoyd (1991), in attempting to illustrate the difficulty African-American researchers often encounter when trying to convince the "gatekeepers of knowledge (i.e., reviewers) of the merit and interpretability of data" about African-Americans, shares a letter she received from an editorial reviewer:

> The primary problem with this study is the use of only black children as subjects. While race as a summary variable for socialization experiences is indeed of interest for developmental investigations, the fact that it may contribute to observed findings raises the possibility that the present results are truly generalizable or interpretable as they reflect upon findings from prior research. In order to achieve its primary goal, the present study should have had two samples of children, one white and one black, in which case the author(s) would have been able to satisfy any intrinsic interest in the black population, tell other investigators something about the effects of those variables assumed to index intrinsic interest and could have spoken to the prior literature to boot. In the present case, this cannot be done and with the possible differences in subjects between this study and prior ones, it is essentially impossible to evaluate it on the dimension providing foundation for its self-justification: the previous literature on intrinsic interest.

If the present study were expanded to include a white population, then, I think the author(s) should be encouraged to resubmit it for further consideration.

The third limitation has to do with the additional burden that the emphasis on sample size places on researchers attempting to do research with African-Americans and ethnic minority populations. As an illustration, assume that you have designed a study that seeks to understand the effects of being away from home on academic performance for freshman college students. One researcher is interested in only European-American college students. Another researcher is also interested in doing the same study but only with an African-American population. The school both researchers have chosen has a European-American population of 10,000 students, whereas the African-American population is 400. The accepted statistical analysis required for this type of study requires an *N* of 100 (100 subjects) for each population. For the researcher studying the European-American student population, a sample of 1% of the total population is needed to obtain the required sample size of 100. The researcher studying the African-American population would have to obtain a sample equal to 25% of the total African-American student population to achieve the same sample size. This, then, places an unfair burden on the researcher interested in doing research with ethnic minorities to obtain a higher proportion of the population to obtain the same results. There is an increased need to develop methods that are sensitive to the value of sampling techniques that are based on the proportion of the population rather than raw numbers. The problem becomes illuminated when one considers that if the researcher working with the European-American student population had to obtain the same proportion of the population as the researcher working with the African-American student population, they would have obtained a sample size roughly 2500 students.

These limitation are by no means exhaustive; however, they do underscore the importance and necessity of journal editorial boards and tenure review committees to expand their structures to include within-group studies as meaningful and critical to the expansion of knowledge production (McLoyd, 1991). Moreover, the increased inclusion of within-group studies with African-American and other ethnic minority populations serves eventually to eradicate the erroneous assumption that European-American populations are the barometers of normality.

Instruments

With regard to the inappropriateness of using instruments normed on European-American populations and applying them to African-American and other culturally different groups, there have been a number of efforts that have articulated the severe limitations with regard to validity and reliability. Among the more prominent are the ongoing debates on the lack of reliability and validity of intelligence testing with

African-Americans (see Williams, 1972; Williams & Mitchell, 1991) and the inappropriate use of personality measures (i.e., M.M.P.I.; Gynther 1972; Davis and Walkins, 1974) with Black populations.

We continue to hold to the position that instruments of assessment and measurement should be normed and standardized on the populations to which they are administered. With respect to African-Americans, the debate continues about whether existing instruments should be modified, or whether new measuring devices should be developed for use. In all cases, instruments need to be scrutinized to determine the degree to which they can meet reliability and validity criteria. In addition, tests developed by and for different populations promote the values, biases, worldview, and assumptions of that cultural group. Users then should be aware of both the constructs measured by the instrument, as well as the inherent biases connected to its design and construction.

In recognition and response to some of the instrument limitations, a number of researchers have developed and continue to develop culturally sensitive measure that seek to portray accurately the African-American psychological experience. In this regard, Jones (1996) has compiled an index of culturally appropriate instruments for use with African-American populations.

His compendium of measures categorizes various instruments according to their stated purpose and the subpopulations they are intended for (i.e., women, men, adolescents, adults). Those interested in utilizing instruments designed to assess or measure constructs relevant to African-American populations would do well to consult his two-volume text.

Design/Data Analysis

One of the problems with design and data analysis is that its emphasis on quantitative measures has proven itself to be less amenable to understanding the range and complexity of human behavior in general and culturally different populations in particular. There are a number of alternate strategies that can be employed that might yield a fuller and more comprehensive picture of African-American culture. Increased deployment of case studies and ethnographic studies or a intelligent combination of both quantitative and qualitative measures that might help researchers enhance the rigor and relevance of their research efforts is one recommendation.

ORI-IRE: FULFILLING OUR DESTINY—A NOTE TO THE NEXT GENERATION

Ori-Ire is a Yoruba term that means to have one's consciousness properly aligned with one's destiny. This term as a gathering notion speaks to a symbiotic balance between one's ideas and actions. In a worldview that asserts that I am because we are, this then suggests that each person's destiny is inextricably linked to the destiny of the whole community. When that destiny is threatened by racial and cultural opression, then, *Ori-Ire* becomes an emancipatory notion that speaks to one's responsibility for the survival, perpetuation, and maintenance of the group. As psychologists, scholars, thinkers, and healers, *Ori-Ire* then speaks to our responsibility to help define, defend, and develop the psychocultural integrity of African peoples. As African-Americans proceed into the 21st century, it is becoming increasingly apparent that African-American psychologists will be presented with a plethora of unprecedented challenges. These challenges will be presented in the forms of a myriad of societal conundrums confronting the African-American community: The increased morbidity and mortality rates, the protracted disintegration of the extended family structure, a shifting and rapidly eroding African-American value orientation, as well as an intensification in impoverishment and disenfranchisement.

Toward this end, the survival of African-Americans in the next millennium will in, large part, be predicated on the ability of African-American psychologists, among others, to recognize and respond to those and other issues that impinge on the quality of life for African-Americans. In this regard, several vital questions arise with regard to the use of Western paradigms, theories, and methodologies: (1) Are African-American psychologists and future mental health care practitioners receiving the training necessary to respond to and emend the specific psychocultural conditions that currently confront African-Americans? (2) Is there anything in the course of their training in Western psychology that will prepare future researchers and practitioners to deal with problems that are created as a result of racism and cultural oppression (i.e., the disintegration of the African family; teenage pregnancy; the open season on African-American men, both young and old; the crack pandemic; or the existential dilemmas) that results from adopting an alien worldview and trying to balance two diametrically opposed cultural orientations? (3) Is it intelligent to expect that theories and methodologies that were designed, developed, and formed to explicate a European psychic reality in a vastly different time and place can simply be transposed on to an African-American reality and still maintain their efficacy and integrity without deleterious implications for African-Americans? (4) Can African-American psychologists use European-American conceptual tools to comprehend correctly African-American psychocultural realities?

Although the renewed call for relativism, pluralism, and inclusivity in some psychological circles (Segall, Lonner & Berry, 1998) may be a recent and welcome phenomenon, it is important to note that from its inception Black psychology has argued and attempted to advance a notion of psychology that was at once emancipatory and inclusive. From Joe White's (1970) appeal for a psychological approach that embraced the humanity of African-Americans to Naim Akbar's call for "The evolution of a human psychology," to Linda J. Myers's articulation of an optimal psychology that is human, healing, and profoundly powerful, African-American psychology has been at the forefront of the call for inclusivity. Perhaps this was because our humanity has always been under scrutiny or perhaps it was something in the historical legacy of African-Americans that would not allow them to deny the humanity of others. Whatever the case, it has been a part of the legacy of Black psychology to be inclusive and pluralistic. African-Americans have always known that Eurocentic assertions that African-Americans were monolithic group was a fiction. Historically, it has been this tolerance for and appreciation of diversity in the midst of a climate of racial hostility, violence, and cultural chauvinism that ensured the survival of the African-American community. The next generation of African-American psychologists would be well served to remember its history. Frantz Fanon once said "each generation out of relative obscurity must seek out its mission and either fulfill it or betray it." If Black psychology is to grow and fulfill its mission, it would do well to remember its past.

8

AFRICAN-CENTERED PSYCHOLOGY IN THE 21ST CENTURY: ISSUES CONFRONTING THE AFRICAN-AMERICAN COMMUNITY

The excitement that characterizes the arrival of the new millennium is instigating thoughts about how best to prepare to meet future challenges. For a people who have had to endure the 19th- and 20th-century horrors of slavery, Jim Crow, segregation, discrimination, racism, etc., the prospect of entering the next century with the promise of a better tomorrow is indeed pleasant.

The fact that significant and noteworthy progress has been made in the African-American struggle for freedom and liberation is undeniable. The political landscape is different in many ways; access to education has improved and the potential for a more economically viable life space has increased. However, despite the real and imaginary progress that some perceive in life, it is clear that continued progress for African-descent people will not come without legitimate struggle. In fact, it was the brilliant poet Langston Hughes who reminded us that indeed, life is not always a crystal stair.

It is in that context that we highlight three issues that we think our community will need to struggle with. In the second edition of this text, we discussed male-female relationships, the endangered

Black male, and the developing social competencies. In this third edition, we want to highlight coping with racism and oppression, confronting the social pathology of the American workplace; and issues impacting African-American women. Like the previous edition, our intention in presenting these topics is not meant to suggest that these issues are the only ones germane to the African-American community. Rather, by including them in this chapter, we acknowledge that in the mental health centers, classrooms, and communities across this country where we work, these topics frequent the discourse. Through this presentation, we hope to challenge each of you to think more critically about the condition of African-descent people and how we can utilize the principles and practices of African-centered psychology to address them in meaningful and effective ways.

COPING WITH RACISM AND OPPRESSION

> "If you don't understand (racism) and White supremacy, what it is, and how it functions, everything else you think you understand, will only confuse you." (Fuller, 1971)

In his text, *The Souls of Black Folks,* it was W. E. B. DuBois himself who prophetically argued that race and the color line would be the problem of the 20th century. Now as we enter the 21st century, many of us wonder whether real and substantial progress has been made in the area of race relations.

There are many who would point to the historical markers of social justice as indicative of progress. Certainly, we may hesitate to argue against achievements like school desegregation, civil rights, voting rights, and affirmative action as reasonable measures. One might also point to the purported declines in overt racism by Whites toward Blacks as evidence of progress in dealing with the color line. Even President Bill Clinton has called for national conversation on race and commissioned a panel of experts to develop a strategic plan for addressing the problem. And yet, there is a restlessness in our spirit that reacts with skepticism to this notion of progress because we know that there are some roads to progress we as a society have not traveled extensively enough. Whether progress is illusory or not will undoubtedly be the subject of continued debate. In this regard, evidence of African-American progress in areas such as education, politics, employment, and economics will be contrasted with arguments citing, for example, Blacks being disproportionately represented in hate crime statistics throughout the counties and cities of this country.

Redefining Progress and Problems

In a Eurocentrically oriented American society that values a material orientation to reality, giving underrepresented people more access to geographical space (i.e., desegregated schools, busses, restaurants, employment) seems like something to celebrate. Yet, the small victories African-Americans have fought for and won obscure what should be the real focus of our analysis. Why has racism been so slow to change? We believe it is because the only people by and large who advocate against it are African-American and other non-White people. As mental health professionals, educators, or concerned citizens, it is important to recognize that the substance and foundation of intolerance cannot be revealed by examining the subjects of imposition. Rather, intolerance must be analyzed by examining the psyche of the imposer. Clearly, the pillars that support intolerant and racist attitudes are not composed of the sensitivities and human frailties of the oppressed. Rather, they are made up of the hardened steel hearts and concretized attitudes of the oppressive group. It is time that our society came face-to-face with the fact that racism is not an African-American or a people-of-color problem; it is a White people's problem. Until Whites decide to clean up their house, little progress will continue to be made. Clearly, it is time that we focus on the victimizer rather than just the victim.

Theoretical Models

In shifting our focus to the larger White community, the psychological and sociological literature has introduced us to some promising theories in this regard. Certainly, Janet Helms's model and Joe Ponterotto's work on White identity development, John Dovidio's concept of the aversive racists, and Michael D'Andrea's model of White reactions to multicultural progress are four noteworthy examples. Others whose work is noteworthy in this regard are Judy Katz in her 1978 work on White awareness and antiracism training; Rita Hardeman in her 1982 writings on White identity development; Jean Phinney in her 1990 work on ethnic identity development in adolescents and adults; and Michelle Fine, Lois Weis, Linda Powell, and L. Mun Wong's 1997 excellent scholarly book entitled *Off White*.

As we seek to employ the constructs of these and other theories, we are struck by how useful these concepts are in categorizing the thoughts, feelings, and behavior of Whites. Helms, for example, in her text *A Race Is a Nice Thing to Have,* argues that White people have difficulty in both admitting that they are White and admitting that they possess racial attitudes associated with their cultural/racial group. She further asserts that in their interactions with African-Americans and other people of color, White people move through a series of stages or phases (*contact* through *autonomy*) that involve a recognition of racism in the evolution of self-protective strategies to contend with it.

However, despite the promise of these theories, their utility seems limited at some level by their failure to provide some necessary insight into the underlying motivation of Whites who are characterized by these models. Using these theories as an interpretive lens, we can clearly label particular attitudes and/or situational responses as belonging to a particular stage or state, or coinciding with a specific principle. What is more difficult, however, is to understand the motives behind the behaviors.

Understanding A Racist Mentality

To begin a constructive dialogue on understanding the racist's mentality will require that we rely on some nontraditional sources to inform our thinking. We cannot afford to become conceptually incarcerated by utilizing a narrow framework of overused definitions that constrict our discourse. What then should we use? We could begin, for example, with James Jones's seminal work *Prejudice and Racism* (2nd edition) as he begins to both define the concept of racism and offer solutions for attacking the problem.

In defining the concept, Jones recognizes that racism is a multidimensional construct in that individual thought, feeling, and response (cognitive, affective, and behavioral) dimensions of one's personality are guided in a direction that negatively impacts upon the lives of others. Furthermore, he illustrates how the process of racism intersects at individual, institutional, and cultural levels, allowing for an analysis of some potentially complex dynamics where Whites are seen as the institutional gatekeepers of a racist system. Thus irrespective of how one comes to understand the concept of racism, there is little doubt that its origins, promotion, and continuation are anchored in the context of how Whites relate to African-descent people and other people of color on individual, institutional, and cultural levels.

In an effort to probe deeper into the psyche of Whites, we could offer up the analyses by Dr. Frances Cress-Welsing or Sister Marimba Ani as well. In her text *The Isis Papers,* Cress-Welsing advances the Cress theory of color confrontation. In it, she posits that the foundation of White people's oppression against African-Americans rests with their anxiety over their numerical inadequacy. This inadequacy around their inability to produce offspring of color, it is believed, instigates in them a sense of defensiveness that manifests itself in an uncontrollable sense of hostility and aggression. Delving further into the psyche of White people, Cress-Welsing discusses a number of defense mechanisms that serve to protect White people's ego from this anxiety and deep-seated fear. Among those considered most salient are repression (of the painful fears) and reaction formation, which is a psychological response that converts something desired and envied into something that becomes the object of degradation and disgust. Racism, then, and a plan of global White supremacy, become the ultimate manifestation of hostility and rejection they (Whites) feel toward themselves.

In seeking to offer a less psychoanalytically oriented but equally penetrating analysis of the White psyche, Marimba Ani introduces us to her text *Yurugu.* In it, she discusses the evolution of White European-American peoples' imposition on African people in America and throughout the Diaspora. In helping us to deconstruct the thought processes of White people, Ani helps us to explain the habitual ways that White people exercise their influence over people of color. While introducing us to a new African-centered vocabulary to facilitate the understanding of White people, Ani concludes that their cultural nature of aggressiveness, distrust, hostility, and competitiveness makes it difficult, if not impossible, to form genuine, authentic relationships with African-Americans and other people of color. The basis for White peoples' response dimensions (thoughts, feelings, behaviors) toward others is then assumed to be the manifestation of an incomplete despiritualized self in search of fulfillment and equilibrium it has yet to find. The chronic disharmony, then, distorts the nature and aim of their spirituality (i.e., life force) such that emotional security becomes anchored in material possession and control and thus instinctive reaction of Whites toward others is an insatiable desire for power and domination.

In contrast we might utilize the writings of Michael D'Andrea and Judy Daniels (both of whom are White) who argue that White racism is rooted in both White people's action and inaction. Their work suggests that Whites are indeed racist, but commonly manifest more unintentional-covert forms of the social ill. They imply that most Whites are not only oblivious to their own racist behaviors, but are hesitant to challenge other Whites or institutions about more systematic manifestations.

Progress on the Horizon

Regardless of which explanation seems most plausible, what seems crystal clear is that little progress on the issue of race and race relations can be made unless and until our White brothers and sisters commit to some deep exploration of their past and current behavior toward African-descent people and other people of color. In fact, the process of examining and analyzing the racism phenomenon in Whites is not unlike the metaphor of "cleaning house." In order to achieve the desired outcome (a clean house), one must first identify the dirt and stains; select the cleaning methods and materials necessary; commit oneself to aggressively scrub, sweep, and vacuum the premises; and then inspect the cleaned areas for residue.

Assuming that some progress in ameliorating racism is a shared goal, the task is too awesome to be approached with attributes like denial, defensiveness, and displacement as White people's interpretative lens. These strategies, like sweeping dust under a rug, only hide what must be considered the real dirt. Instead, we need active listening, honest self-disclosure, respectful questioning, intelligent debate, and some collective goal setting from our brothers and sisters in the White community.

With respect to honest self-disclosure and active listening, there is a ray of hope. Among the more promising movements to come along in awhile may be the "Annual Conference on Whiteness." And although the institutions of higher education or society at large have yet to see some tangible outcome from this work, at least those conference participants and supporters are reflective enough to admit that racism exists. They understand that they are contaminated with racist mentalities and desire to examine how their attitudes and behaviors disadvantage others. However cathartic their annual testimonies may be, I hope that their individual and collective struggles with guilt, regret, and blame do not derail their discussions about how to rectify the historical and contemporary disadvantages that their society has scripted for people of color. Assuming their hearts and minds are in the proper place, we should all wish them well in their explorations.

With regard to "respectful questioning," another promising element of the discourse on race are the discussions on the concept of "White privilege." Although Michelle Fine and her coauthors of the text *Off White* provide an excellent example for expanding the discourse on race, I believe it was Peggy McIntosh, among others, who introduced the concept into our thinking. She articulated what others intuitively knew, that racism is not restricted to acts of hatred and meanness. Rather, she asserts that racism helps to create and perpetuate invisible systems that confer statuses and privileges, or otherwise unearned assets, that most Whites take for granted.

White privilege is not at all a function of genetic endowment, but more a function of conscious and unconscious entitlements that exist to support life in day-to-day White America. As such, educators and other professionals alike must be invited to examine ways they benefit from privilege statuses while African-Americans and other folks of color do not. However progressive this line of thinking may be, discussions of White privilege will not magically transform conversations into havens of self-disclosure. In fact, we suspect that such discussions will be met with levels of defensiveness similarly found in the more hard-core discourse on racism and White supremacy. We believe, as Aida Hurtado and Abigail Steward have previously noted, that White privilege is difficult to define for most Whites because its existence rarely has to be brought into consciousness until its continuation is threatened. Then, Whites may more easily focus on a status no longer conveyed or an identity exposed as being unintentionally racist. Clearly, the obstacles that reinforce our ostrich-style approach to dealing with issues of race and White privilege include: (1) Whites not viewing themselves as having a "race"; (2) Whites not wanting to confront the realities of how they profit from racism and White privilege; and (3) denial of the extent to which many Whites, even unintentionally racist ones, contribute to the perpetuation of systemic racism.

Concluding Thoughts

The problems of race and racism continue to plague this nation. Those of us in the field of mental health or even institutions of higher education are uniquely trained and positioned to assist society in examining its biases and prejudices. Yet, we must be careful as well about our own level of wellness, for if we as educators and professionals are ill, then our ability to contribute to the healing of this nation will be at best compromised.

The challenge of confronting the social ills of our day requires the adoption of specific roles and responsibilities. As African-American psychologists, educators, graduate students, and community residents, our challenge is to continue to teach our children and African-American people generally about the nature of racism and White supremacy such that they learn to negotiate successfully the pathways to productivity and success. Indeed, we are committed to helping our people in the struggle for mental liberation. Further, our challenge is to not allow the historical and contemporary realities of racism to contaminate our consciousness so thoroughly that we lose hope in the possibility of substantive change. However, what remains crystal clear to us is that confronting racism and systems of White supremacy are not the sole responsibility of African-American people or a few liberal-minded, socially conscious, progressive Whites. National conversations on race are a good start, but our nation is in need of more than conversations and meetings, and our White brothers and sisters must take on that burden of providing more leadership. Our educational systems need to infuse some antiracism content into the curriculum; our workplaces could benefit from continued diversity training; our churches could benefit from discussions on how to achieve greater levels of congruence between what is preached and what is practiced by their congregations; and our research and writing on racism need to be expanded to include an analysis of the privileges Whites inherit and enjoy because of their racial background, and not simply the ways African-Americans and other folks of color are disadvantaged by racist systems. Indeed, we would invite our colleagues in the White community to understand that an opportunity to eliminate and dismantle racism is a threat to those who only see failure, but a challenge to those who see the benefits of creating an equitable and more humane society. Cornell West, in his text *Race Matters,* was clear on the point that to engage in a serious discussion of race in America, we must begin not with the problems of Black (and other oppressed) people, but with the flaws of American society itself. One of those flaws, we would submit, is the refusal by the larger White community to take responsibility for eradicating racism. Isn't it about time for that change to come?

CONFRONTING THE SOCIAL PATHOLOGY OF THE AMERICAN WORKPLACE

Traditionally, the American workplace has held the promise of actualizing the career-related dreams and aspirations of an energetic workforce. Whether the setting was a corporation or agency; local, state, or federal government office; or institution of higher education, people engaged their craft as a way of providing a meaningful service to others, as well as a means of supporting themselves and their families, and as a means of obtaining some level of self-actualization.

Historical and Contemporary Realities

In adjusting to the culture of the workplace, individuals have tried to understand what it takes to be a success in whatever enterprise they choose. The experiences they come to know as "reality" are shaped by an underlying belief system that serves as the organizing principle for their experience. In a workplace dominated by Eurocentric values, the cornerstone of that belief system or worldview includes a materialistic orientation, where self-worth is based on acquisition of objects and development and success are rooted in economic realities, supported by a posture of individualism and competition (Myers, 1988). The lessons learned have come from a myriad of sources, including bosses, managers and supervisors, co-workers, mentors, professional colleagues, family, elders, books and periodicals, and even workplace stereotypes. What these sources attempt to relate to workers are the norms, customs, habits, expectations, and traditions of the organizational cultures they inhabit.

In confronting the social pathology, it is necessary to examine our use of the term, and how this phenomenon manifests itself within the workplace. *Social* is a term used to describe the interaction between individuals and/or groups. *Pathology* is the study of the essential nature of disease and the structural and functional changes produced by them. Our use of the term *social pathology* is meant to describe our observations of the workplace environment, which we believe is experiencing disease, particularly in the way management treats employees, employees respond to management, and workers generally respond to each other. This disease is instigating reactions to changes in the workplace that are unhealthy, and the irony of the situation is that it is a climate of "democratic sanity" that prevents the workplace from knowing it's sick because everyone acts in similar fashion.

Indeed, there is a sickness sweeping across America's workplace, and as psychologists, it is our task to lend our individual and collective expertise in helping the workplace to experience a greater level of wellness and health. And so the need to confront the social pathology of our day emerges out of the same desire to assist our clients and patients in adjusting to and overcoming the debilitating effects of life's challenges and obstacles. But the question we ask this day is: What is the condition of the workplace in urban America, and why does it need the assistance of psychology?

Now, assuming that lessons learned were and are incorporated into the workday experiences, employees generally understood that they were expected to be reliable, stable, hard working, honest, loyal to the company, individually achieving, highly productive, interpersonally skilled, ethical in their professional practices, efficient, and hesitant about expressing discomfort with organizational policies and practices, or otherwise rocking the workplace boat.

For workers in urban America, particularly those who come from African-American communities, the rules of the workplace were learned from a different perspective, one which by necessity incorporated lessons about the social ills of America. Racism, sexism, classism, discrimination, and other ills have become an integral part of the workplace culture regardless of the setting. Indeed, the reality African-Americans perceive is very different from their European-American counterparts. Although many Whites ponder career choices to select from, most African-Americans have worried about gaining access to any opportunities at all. For many White males who contemplate their next promotional advancement, most African-American women have worried about developing strategies to break the glass ceilings that have been placed in their way. Although most able-bodied people navigate the workplace environment with ease, most physically challenged persons must worry about access to opportunities as well as negotiating around physical barriers in the workplace. Now, although the social ills many African-Americans and urban dwellers confront are formidable, these workers are no less committed to conforming to organizational and institutional workplace norms. In fact, that willingness to conform is quite remarkable given that most of them will find their worldview and cultural norms in conflict with those of the workplace.

In exchange for their cooperation and adherence to organizational norms, African-American workers and those from other cultures generally enter into an implicit, and sometimes explicit, social contract with their employers. The benefits they bargained for included reasonable working conditions, appropriate compensation for their efforts, positive feedback for a job well done, incentives for above-average to superior performance, accommodations for necessary leaves, opportunities for advancement, long-term security and stability of employment, and adequate resources to provide health care and on which to retire. That picture was the traditional workplace.

Unfortunately, the workplace of yesterday has undergone a radical transformation, and what workers historically accepted as truth can no longer be counted on as gospel. A review of many workplace environments throughout this country reveals that working conditions are poor; compensation is at best stagnate and at worst being cut; benefits are being reduced; merits and incentives for performance are only hollow promises; there is little validation for a job well done; and morale is extremely low. What is clear about the current workplace changes is that employers, employees, and the institutions they occupy are feeling the pinch of hard economic times. If the 1980s were considered an age of prosperity, then the 1990s are certainly considered an age of cutbacks, belt-tightening, downsizing, mergers, acquisitions, hostile takeovers, and general workplace uncertainty. What is more distressing, however, in the year 2000 and beyond is how employers and employees are now responding to each other in the context of these workplace transformations.

The central theme in the workplace over the last 5 to 10 years has been economics. This is not surprising given the materialistic orientation to reality. And although historical social contracts allowed for employers and workers alike to share in the earnings and profits, the new order of business is discernibly different. Specifically, there is a simmering frustration sweeping across this country because weekly wages and annual salaries, as well as benefits, have declined significantly for workers (both managers and staff), whereas the wealth and earnings of the corporate elite have risen steadily. As these economic divisions grow, those who find themselves "wanting" begin to look with envy, jealousy, contempt, and anger at those they perceive to be more privileged; in contrast, those who "have" continue to justify why their perceived greed and such trends are necessary for corporate survival. And if there is any truth to the saying "You reap what you sow," then the seeds frustration and bitterness are sprouting in our African-American communities and other urban and suburban areas.

Why? Because the urban centers of our nation are experiencing similarly tough economic hardships, but the effects are felt more dramatically in these areas (Oliver & Shapiro, 1995). It is often said that when America generally finds itself sneezing, African America has already caught a vicious cold. They have experienced an exodus of industrial and manufacturing jobs from urban centers to cheaper labor markets here and abroad; housing patterns that have been redisbursed in such a fashion as to create people-of-color inner cities and White suburbs; federal programs that provide meaningful family supports have been cut; available jobs for traditional urban residents and the growing numbers of immigrants in the plant and manufacturing areas are decreasing; and the workplace climate that tolerated their presence under the guise of affirmative action, equal rights, and social progress has now turned hostile in light of the current scarcity of jobs and other economic resources. Additionally, because of material orientation and focus on monetary issues, general chaotic conditions in the workplace were assumed to be related to economic realities in the country and around the world. Consequently, workplace conditions may be expected to improve when economic realities become better. However, the real culprit may be a crisis of spirit that is instigated by a lack of spirituality and general disregard for the humanity of others, particularly those who occupy our urban centers across this nation.

Now, when we begin to analyze the dynamics of the workplace, we ourselves (as psychologists) must be clear about the need to examine the utility of our own psychological theories, models, and practices. It is not unusual, for example, for clinicians and counselors to treat individuals impacted by the changes in the workplace. In fact, clients who are anxious about their futures, frustrated about their working conditions, or depressed about their inability to provide for their families, are all a part of many therapists' caseloads. However, if we as African-centered psychologists are only successful in helping people adjust to the intrapsychically related cognitive, emotional, and behavioral dimensions of their workplace problems, all we have really done is help to restore a level of mental health to people who are still vulnerable to the same social pathology that instigated their distress in the first place. For our part, we must recognize that all client distress is not intrapsychic; much of it, particularly for African-American people in the workplace, is social/cultural and environmental (White & Parham, 1997).

It is also not unusual for psychologists to serve as consultants to agencies, business, academic institutions, and corporations under the guise of helping them manage workplace environments that are increasingly more hostile and violent. *USA Today* (August 8, 1996) reports that the workplace is hungry for so-called job violence experts who can instruct workplace officials in the latest violence prevention techniques. However, if we as psychologists are only successful at helping institutions manage the physical plant of the work environment (i.e., better locks, electronic security, bulletproof glass), then all we have really done is help these institutions reinforce their denial systems that nothing is structurally and functionally wrong with them. For our part, we must help them acknowledge their own pathology associated with the workplace culture and climate that they have created. Consequently, if we assume that the etiology of client distress is a worker's interaction with the workplace environment, then by necessity the targets of our intervention must include the workplace environment itself.

You see, we would argue that in order to engage in meaningful discourse about workplace issues in urban America, we must begin not with the problems of the urban dwellers, but rather with the flaws of the workplace itself. Indeed, the workplace will have to confront issues of poverty, substance abuse, homelessness, violence, child care, and poor schools in working with urban residents. But the workplace must heal itself first if these issues are to be addressed.

Flaws of the Workplace

The *first* flaw we wish to discuss is the construction of a workplace *value system* that sees profits as the bottom line, individual competition as a means of achieving it, and employee satisfaction as a term reserved only for human resources manuals. There is an exercise of power over the environment and employees, but rather than actualize the power to do good, employers exert power in order to control people, materials, and circumstances.

We have also observed that the physical/material orientation to the world invites employers to treat workers as objects of control and manipulation. Workers are hired, fired, promoted, demoted, and transferred like tokens on a Monopoly board, all with very little regard for their emotional and spiritual well-being, or the impact that such changes have on their families and significant others in their lives. The pathology associated with this worldview and value system is even more pronounced when you consider that the devaluation of the African-American worker (or any worker) can never result in him or her achieving the fullest expression of themselves, because the workplace refuses to recognize their true nature and essence. At issue as well is the corporate culture that forces workers into postures of defensiveness, confrontation, and destructive competition in the face of harsh economic realities. Thus, rather than cooperate across sections or divisions, each competes with the other for perceived "favorite status" positions and/or resources in an attempt to avoid the dreaded "right-sizing" ax. *We must challenge that value system!*

The *second* flaw of the workplace is its *failure* to understand and effectively *manage the diversity* of the workforce. Because the workplace seems to employ a "difference equals deficiency" logic in its orientation and culture, it is difficult for African-American people in the workplace to be appreciated both for their real value as human beings and their ability to contribute effectively to the particular organization or institution. We would argue, as Loden and Rosener (1991) have before us, that most American institutions and managers, whether in academic or corporate arenas, continue to relate to employee diversity based on several traditional assumptions. These assumptions include: (1) otherness is a deficiency, (2) diversity poses a threat to the organization's effective functioning, (3) expressing discomfort with the dominant group's value is oversensitivity, (4) members of all diverse groups want to become and should be more like the dominant group, (5) managing diversity means changing the people, not the organizational culture.

Now, the diversity flaw is further compounded by the fact that the structures of intolerance that characterize the workplace of urban America are anchored in a racist and sexist ideology that has a long history of discrimination and oppression. And tragically, the workplace's failure to acknowledge this truth and/or deny the presence of such practices and sentiments will make treating the problem very difficult.

Another distressing aspect about the diversity issue is that the workplace has never learned to distinguish between the concepts of *desegregation* and *integration*. In fact, we are constantly amazed at how many people believe that the workplace is integrated, as is the larger society. We would argue that our workplace, and society at large, focuses too much on demographics and frequency distributions as measures of progress toward diversity. You see, *desegregation* suggests that people have the right to occupy the same geographical space. Although *integration* suggests that all individuals should be able to see themselves reflected in the policies and practices of that institution's, what we have in the workplaces of America, whether suburban or urban, is merely a desegregated environment. *We must change this!*

A *third* flaw in the workplace is its *failure to understand that management styles* must involve a greater focus on interpersonal relations, and not simply oversight and accountability for the production of products. It is our observation that in the workplace of today, many managers adopt a style of being a paper pusher, or a people pusher.

Paper pushers tend to be very detached from their workers, communicate through memos (more often than not), insisting on everything being written down, provide directions via written correspondence, and are very task-oriented. This style sometimes has a record of being perceived as aloof, unsympathetic, and even disrespectful. In contrast, people pushers are in touch with their workers, communicate face to face (more often than not), insist on developing relationships with their supervisees and co-workers, provide directives via verbal instructions, are strong communicators, and are high relationship-oriented. In my opinion, the most effective type of manager is a people pusher, particularly in the case of urban dwellers who sometimes put a higher premium on interpersonal dynamics. It is vitally important for the workplace to realize that what they manage are human resources, and people's needs for affiliation are strong and can only be satisfied through personal relationships.

It is also important for the workplace to understand that the crisis in leadership that the literature talked about in the 1980s is still present to this day. In our opinion, African-Americans are no different than their White counterparts in wanting leaders who are interested, involved, and caring. The problem with the workplace in the 1990s is that too few of our workers, especially urban dwellers, believe that the leadership in the organizations and institutions they occupy are interested in them as people, are involved in their efforts to work for them, and care enough about them as people to forge genuine relationships. These perceptions are further reinforced by the larger society, which supports a climate of, at best, indifference, and at worst, hostility, insensitivity, and blatant disregard for urban dwellers.

A *fourth* flaw in the workplace is the *failure to confront and positively impact the factors* that contribute to an underrepresentation of African-American people in particular occupational categories. It is our observation that many African-Americans must face a host of obstacles that hamper their ability to participate fully in the occupational mainstream. Yet not enough corporations and institutions are involved in helping to address some of these issues.

A *fifth* flaw in the workplace is its *failure to acknowledge the truth* that racism, sexism, and discriminations of all types occur in the workplace. In addition, the workplace has failed to set a stronger tone for policing the social ills that exist and taking very visible and dramatic steps to rectify these intolerable conditions. In some respect, the workplace relates to social pathology by denying its existence, or engaging in an "ostrich-style mentality," hoping that if they bury their heads long enough, problems will just go away. Imagine what this does for the perception of integrity in the minds of many urban workers.

Roles for African-Centered Psychologists

Because our society has put such a premium on the attainment of educational degrees, doctoral-level Black psychologists are blessed with a measure of privilege and influence that few in our society will attain. However, it is important for us to develop a greater awareness of our gifts and the proper purpose for which they were intended. In our opinion, the test of our integrity as psychologists will not be based on whether we individually achieve fame and fortune, or obtain higher reimbursements from managed care agencies and insurance companies to treat urban and suburban clientele. Rather, we suspect that we will be judged, among other things, on how we use our privilege and influence to better the quality of living for those who struggle with life's challenges. One of those challenges, of course, is the workplace. Indeed, I believe that if our gifts are not sustained on the basis of righteous character, meaning how do we promote truth, justice, righteousness, and harmony in the workplace, then our gifts of knowledge, privilege, and influence are in vain.

Lessons Learned

Given the multiple roles African-American psychologists play in today's society, it is not unusual for us to be placed in the role of teacher. And teacher is precisely where we ought to be because the workplace has some specific lessons it needs to learn about issues in African America, and we must be in the position of influencing organizational dynamics.

The *first lesson* we must teach the workplace is helping them to appreciate the real value of their workforce. We must teach them that they can never subordinate the real value of their African-American employees by only being concerned with their ability to contribute to the profit margins, and leaving their intellectual, moral, and spiritual sides uncultivated. The African-American workers they employ are divinely inspired seeds of human possibility that require certain amounts of cultivation and nurturance in order to grow. It is our job as African-centered psychologists to teach them how to access that spiritual core that is so vital to the human condition. In addition, we must help them to teach their workers that as employees, they have value and worth regardless of their level of salary or position in an organization. Anchoring a self-worth in the contingency seas of material attainment is a pathology we must confront.

The *second lesson* we must teach them is that the diversity that characterizes America's urban centers has a wealth of potential. But the potential only exists if managers, CEOs, and even line workers have the courage to remove the blinders that hide the fears and stereotypes they have acquired in their lifetimes. Indeed, we must teach the workplace to understand that the opportunity to appreciate diversity is a threat to those who see only deficiencies, but it is a challenge to those who see the benefit of cultivating a greater level of human potential. And we must teach them that diversity will no longer be defined by demographics, but rather "have the policies and practices of the institution changed as a function of changes in demographic makeup?"

A *third lesson* we must teach them involves the need to examine the value system that permeates the workplace and how a different set of values might be more beneficial to all those who currently occupy it. It will be difficult to argue against profitable bottom lines and competitive styles as a means of achieving them. However, to exclude more African-centered outcomes and values that focus on the need to make a difference in someone's life, compassion for those less fortunate, respect for difference, or styles that practice greater levels of cooperation rather than destructive competition is a mistake the workplace can no longer afford to ignore. In addition, we as African-centered psychologists must invite the workplace to consider modifying, or in some cases eliminating, values and practices that do not contribute to the cultivation of each worker's human potential. There are alternate orientations to the world that can help the workplace define new measures of success, without exacting the high price current values take on diminished self-worth, angry and frustrated spirits, and destructive behaviors. Indeed, the current levels of violence affecting the workplace are strong evidence that something is terribly wrong with our workplace practices. And solutions that only focus on protection and safety issues (i.e., bulletproof glass, limited access, and locks) will be limited in their effectiveness because they only treat one dimension of the problem.

The *fourth lesson* we must teach the workplace is how to become risk takers with African America. The risk taking we speak of here has more to do with the dynamic orientation that may require the risk of losing something certain (i.e., the status quo) for the possibility of achieving something much greater than that. In the context of risk taking, the workplace needs to be taught how to take *mental risks* where their attitudes and opinions about African America are stretched beyond their current biases and stereotypes. They need to be taught to take *verbal risks,* which invite them to engage in specific dialogue with African-American people about what they have to contribute to the workplace. And the workplace needs to learn about taking *behavioral risks* that might allow it to break with traditional practices in order to explore the possibility of genuine collaboration with African-Americans that might produce significant and meaningful innovations.

In short, we must help the workplace understand that the real task is not simply the construction of buildings and other infrastructure, but the confrontation of the social pathology that serves as a foundation for the chaos we have come to know as the contemporary workplace.

"WE ARE THE ONES WE'VE BEEN WAITING FOR": CONTEXTUALIZING BLACK WOMEN'S PSYCHOSOCIAL EXPERIENCES AND RESISTANCE TO OPPRESSION BY HELEN A. NEVILLE, PH.D.

Black feminist scholars have long argued that Black women's experiences reflect a complex interrelationship among race, class, and gender. It is evident that race plays a critical role in Black men and women's psychosocial experiences. For example, as African-Americans, we share many similar cultural traditions as well as encounter similar systemic racial oppression. Race does not fully account, however, for the unique experiences that Black women face across class backgrounds or the unique position of poor and working-class Black women. For example, African-American women have cultural practices based on their unique social experiences (e.g., the culture developed around hair-care practices, or being mothers raising Black children). Extending Thompson and Neville's (1999) work on racism and mental health, we assert that the interlocking systems of race, class, and gender influence the ideological representation of and institutional practices toward Black women in a number of important ways. In this section, we define these terms and outline how the dialectic between ideology and structure (social practices) impact the lives of Black women. We also discuss specific ways in which Black women have worked collectively to better their conditions, and also the role the community can play to eliminate environmental barriers and to promote mental health among all sectors of the African-American community.

Ideological (Mis)Representation

False and stereotypical images, or ideological (mis)representations, of Black women are used to help justify their mistreatment and oppression, including economic exploitation and sexual abuse, which will be discussed later. According to Collins (1990), the most pervasive controlling images in the media and popular discourse include the following interrelated representations:

- Jezebel—One of the oldest images of Black women is of the Jezebel or someone who is sexually loose, wanton, and lascivious. The portrayals of Black women as hypersexual and animal-like reflect this image. For example, a recent content analysis of visual images in women's journals found that Black women are shown in animal print significantly more often than White women.
- Mammy—The quintessential mammy image of the asexual, subservient, mother figure that appreciates her position in life was captured in Hatty McDaniel's Oscar winning performance in the 1939 film "Gone with the Wind." The image of the mammy was so popular among Whites during and after slavery that the Daughters of the Confederates wanted to erect a monument in honor of her likeness in the early 1900s. Mammy, for them, represented a nonthreatening person who accepted the status quo and was willing to socialize her children to adopt similar beliefs.
- Matriarch—The image of the matriarch is in direct opposition to that of the mammy. The matriarch is viewed as the bad mother, someone who is lazy, unfeminine, and emasculating. She is considered the person who runs Black men away from family responsibilities and teaches her children to be idle and sexually promiscuous. The image of the matriarch in the 1960s is closely tied to the current image of Black women as Welfare Queen, with the exception that the latter is also viewed as a "baby factory."
- Sapphire—Sapphire, named after Kingfish's wife on the popular "Amos and Andy" radio and television series in the 1930s to 1950s, is emasculating, sassy, and loud. Her image is similar to that of the matriarch with respect to core personality traits (e.g., unfeminine). However, Sapphire is also verbose and is viewed for her "entertainment" value. The character Dee on the popular 1970's television sitcom, "What's Happening" embodies this image.

In her important work deconstructing cultural (mis)representations, Jewell (1993) underscores that the above images are stereotypes and do not reflect how Black women really are. Although these images are completely false and were initially constructed outside of the Black community, they have been used for detrimental purposes. Controlling images have served to legitimize social policy (e.g., welfare reform) and also personal mistreatment of Black women by a variety of people, including Black men and other Black women. In the first instance, the image of lazy Black women having babies out of wedlock and getting rich off of public assistance informed recent welfare reform; more specifically, the Personal Responsibility and Work Opportunity Reconciliation Act of 1996. In fact, the first line of this law states that "Marriage is the foundation of a successful society," and then proceeds to blame single-motherhood for social ills such as poverty and crime. Important issues such as the lack of available jobs paying a livable wage were not addressed; in 1996, the unemployment rate for young African-American women with high school diplomas was an amazing 21% (Economic Policy Institute, 1997). In the second instance, the internalization and perpetuation of the images of Black women as Jezebels and Sapphires are best reflected in the common reference to Black women as "bitches" and "hoes" in rap songs and everyday discourse among our youth.

Institutional Practices

According to Thompson and Neville (1999), institutional practices are influenced by social structures or the systems that society is organized, including political, economic, and social institutions (e.g., education, law enforcement, military, and prison). From this perspective, Black women's lived experiences are affected by racism and sexism because these structures help to further maintain and perpetuate the political and economic domination of men, especially White elite men and, conversely, discriminate against racial and ethnic minorities, especially women, in institutional participation. Simply put, racism and sexism have real and lasting implications on Black women's lives. The conditions of Black people differ depending, to a large extent, on the interconnected forces of race, class, and gender. For example, working and poor Black women are confronted with the greatest levels of structural racism and sexism; they are superexploited economically and are the most alienated from political and social institutions. Black women are also overrepresented among the poor, and consequently have limited access to quality, affordable health care.

It is important to note that ideology and structure are not independent forces. Instead, there is a dialectic relationship between the two such that they co-influence one another. Ideology (or representations) is used to further reinforce structural oppression (e.g., limited access to resources), and structures of society (e.g., media, educational system) further reinforce and perpetuate (mis)representations of Black women. Using the Welfare Queen example, the image of Black women as lazy people who have babies to avoid work shaped how welfare has been discussed in our society and also the solutions identified to address this "social problem" (e.g., establishing laws to limit poor Black women's reproduction such as family cap laws). On the other hand, institutional practices like welfare reform help create an ideology that blames women, particularly Black women, for not having full employment and for high rates of crime in poor and low-income neighborhoods. Below we describe specific institutional and social practices that influence Black women's psychological and behavioral health. We also discuss how controlling images serve to perpetuate these practices.

Economic Exploitation

Since the time Black women were brought to America, their labor has been exploited. Obviously, slavery represented the ultimate form of economic exploitation, as Black men and women were not paid for their labor or the products that they produced. African-American women have been relegated to completing the dirtiest and most labor-intensive "women" jobs at every historical juncture. In summarizing Black women's work in the earlier part of this century, historian Paula Giddings (1984) commented that because Black women "were thought to be able to withstand more heat [an ideological (mis)representation], they got the most heat-intensive jobs in the candy and glass factories. In the bakeries it was Black women who cleaned, greased, and lifted the heavy pans. In the tobacco industry, Black women did the stripping of the tobacco, the lowest-paid and most numbing work" (p. 144). Even today, Black women, on average, are represented in the lowest-paid service occupations. For example, in the health-care industry, Black women are represented in the least-secure positions such as nursing assistants, licensed practical nurses, and health-care aides. They are the ones doing the least desirable duties for the least amount of money, like changing bedpans and cleaning up vomit.

The fact that Black women tend to earn significantly less than Black men and White men and women further supports their current exploitation. For example, the average salary of an African-American woman with a college degree is significantly less than a White male with a high school diploma (Rix, 1990). Also, it has been found that Black women earn nearly 83% and 59% of what Black and White men make, respectively (Amott & Matthaei, 1996). Moreover, the jobs Black working and poor women have are insufficient to provide their families a sustainable living or to lift them out of poverty. A person working 40 hours for 50 weeks at $5.30/hour would only earn a mere $10,600; hardly enough to support one person, let alone a family.

Although recent trends suggest a slight increase in the median household income of African-Americans, a little over one-quarter of Black people still live in poverty (Census Bureau, 1997). Black women, especially single parents, are the most overrepresented among the poor. Approximately, 45% of African-American-woman–headed households live in poverty. Myths about poor women, especially poor Black women, serve to support the Welfare Queen image and to rationalize their predicament. Some of the common myths surrounding this image include "welfare causes dependency" (75% of Aid to Families with Dependent Children [AFDC] recipients left welfare in less than two years; [Statistical Abstract of the United States, 1996]) and "women are poor because they are having too many babies" (72% of all families that received AFDC had two or fewer children [Statistical Abstract of the United States, 1996]). It is important to realize that the economic conditions of poor women and their family's play an important role in availability of resources, including quality, safe living environments, schools, and health care. Also, household income has been found to be related to both mental and physical health, such that those individuals with lower incomes report greater health concerns (Williams, Yu, & Jackson, 1997).

Justice System Abuse

Although women prisoners account for a small percent of the total prison population (less than 10%), there has been an increase in Black women prisoners over the past decade and a half. Between 1984 and 1994, the imprisonment rate of Black women increased by an amazing 226% (Stuart, 1997). These women were primarily sentenced for nonviolent, drug-related offenses. For example, Black women's drug offense incarceration rate rose 828% from 1986 to 1991, compared to an increase in 241%, and 328% among White and Hispanic women, respectively (Bush-Baskette, 1998). Although Black women make up a little over 12% of the U.S. women population, they constitute over 50% of the women's prison population (Stuart, 1997). What we are finding is that poor Black women have the greater chance of being imprisoned. The majority (60%) of women incarcerated were on some type of public assistance prior to incarceration and the overwhelming majority of women reported incomes at or below poverty levels at the time of their arrest

Scholars have identified several trends suggesting differential treatment of Black women within the penal system that may help to explain some of these trends. Black women are overarrested, underdefended, and oversentenced. There is a greater proportion of White women arrested, yet they are sent to prison much less frequently than are Black women. For example, the prosecution rate of White women is 19%, and it is 30% for Black women. Black women are also generally sentenced for longer periods of time for committing the same crime. In Missouri, Black women end up serving one-third more time than White women for the same offenses and, in general, Black women are twice as likely to be convicted of killing their abusive husbands than White women. The point here is not to valorize criminals, but rather to consider the inconsistencies in practices within our penal system.

Feminist scholars have also discussed the differential treatment that women inmates experience in prison compared to their male counterparts. In general, women prisoners are exposed to fewer programs such as medical education and they have limited or insufficient prenatal services (e.g., nutritious food, exercise, sanitary conditions, and supplements afforded by Women's, Infant, Childrens Nutrition Program [WIC]). Because there are fewer facilities housing women, prisoners are more likely to be relocated far from their families, including their children. This is of particular importance considering that the majority (nearly 70%) of Black women prisoners are mothers of children under the age of 18 (Stuart, 1997).

Sexual Violence Against Women

Consistent data suggest that between 14% and 25% of women across racial and ethnic lines will be sexually assaulted (experience rape or attempted rape) in their lifetimes (Koss, 1993). This is important because sexual assault survivors experience many short- and long-term deleterious effects, including depression, anxiety, posttraumatic stress symptoms, eating disturbances, and sexual dysfunctions months and, in some instances, years following the assault (Neville & Heppner, 1999). For example, nearly one-third of rape survivors develop post-traumatic stress disorder sometimes in their lifetimes and about 40% of survivors indicate clinical levels of depression following the assault. In addition, women report feeling as though the course of their lives had been completely altered as a result of the trauma. It is not uncommon for survivors to make comments such as the following: "It crippled me"; "It ruined my life"; "I'll never get rid of it."

It is important to note that the prevalence of sexual assault of African-American women is comparable to other populations in the United States. These data help to refute the myth of the Black male rapists. If almost all (97%) of rapes are intraracial, and Black women are assaulted at a similar rate as other women, then Black men are not going around sexually assaulting women at a disproportionately higher rate than other men. These statistics thus provide data countering the controlling image that Black males are hypersexual, violent criminals. The controlling image of the Black male rapist had been especially harmful after slavery and at the turn of the century, as it was used to legitimize the lynching of Black men. All of this said, the fact remains that upwards of one-fourth of all African-American women will experience some form of sexual assault, most likely at the hands of Black male; this is unacceptable.

Black feminist scholar-activists such as Angela Davis link the rape of Black women to race, gender, and class oppression. The controlling image of Black women as Jezebel reflects the interplay between these structures and helps to contexualize Black women's historical experience with sexual assault. During slavery, characterizations of Black women as sexually promiscuous were used to justify the routine rape of women slaves by White men. The logic here was that Black women could not be raped because they were always desirous of and enjoyed sex. Unfortunately, this image also influenced laws and social practices after slavery. For example, juries historically were reluctant to convict someone (Black or White) of raping a Black woman, citing the difficulty in believing the victim's story. A recent study found that college students perceived an incident of rape to be more serious when the victim was White (Foley, Evancic, Karnik, King, & Parks, 1995). Specifically, the perpetrator's behavior in a rape scenario involving a Black victim was more likely to be perceived as alright or as an act of love when compared with a White victim. On the other hand, when the victim was White, students were more likely to perceive the rape as a crime that should be reported.

The Jezebel image may also be related to how Black women understand why they were sexually assaulted. Initial research findings suggest that Black women identify race-related attributions (e.g., "Black women are portrayed as sexually loose.") as more important in making sense of their assault than general attributions (e.g., "I was too trusting."). In addition, data suggest that Black women rate these race-related attributions as more significant than their White counterparts. Interestingly, though, race-related attributions have not been found to be related to self-esteem, whereas general attributions have (Neville & Heppner, 1999).

Resistance

White and Parham (1990) perceptively noted that Black people are not just passive victims of oppression. Black people, like all social groups, have demonstrated agency throughout our history. By agency, we mean the ability to act on and influence as opposed to being acted upon. I titled this section "we are the one's we are looking for" after cultural activist's Bearnice Johnson Reagon's statement, because the phrase underscores African-Americans' agency in identifying and acting on our own behalf. Throughout history, Black people have challenged, actively resisted, and changed social structures as exemplified in the slave revolts, abolition efforts, and the civil rights and Black power movements. In addition to fighting the forces of oppression, the African-American community also created positive intellectual, cultural, and psychological traditions, building on strengths peripheral to institutional barriers.

Although often working within multiracial and/or mix-gendered coalitions, Black women have individually and collectively brought about social change via two primary channels: (1) undermining structures by changing ideological and cultural representations and (2) actually changing the multiple interlocking systems of oppression. The Black Women's Club Movement was popular at the turn of the century and played an active role in redefining what it means to be a Black woman, and thus resisting ideological pigeon holes while creating new representations. Efforts designed to provide internal definitions of the collective self, such as the above, have been instrumental in our group survival, especially on a psychological level. For example, dominant information media in the United States characterize the ideal body type for women as being thin. These cultural expectations of women have had negative effects on White women and have been identified as factors associated with body and eating disturbances within this population. This is not the case for Black women. Black women appear to use a different yard stick of beauty, with standards reflecting internal cultural norms. As a result, Black women, on average, maintain a positive body image despite the fact that as a group they are heavier. Also, across geographical location, age, and population (e.g., student, community member), Black girls and women as a group report feeling better about their overall appearance and are more accepting of their bodies than White women (Falconer, 1998). With respect to social transformation, Black women's critical participation in almost every type of social movement in this country (e.g., antilynching campaigns to the current welfare movement) have been instrumental in helping to eliminate, or at the minimum, to challenge discriminatory practices that Black men and women face in the law, employment, housing, education, as well as in our personal spheres.

Challenges for the Black Community in the 21st Century

Nearly 100 years ago, W. E. B. DuBois noted that the problem of the 20th century would be that of the color line. It is amazing that as we enter a new millennium, the color line or racial issues remain one of the central contradictions in U.S. society. However, society's understanding of the color line is much more complex. We now realize that gender and class add new dimensions to Black people's lived experience. Thus, the primary challenge for the Black community in the new millennium is to create a vision of a society that will support the development (psychological, physical, material) of all of its citizens. Naturally, such a vision should consider the multiple and interlocking roles of race, class, and gender in our lives. Black psychologists can play a unique role in this process by intervening on various individual and system levels to enhance mental and behavioral well being of our community. We use the ideological representations and institutional practices discussed above to guide our discussion of specific interventions Black psychologists can implement.

Individual- and Microlevel Interventions

Black psychologists can play an active role in intervening to assist individuals and small groups and family units to develop better coping skills or social competencies to negotiate the cumulative stressors of daily life of African-American girls and women. Recently, increased attention has been given to providing parenting training to educate parents about general child development issues and to teach parents to respond to children in developmentally appropriate ways. We argue that parents must also understand the role of social identities on the development of their children. Building on Greene's (1994) discussion of racial socialization, psychologists can develop, implement, and evaluate the effectiveness of race-gender-parent socialization training programs. The purpose of such training efforts should focus on teaching parents how to nurture their girl children to understand, accept, and value being Black and female. Specific activities would center on providing parents with the tools necessary to teach their girls social competencies, such as how to: (1) correctly identify race-gender experiences and discrimination in a variety of contexts; this could include providing an interpretive lens to critically analyze media (mis)representations; (2) identify an array of appropriate and effective ways to respond to such incidents, with an emphasis on empowerment; (3) honestly analyze the psychological impact of the incident(s) and to repair self-confidence if necessary; (4) develop a positive internal, as opposed to external, definition of what it means to be a Black girl and eventually a Black woman; (5) understand the positive contributions of Black girls and women throughout history; and (6) explore all forms of career options, not just those limited to them by race, gender, and/or class.

Black women who have not experienced the type of race-gender socializing discussed above growing up may be susceptible to internalizing (1) negative stereotypes [ideological (mis) representations] (e.g., Black women are too aggressive, Black physical characteristics are unattractive, such as darker skin) or (2) restricted race-gender roles (e.g., Black women have to be strong for everyone in the family, Black women should not show any signs of vulnerability). Designing individual and group programs to counter these processes is important because internalized racism has been found to be related to a host of psychological and behavioral health concerns, including increased alcohol consumption, greater levels of depression, and decreased perceived coping efficacy (Howard, 1999). Interventions targeting these issues should provide women a space to (1) identify their socialization as a Black women, (2) normalize their psychological and behavioral responses to this socialization, (3) place this experience in a sociohistorical context, and (4) create a new more positive definition of race-gender identity.

Earlier we discussed the deleterious effects of sexual violence on women and we alluded to specific issues that could be included in treatment efforts with Black women. Primarily, we suggested that counselors should consider the impact of controlling images (e.g., Jezebel) on the recovery process of Black women; this should include an examination of not only how Black women interpret the trauma, but also how others treat them after the crime. In addition to identifying other specific race-related variables influencing the postassault process, psychologists must also design culturally appropriate interventions to prevent the incidence of rape in our communities. Some initial empirical work has been done in this area. Heppner and colleagues (1999) evaluated the immediate and long-term effectiveness of a systematic rape prevention program on Black and White fraternity college students. Results suggest that Black participants who were part of a culturally inclusive treatment program (e.g., Black cofacilitator, inclusion of statistics and information related to African-American community) found the treatment more cognitively engaging than Black participants in a colorblind condition, in which race was never discussed. More efforts are needed to reach a broad sector of the Black community (students, church members, community residents, etc.). It appears that making the training specific to the experience of African-Americans is helpful, but we need additional information about the race-related rape myths among Black men and other factors that have been found to be related to why men rape.

System-Level Interventions

As noted earlier, Black women's lived experiences are shaped by multiple interlocking systems. Psychologists can and should intervene to increase the optimal level of functioning. However, Black psychologists should also play a critical role in articulating a new vision for society (a society free of racial, gender, and class exploitation) by working with others in mass organizations such as the Black Radical Congress and the NAACP. In addition, Black psychologists can serve as social change agents. The Association of Black Psychologists provides leadership in shaping ways psychologists can work collectively to affect institutional change, such as activism around AIDS. Black psychologists can also function independently to assist communities or specific populations in their efforts to empower themselves. The philosophical assumptions in this approach is that (1) human behavior is in part determined by the social forces in one's life (e.g., poverty, lack of educational resources) and that (2) changing or eliminating environmental stressors will increase the psychological and behavioral health of individuals and groups. There are several steps psychologists can undertake in their role as social change agents, including the following:

- Educating themselves about national trends affecting Black girls and women (e.g., health-care concerns such as AIDS, rising imprisonment rates, welfare reform).
- Becoming aware of specific local and national legislation affecting Black women (e.g., family cap laws, Personal Responsibility and Work Opportunity Reconciliation Act).
- Understanding how trends and legislation affect poor Black women in particular, because they are the most disenfranchised and marginalized population; a population that could benefit from empowerment activities.
- Educating themselves about local activities or groups whose goal is to counter negative forces and to enhance the quality of life for Black girls and women (e.g., Chicago Legal Aid to Incarcerated Mothers).
- Designing community forums to educate people about trends, legislation, available resources, and organizations.
- Working with community members or specific Black women's groups to help them to (1) identify the major concerns they would like to change and (2) strategize about effective interventions to change or eradicate the concern. The key here is that interventions are community or group-centered. This is an important step in creating an environment in which Black women can empower themselves.

In conclusion, the quality of life of African-American women is influenced by the interlocking systems of race, class, and gender. Although oppression based on these social categories negatively affects women's health, Black women are involved in a variety of activities to resist and eradicate these forms of ideological and structural domination. Moreover, it is important to understand that Black women are more than an oppressed group; they are strong survivors and have many traditions and contributions that are peripheral to being oppressed. Black psychologists can play an important role in enhancing the material conditions and also the psychological and behavioral health of Black women. First, Black psychologists can help to articulate a vision for a society free of all forms of oppression. More concretely, Black psychologists should provide culturally sensitive interventions to promote positive personal and social competence as well as become effective social agents, where they assist Black women in empowering themselves to enact changes they define as critical.

9

AFRICAN-AMERICAN PSYCHOLOGY: THIRTY YEARS IN THE EVOLUTION OF AN IDEA—CONCLUSION

In writing this third edition of the *Psychology of Blacks: An African-Centered Perspective,* we have attempted to capture the essence of the African ethos in each chapter. It is our hope that the information contained within this text will be both informative and challenging as you navigate the waters of culturally specific psychological theories and practices. Although we take some measure of pride in offering these ideas to the discipline of psychology and various African-American communities across America and the diasposa, we are nonetheless cognizant of the fact that the knowledge we present is but a sampling of what one must know to develop a deep understanding, sincere appreciation for, and working knowledge of the culture of African-descent people.

The most difficult challenge in advancing these theories and constructs is not what to present. The plethora of written resources in the field of Black psychology leaves one with sufficient material to substantiate, and in some cases augment, our thinking. The most challenging aspect of our work remains one of relevance. We believe that the authenticity of these principles of African-centered psychology must be measured against our ability to apply them to people's lives in meaningful ways. If that can be done, if people's lives are better or somehow transformed or service providers are more effective by using our work, then the question of authenticity will have been answered.

The strength and resolve of our determination to produce this book have been fortified by a belief that one should be cautious about criticizing what exists unless one is able to put something more constructive in its place. We are clear that the principles and practices of Euroamerican psychology has severe limitations when applied to African-descent people. In contrast, we believe that anchoring one's analysis in an African-centered worldview is a more enlightened approach in seeking to understand the spiritual, cognitive, affective, and behavioral dimensions of African-American people's lives and experiences. However, those who accept the challenge of integrating African-centered perspectives into their work with African-American people must come to grips with several issues. The first of these centers around the necessity to develop a personal comfort level and commitment with the worldview itself.

The socialization each of us receives through society's institutions often conditions us to be uncomfortable with our unique cultural heritage. In some cases our thinking is so contaminated that we accept society's notions that to be in support of African-centered principles and practices, one must by necessity be in opposition to Euroamerican people and ideas. As a consequence of our discomfort and confusion, we, at worst, distance ourselves from ideas and people that are African-centered, and at best, only tangentially commit ourselves to embracing the personalities of those who are considered important in the field. Neither of these perspectives is acceptable if you expect to be successful in working with African-American people. Those who are serious about effectively intervening with African-American population must be: (1) less focused on "personalities" in psychology, (2) more focused on the "principles" our scholars advance, and (3) more committed to achieving greater congruence between what we profess in principle and what actually occurs within the institutions that serve the mental health needs of African-descent people.

The second issue involves identification and study of the original sources of knowledge and truth. Throughout this text, we have deliberately looked back to the past for the information that will assist us in the future. The reclamation of African-centered principles that emerged from ancient Kemetic and historical African times provides all of us with the conceptual anchors necessary to embrace the original human psychology. Once reclaimed, this knowledge can be used to assist African-descent people, and those who serve them, with promoting greater levels of order, harmony, mental health, and wellness in their lives. The challenge, of course, becomes how to translate and adapt this ancient and historical knowledge and truth into strategies for intervention. Each of you must play a part in this as well.

The third issue involves the necessity for helpers to integrate African-centered principles into their own lifespace. We believe that it will be difficult to effect meaningful change in the lives of our clients, students, and others unless service providers are themselves culturally grounded. The power to become a healing presence in someone's life, or a contributor to someone's growth and nurturing can never be achieved by the superficial application of African-centered knowledge and truth. These principles are not something that can be pulled down off of a shelf and accessed when it is convenient. African-centered psychology is about the life-affirming principles that bring order and harmony to the lifespace of both client and healer. Consequently, the healer cannot facilitate spiritual enlightenment and illumination, or any other health state, unless and until he or she is in a state of health and enlightenment himself or herself. Hopefully, this text will aid each reader in the processes of knowledge acquisition and self-discovery; once achieved, we grow in confidence in knowing that our sensitivity, awareness, and understanding is congruent with the principles of human psychology and mental and spiritual liberation.

In advocating for greater levels of awareness and understanding, we are clear that enlightenment does not occur overnight; and while you the reader flatter and honor us by utilizing our text as a resource in your learning process, we are also clear that a single text will not suffice. African-centered perspectives cannot be learned in one book, in one course, in a finite amount of time. Serious study does not mirror television programs where resolution is achieved after 30 minutes, with or without commercial interruption. Indeed, mastery and competence are levels to which we aspire, not plateaus we arrive at because we have read a certain book or attended a particular seminar.

Consequently, we conclude this third edition with an invitation to solidify your exposure to African-centered perspectives in psychology by reading and studying other resources. The recommendations of reading materials are not meant to be exhaustive. They are considered essential reading for anyone wanting to engage in serious study, and acquire a greater mastery of the knowledge required to understand and facilitate mental health with African-American people.

A SELECTED ANNOTATED BIBLIOGRAPHY

African American Psychology:
Thirty Years in the Evolution of an Idea
A Selected Annotated Bibliography

Historical Antecedents

Ani, M. (1996) ***Let the Circle Be Unbroken.*** **Trenton: Red Sea Press.** An excellent and user-friendly book for anyone interested in understanding the African worldview.

Carruthers, J. H. III, and Leon Harris (Eds.). (1998) ***Association for the Study of Classical African Civilizations World History Project: Preliminary Challenges.*** An important overview concerning the creation of an African-centered general history of Africa by some of the pre-eminent thinkers in the African centered movement today.

Diop, C.A. (1959) ***The Cultural Unity of Black Africa.*** **Chicago: Third World Press.** One of the most important books ever written on the notion of an African cultural unity. Diop explores and makes a cogent argument for the social, cultural, and linguistic unity of African peoples.

Jackson, J.G. (1980) ***Introduction to African Civilization. New Jersey:*** **Citadel Press.** A classic introduction to the vast history of Africa and her peoples, from ancient Kemet (Egypt) to the nation states of Ghana, Mali, and Songhay.

James, G.G.M. (1976) ***Stolen Legacy.*** **San Francisco: Julian Richardson Associates.** Professor James suggests that what is currently known as Greek philosophy was in fact stolen from the ancient Africans.

Williams, C. (1974) ***The Destruction of Black Civilization: Great Issues of a Race 4500 B.C. to 2000 A.D.*** **Chicago: Third World Press.** One of the most important historical studies of African history and culture to date. Essential reading for anyone interested in an easy-to-read study of African history.

Wobogo, V. (1976, Winter) "Diop's Two Cradle Theory and the Origin of White Racism." ***Black Books Bulletin, 4*** **(4), 20–29,72.** One of the most important early writings on the history of European cultural chauvinism.

The History and Evolution of Black Psychology

Akbar, N. (1985) Nile Valley Origins of the Science of the Mind. In Ivan Van Sertima (Ed.), *Nile Valley Civilizations,* New York: Journal of African Civilizations. A historico-philosophic discussion of the ancient African foundations of Western psychology.

Akbar, N. (1986) "Africentric Social Sciences for Human Liberation." *Journal of Black Studies,* 14 (4), 395–414. An important discussion of the ways in which worldviews inform psychology and the role that an Africentric worldview can play in helping to humanize psychology.

Clark, C.X., Nobles,W., McGee, D.P., and Weems, X.L. (1975) "Voodoo or I.Q.: An Introduction to African Psychology." *The Journal of Black Psychology,* 1 (2), 1975. Voodoo or I.Q. is the article that launched a movement. This is the seminal article that literally changed the face of Black psychology. In many ways this article was ahead of its time in its dealing with the importance of African culture as a means of psychological order.

Guthrie, R. (1976) *Even the Rat Was White.* New York: Harper & Row. A historical analysis of the racist use of Western psychology and the African-American pioneers in Western psychology.

Jones, R. (Ed.) (1991) *Black Psychology* (3rd ed.). Hampton, VA: Cobb and Henry. This book is the culmination of nearly thirty years of theory, research, and practice in the area of Black psychology. This is a must have book for anyone seriously interested in the writings of some of the seminal thinkers in the field.

Myers, L.J. (1988) *Understanding the Afrocentic Worldview:* Introduction to an Optimal Psychology. Dubuque, IA: Kendall/Hunt. A theoretical discussion of the humanizing potential that an Afrocentric psychology can have on the continued development of psychology.

Nobles, W.W. (1972) African Philosophy Foundation for a Black Psychology. In R. Jones (Ed.), *Black Psychology.* New York: Harper Row. Nobles posits that there exists a core African philosophy that should be the basis for a Black psychology. In many ways this article helped to launch the Afrocentic psychology movement.

Nobles, W.W. (1986) *African Psychology: Toward Its Reclamation, Reascension and Revitalization.* Oakland: Institute for the Advanced Study of Black Family Life and Culture. The first text to explore in detail the basis for an African psychology. This text builds on the earlier ideas articulated in Voodoo or I.Q.

White, J.L. (1972) Toward a Black Psychology. In R.L. Jones (Ed.), *Black Psychology*. New York: Harper and Row. The seminal work in the field of Black psychology. In many regards this work is seen as the foundation for much of what is useful in Black psychology.

Personality and Identity Development

Akbar, N. (1976) "Rhythmic Patterns in African Personality." African Philosophical: *Assumption and Paradigm for Research of Black Persons,* In L.M. King, V.J. Dixon, W.W. Nobles (Eds.), *Africa Phil.*: Fanon Center Publications. A unique look at the interconnectedness of African culture and its implications for the development of a theory of African American personality.

Cross, W.E. (1991) *Shades of Black.* Philadelphia, Phil. Temple University Press.

Cross, W.E. (1971) "The Negro to Black Conversion Experience: Towards the Psychology of Black Liberation." Black World, 20, 13–27. Foundational reading for any one interested in Black identity development. This invaluable work gave rise to two generations of scholarship on Black identity.

Dubois W.E.B. (1903) *The Souls of Black Folks.* Chicago: McClary.

Kambon, K. (1992) *The African Personality in America: An African Centered Framework.* Tallahassee: Nubian Nation Publications. An African-centered theory of personality in an American context.

Nobles, W.W. (1998) To Be African or Not to Be: The Question of Identity or Authenticity—Some Preliminary Thoughts. In R.L. Jones, (Ed.), African American Identity Development, A look at the importance and value of asserting an African agency based on a notion of human authenticity.

Parham, T.A. (1989) Cycles of Psychological Nigrescence. Counseling Psychologist, 17, 226. Building on the Cross nigrescence model, Parham offers a seminal examination of the Black identity development as a lifespan phenomenon.

Thomas, C. (1971) *Boys No More.* Beverly Hills: Glencoe Press. Articulates the concept of Negromachy, which is a confusion of self-worth, where the individual in appropriately depends on White society for self-definition.

Assessment and Appraisal

Banks, W.C. (1982) Deconstructive Falsification: Foundations of Critical Method in Black Psychology. In E. Jones & S. Korchin (Eds.), *Minority Mental Health.* New York: Praeger. Banks advances a notion of a self-reflective critical method in Black psychology that seeks to interrogate and expand knowledge production in Black psychology.

Banks, W.C. (1992) "The Theoretical and Methodological Crisis of the Africentric Conception." *Journal of Negro Education,* 61 (3). An in-depth discussion of the current theoretical and methodological state of the field in Black psychology.

Banks, W.C. (1976) "White Preference in Blacks: A Paradigm in Search of a Phenomenon." *Psychological Bulletin,* 83. A ground breaking discussion of the ways in which method in psychology has been used as a tool to maintain and perpetuate oppression.

Gynther, M. D. (1972) "White Norms and MMPI's: A Prescription for Discrimination?" *Psychological Bulletin,* 78, 386–402.

Hilliard, A.G. III. (1981) I.Q. as catechism: Ethnic and cultural bias or invalid science." *Black Books Bulletin,* 7 (2). A deconstructionist examination of ways in which intelligence testing has been used to assert, maintain and justify racism.

Hilliard, A.G. III. (1994) "What Is This Thing Called Intelligence and Why Bother to Measure It?" *Journal of Black Psychology,* 20 (4), 430–444. An examination of the limitations of intelligence as a construct.

Nobles, W.W. (1978) *African Consciousness and Liberation Struggles: Implications for the Development and Construction of Scientific Paradigms.* Presented at the Fanon Research and Development Institute, Port of Spain, Trinidad. An examination of the relationship between culture, worldview, and the development and use of science.

Education

Akoto, K.G. (1992) *Nation-Building: Theory and Practice in Afrikan Centered Education..* Washington, D.C.: Pan Afrikan World Institute. A look at the theory and practical application of Afrikan centered educational model.

Erny, P. (1973) *Childhood and Cosmos: The Social Psychology of the Black African Child.* New York: New Perspectives. An early study on the African conception of childhood.

Hilliard, A.G. III. (1997) *SBA: The Reawakening of the African Mind.* Gainesville: Makare Publishing. Professor explores the ancient African foundations of wisdom, and their implications for contemporary education and teacher training.

Shujaa, Mwalimu, (Ed.) (1994) *Too Much Schooling, Too Little Education: A Paradox of Black Life in White Society.* Trenton: Africa World Press. A compilation of 17 Afrocentric essays exploring the contours and complexities of education in African America.

Tedla, E. (1995) *Sankofa: African Thought and Education.* New York: Peter Lang. A look at the basis for a model of education that is rooted in African thought and wisdom.

Woodson, C.G. (1990) *The Miseducation of the Negro,* Trenton: Africa.

Counseling/Clinical Therapeutic Interventions

Adebimpe, V. (1981) "Overview: White Norms in Psychiatric Diagnosis of Black Patients." *American Journal of Psychiatry,* 138 (3), 279–285.

Akbar, N. (1981) "Mental Disorders Among African Americans." *Black Books Bulletin.* Naim Akbar challenges some of the prevailing traditional conventions regarding mental disorder, while introducing the reader to an African centered conception of mental order and disorder.

Azibo, D.A. (1989) "African Centered Theses on Mental Health and a Nosology of Black/African Personality Disorder. *The Journal of Black Psychology,* 15(2), 173–214. Azibo discusses the implications for an African-centered conception of personality disorder while offering a nosology that attempts to categorize 18 personality disorders not found in the DSMIV and endemic to African-Americans.

Parham, T.A. and Helms, J.E. (1981) "Influences of Black Students Racial Identity Attitudes on Preference for Counselor Race." *Journal of Counseling Psychiatry,* 28 (3), 250–256. Parham and Helms explore the ways in which the nigresence model might be used to understand counselor race influences on Black students' racial identity and attitudes on preference.

Black Family

Billingley, A. (1968) *Black Families in White America.* Englewood Cliffs, NJ: Prentice-Hall. A psychosocial study of the Black family in America.

Boyd-Franklin, N. (1989) *Black Families in Therapy.* New York: Guilford Press. A theoretically sound and practically relevant guide to working with African-American families in a Family Systems approach.

Clark, R. (1983) *Family Life and School Achievement.* Chicago: University of Chicago Press. An ethnographic study out of Chicago that makes the essential point that it is not family composition but parental disposition that makes the biggest difference in facilitating educational achievement in Black children.

McAdoo, H.P. (Ed.) (1981) *Black Families.* Beverly Hills; Sage. A comprehensive look at the mutidimensionality of the Black family.

Nobles, W.W. (1974) "African Root American Fruit: The Black Family. *Journal of Social and Behavioral Sciences,* 20, 66–75. A look at African cultural retention's as a source of strength and vitality for African Americans; and the implications for the study of the African American family.

Nobles, W.W. (1985) *Africanity and the Black Family: Toward a Theoretical Model.* Oakland: Black Family Institute. In many ways this text represents the amplification of his earlier work on African cultural retention's as a source of strength and vitality for African-Americans.

Cultural Oppression

Ani, M. (1994) *Yurugu: An African Centered Critique of European Cultural Thought and Behavior.* Trenton: African World Press. Ani offers an African examination and analysis of Plato and his impact on European culture and behavior and the ways in which European cultural thought and behavior have created a system of global domination and oppression.

Bulhan, H.A. (1985) *Frantz Fanon and the Psychology of Oppression.* New York: Plenum. Pehaps the most comprehensive review and distillation of Frantz Fanon's thinking to date.

Cress-Welsing, F. (1990) *The Isis Papers: Keys to the Colors.* Chicago: Third World Press. A penetrating and provocative thesis about the European psyche and the perpetuation of global white supremacy.

Fanon, F. (1967) ***Black Skin, White Mask.*** **New York: Grove Press.** Fanon's classic study of the impact of oppression on the development of identity.

Jones, J. (1997) ***Prejudice and Racism*** **(2nd ed.). New York: McGraw-Hill.** A compelling analysis of racism and prejudice and how they impact the lives of all people.

Nobles, W.W. (1974) "Black People in White Insanity: An Issue for Black Community Mental Health." ***Journal of Afro American Issues,*** **4, 21–27.** A look at the negative psychological effects of Western culture on the psychosocial well-being of African-Americans.

Wilson, A. (1993) ***The Falsification of Consciousness: Eurocentric History, Psychiatry and the Politics of White Supremacy.*** **New York: Afrikan World Infosystems.** A look at the colonization of African history by Europeans and it negative impact on the psychological functioning of African peoples.

General Studies

Asanti, M. (1997) ***The Afrocentric Idea.*** **Philadelphia: Temple University Press.**

Jenkins, A. (1982) ***The Psychology of the Afro-American: A Humanistic Approach.*** **New York: Pergamon Press.**

Self-Healing

Powell-Hopson, D. and Hopson, D. (1998) ***The Power of Soul: Pathways to Psychological and Spiritual Growth for African-Americans.*** **New York: Wm. Morrow & Co.**

Vanzant, I. (1998). ***One Day My Soul Just Opened Up.*** **New York: Simon & Schuster (Fireside).**

AFTERWORD

"Remembering Sadie": A Son to His Mother

Statistical probability says that a Black female, raising four children by herself, would be overwhelmed by life's obstacles and challenges. Statistics could measure your income and classify your ethnicity and age, but they couldn't possibly measure your heart.

You gave years of outstanding service as our government worked you for 33 of them. You trained countless others less knowledgeable and capable than you to do their jobs, and watched them get promoted into positions you were rarely, if ever, considered for, but you never complained. You simply performed your job with pride and dependability, and never let resentment creep into your consciousness, because asserting yourself was less important than providing for your family. They could try and measure your temperament, but they could never really measure your heart.

Separation and not-continued marriage was a path you chose, when the perception of alcoholism and related consequences were risks you were unwilling to subject your children to. And so you checked your adult dreams, wants, and desires at the door of responsibility, and while many parents were exploring ways to get their groove on, you looked for ways to ensure the proper feeding, clothing, nurturing, and protection of your children, who were the center of your life. They could calculate the dreams deferred, but they could never measure your heart.

Physical illness and childhood sickness were a constant companion in our family; and when rocking back and forth/back and forth in the middle of the night was the only relief from the asthmatic wheezing and shortness of breath, you were there with us all night with home remedies and TLC. Statistics could measure the hours of lost sleep, but they couldn't measure your heart.

The RTD bus was our source of transportation in the days when a quarter and a transfer would get us to our destination. Day or night, bus stops safe and not, on the go with four children always in toe. Others might complain about the inconvenience, but not you. They could measure the miles you traveled, but they could never measure your heart.

Hawaii was never quite your style, as sitting on the beach watching the sunset or sipping on a piña colada could never match the thrill of a nickel slot machine at Vegas or Tahoe. The Flamingo Hilton held a certain appeal and not even the splendor of the new MGM Grand or the Luxor could match the anticipation of that certain machine you knew was ready to hit and pay off, and help to extend your daily allotment of money to spend, even if only $20.00.

Always ready to share a meal or some motherly advice, when four children were extended by friends who became adopted sons and daughters. There were Carlos and Alfred, Pat, Redmond, and Michael Green; Chris Dansby, Bobby, Hush, Gordon, Julia, and Jeff Whitt. Numbers might estimate the meals you cooked or the advice and care you gave, but they could never measure your heart.

You never finished college, but there was no question about your expectation for us to exceed your own goal attainment. And, as proud as you were of our academic and professional accomplishments, expectations of self-sufficiency and a strong faith in God were the markers you set for "true" success, and you kept us humble.

Devoutly religious, your relationship with God remained strong even after the arthritic deformities and joint pain made it impossible to continue attending regular church services. Always remembering to give thanks for even the smallest blessing, your faith was solid as a rock.

In your final months, weeks, days, and moments, medical technology tried to measure your heart rate, oxygen saturation level, arterial blood gases, and your blood pressure. But you know that they could never truly measure your heart. But we who knew you and loved you know better.

If they had an adequate instrument or device to measure your heart, what would it reveal in its truest form. Beyond the ventricles and mitral valves are found:

1. Strength
2. Unlimited love
3. Pride
4. Determination
5. Discipline
6. Willingness to persevere through whatever adversity came your way
7. Faith in God

Mom, we love you and will miss you, but your heart will always be with us.

Thomas Parham
July 20, 1998

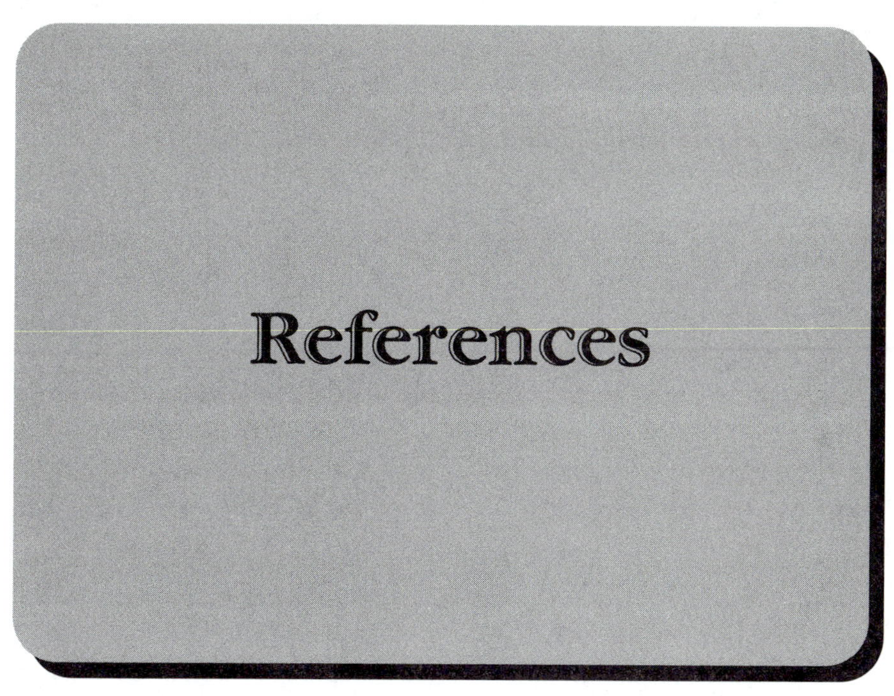

References

Abrahams, R. (1970). *Deep Down in the Jungle*. Chicago: Adline Publishing Company.

Adams, W.A. (1950). "The Negro Patient in Psychiatric Treatment," *American Journal of Orthopsychiatry,* 201, 305–308.

Adebimpe, V. (1981). "Overview: White Norms in Psychiatric Diagnosis of Black Patients," *American Journal of Psychiatry,* 138(3), 275–285.

Akbar, N. (1989). "Nigrescence and Identity: Some Limitations," *The Counseling Psychologist,* Vol. 17(2), 258–263.

Akbar, N (1984). "Africentric Social Sciences for Human Liberation," *Journal of Black Studies,* Vol. 14(4), 395–414.

Akbar, N. (1981). "Mental Disorders Among African Americans," *Black Books Bulletin,* 7(2), 18–25.

Akbar, N. (1994). *Light from Ancient Africa*. Tallahassee: Mind Productions.

Ajamu, A.A. (1998). Ubunye Umuzi; Distinguishing essence from expression, the African American contribution. *The Black Studies Journal,* San Francisco: San Francisco State University. Winter, Vol. 1, 1–9.

Ajamu, A.A. (1998). From Tef Tef to Mdw Nfr: The Importance of Utilizing African Terminologies and Concepts in the Rescue, Restoration, Reconstruction and Reconnection with African Ancestral Memory. In the African World History Project: Preliminary Challenges, Jacob H. Coruthers Jr. and Leon Harris (eds.).

Ajamu, A.A. (1998). Ubunye Umuzi: Distinguishing Essence from Expression—The African American Contribution. *San Francisco State Journal of Black Studies*. ADISA.

Akoto, K.A. (1992). *Nationbuilding: Theory and Practice in Afrikan Centered Education*. Washington: Pan Afrikan World Institute.

American College Dictionary (1987). New York: Random House.

Ames, R. (1950). "Protest and Irony in Negro Folksong," *Social Science,* 14, 193–213.

Ani, M. (1994). *Yurugu: An African Centered Critique of European Cultural Thought and Behavior*. Trenton: African World Press.

Ani, M. (1989/1997) *Let the Circle Be Unbroken: Implications of African Spirituality in the Diaspora*. Trenton: Red Sea Press.

Aries, P. (1980). *The Hour of Our Death*. New York: Knopf.

Arnez, N.L. (1972). "Enhancing Black Self-Concept Through Literature." In J. Banks and J. Grambs (eds.), *Black Self-Concept*. New York: McGraw-Hill.

Azibo, D. (1989). "Advances in Black/African Personality Theory." Unpublished manuscript.

Azibo, D. (1983). "Some Psychological Concomitants and Consequences of the Black Personality: Mental Health Implications," *Journal of Non-White Concerns* (January), 59–66.

Baldwin, A.L. (1980). *Theories of Child Development* (2nd ed.). New York: Wiley.

Baldwin, J.A. (1985). "African Self-Consciousness Scale: An Afrocentric Questionaire," *Western Journal of Black Studies,* 2(9) 61–68.

Baldwin, J.A. (1963). *The Fire Next Time*. New York: Dell Publishing Company.

Banks, W.C. (1992). "The Theoretical and Methodological Crisis of the Africentric Conception," *Journal of Negro Education,* Vol. 6(3).

Banks, W.C. (1982). "Deconstructive Falsification: Foundations of Critical Method in Black Psychology." In E. Jones & S. Korchin (eds.), *Minority Mental Health*. New York: Praeger.

Banks, W. and Grambs, J. (1972). *Black Self Concept*. New York: McGraw-Hill.

Barnes, E.J. (1972). "The Black Community as the Source of Positive Self-Concept for Black Children: A Theoretical Perspective." In R.L. Jones (ed.), *Black Psychology*. New York: Harper & Row.

Basch M. (1980). *Doing Psychotherapy*. New York: Basic Books.

Beale-Spencer, M. (1997). "A Phenomenological Variant of Ecological Systems Theory (PVEST): A Self Organization Perspective in Context." *Development and Psychopathology,* 9, 817–833.

Beale-Spencer, M., Kim, Soo-Ryon, and Marshall, Sheree (1987). "Double Stratification and Psychological Risks: Adaptational Processes and School Achievement of Black Children." *Journal of Negro Education*, Vol. 56(1), 77–87.

Beez, W.V. (1969). "Influence of Biased Psychological Reports on Teacher Behavior and Pupil Performance." Proceedings of the 76th Annual Conventions of the American Psychological Association, No. 3, 605–606.

Berry, G. (1982). "Television, Self-Esteem and the Afro-American Child: Some Implications for Mental Health Professionals." In B.A. Bass, G.E. Wyatt, and G.J. Powell (eds.), *The Afro-American Family: Assessment, Treatment and Research Issues*. New York: Grune & Stratton.

Betancourt, H. and Lopez, S.R. (1993). "The Study of Culture, Ethnicity and Race in American Psychology." *American Psychologist,* 48, 629–637.

Billingsley, A. (1968). *Black Families in White America*. Englewood Cliffs, NJ: Prentice-Hall.

Blassingame, J. (1972). *The Slave Community*. New York: Oxford University Press.

Block, C. (1980). "Black Americans and the Cross-Cultural Counseling Experience." In A.J. Marsella and P.B. Pederson (eds.), *Cross-Cultural Counseling and Psychotherapy*. New York: Pergamon.

Bourne, P. (1973). "Alcoholism in the Urban Population." In P. Bourne and R. Fox (eds.), *Alcoholism: Progress in Research and Treatment*. New York: Academic Press.

Boyd-Franklin, N. (1989). *Black Families in Therapy*. New York: Guilford Press.

Boykin, A.W. (In Press) "Talent Development, Fundamental Culture and School Reform: Implications for African Immersion Schools." In D. Pollard and C. Ajirotutu (Eds.) *Sankofa Issues in African Centered Education*. Westport, CT: Greenwood Press.

Boykin, A.W. (1997). "Culture Matters in the Psycho-Social Experiences of African Americans: Some Conceptual, Process and Practical Considerations." Unpublished manuscript.

Boykin, A.W. (1994). "Afrocultural expression and its implications for schooling." In E. Hollins, J. King, and W. Hayman (Eds.) *Teaching Diverse Populations: Formulating a Knowledge Base*. Albany: State University of New York Press.

Boykin, A.W. (1994). "Harvesting Culture and Talent: African American Children and School Reform." In R. Rossi (Ed.) *Schools and Students at Risk: Context and Framework for Positive Change*. New York: Teachers College Press.

Boykin, A.W. (1983). "The Academic Performance of Afro-American Children." In J. Spence (Ed.), *Achievement and Achievement Motives*. San Francisco: W. Freeman.

Boykin, A.W. (1979). Black Psychology and the Research Process: Keeping the Baby But Throwing Out the Bath Water. In Boykin, W., Franklin, A.J., & Yates, F. (Ed.), *Research Deviations for Black Psychologists*. Thousand Oaks: Sage.

Boykin, A.W. and Ellison, C. (1995). Rhythmic-Movement Facilitation of Learning in Working-Class Afro-American Children. *Journal of Genetic Psychology,* 149, 335–348.

Brayboy, T. (1971). "The Black Patient in Group Therapy." *International Journal of Group Psychotherapy,* 2(3), 288–293.

Brigham, J.C. (1974). "Views of Black and White Children Concerning the Distribution of Personality Characteristics," *Journal of Personality,* 42, 144–158.

Brofenbrenner, U. (1963). "Development Theory in Transition." In H.W. Stevenson (ed.), Child Psychology. *Sixty-Second Yearbook of the National Society for the Study of Education*, Part 1. Chicago: University of Chicago Press.

Campbell, D.T. (1976). "Stereotypes and the Perception of Group Differences," *American Psychologists,* 22, 817–829.

Caplan, N. (1970). "The New Negro Man: A Review of Recent Empirical Studies," *Journal of Social Issues,* 26, 57–73.

Carter, R. and Helms, J.E. (1987). "The Relationship of Black Value-Orientations to Racial Attitudes," *Measurement and Evaluation in Counseling and Development,* 17, 185–195.

Carruther, J.H., Jr. (1972). *Science and Oppression.* Chicago: Northeastern Illinois University, Center for Inner City Studies.

Carruthers, J.H. (1972,1996). "Science and Oppression." In *African Psychology in Historical Perspective and Related Commentary.* Daudi Azibo (ed.). ADISA.

Claiborn, W.L. (1969). "Expectancy Effects in the Classroom: A Failure to Replicate," *Journal of Educational Psychology,* 60, 377–383.

Clark, C. (1975). "The Shockley-Jensen Thesis: A Contextual Appraisal." *The Black Scholar,* 6, 2–5.

Clark, C.X.; Nobles,W.; McGee, D.P.; X, Luther Weems (1975). "Voodoo or I.Q.: An Introduction to African Psychology." *The Journal of Black Psychology.* Vol. 1(2).

Clark, K. and Clark, M. (1947). "Racial Identification and Preferences in Negro Children," *Readings in Social Psychology.* New York: Holt.

Clark, R. (1983). *Family Life and School Achievement.* Chicago: University of Chicago Press.

Cole, M. (1995). "From Cross-Cultural to Cultural Psychology." *Swiss Journal of Psychology,* 54, 262–276.

Cole, M. (1984). "The World Beyond our Borders: What Might our Students Need to Know About It." *American Psychologist,* 39, 998–1005.

Coleman, K. (1996). "The Influence of a Commural Learning Context on African American Elementary Students' Creative Problem Solving." Masters Thesis, Howard University, Washington, DC.

Cottle, T.A. (1975). "A Case of Suspension," *National Elementary Principal,* 5, 69–74.

Counter, S.A. and Evans, D.L. (1981). *I Sought My Brother: An Afro-American Reunion.* Cambridge: MIT Press.

Cross, W.E., Parham, T.A., and Helms, J.E. (eds.) (1998). "Nigrescence Revisited: Theory and Research." In R.L. Jones (ed.), *African American Identity Development.* Hampton, VA: Cobb & Henry Publishers.

Cross, W.E. (1971). "The Negro to Black Conversion Experience: Towards the Psychology of Black Liberation," *Black World,* 20, 13–27.

Dance, D. (1978). *Shuckin' and Jivin': Folklore from Contemporary Black Americans.* Bloomington: Indiana University Press.

Dansby, P. (1972). "Black Pride in the Seventies: Fact or Fantasy." In R.L. Jones (ed.), *Black Psychology*. New York: Harper & Row.

Davis, L.G. (1994). The Changing Black Family. In R. Staples (ed.), *The Black Family: Essays and Studies*. Belmont, CA: Wadsworth Publishing Company.

Davis, R. (1981). "A Demographic Analysis of Suicide." In L.E. Gary (ed.), *Black Men*. Beverly Hills: Sage Publishing Company.

Delpit, L. (1995). *Other People's Children*. New York: The New Press.

Dill, E. (1996). The Influence of Commural and Peer-Tutoring Context on the Text Recall Learning of Low Income African American Students. Masters Thesis, Howard University, Washington, DC.

Diop, C.A. (1991). *Civilization or Barbarism: An Authentic Anthropology*. Brooklyn, NY: Lawrence Hill Books.

Diop, C.A. (1974). *The African Origin of Civilization: Myth or Reality*. Westport, CT: Lawrence Hill & Co.

Diop, C.A. (1959). *The Cultural Unity of Black Africa*. Chicago: Third World Press.

Dixon, R. and Lerner, R. (1994). "A History of Systems in Developmental Psychology." In M. Bornstein and M. Lamb (eds.), *Developmental Psychology; An Advanced Textbook*. (3rd ed.). Hillsdale: LEA.

DuBois, W.E.B. (1903). *The Souls of Black Folks*. Chicago: McClurg.

Dyke, B. (1983). "Pre-Therapy Education Techniques for Black Families: Expectancies and Cognitions." Unpublished Doctoral Dissertation, University of Pennsylvania.

Ellison, R. (1952). *Invisible Man*. New York: Random House.

Erny, P. (1973). *Childhood and Cosmos*. New York: Black Orpheus Press.

Fanon, F. (1967). *Black Skin, White Masks*. New York: Grove Press.

Fanon, F. (1966). *Wretched of the Earth*. New York: Grove Press, Inc.

Feyerabend, P.K. (1978). *Science in a Free Society*. London: NLB.

Fiester, A.R. and Rudestam, K.E. (1975). "A Multivariate Analysis of the Early Drop-Out Process," *Journal of Consulting and Clinical Psychology*, 43(4), 528–535.

Fisher, J. (1969). "Negroes and Whites and Rates of Mental Illness: Reconsideration of a Myth," *Psychiatry*, 32, 428–446.

Fleming, E.S. and Anttonen, R.G. (1971). "Teacher Expectancy or My Fair Lady," *Aera Journal*, 8, 241.

Forde, D. (1964) *African Worlds*. London: Oxford University Press.

Frazier, E.F. (1962). *Black Bourgeoisie*. New York: Crowell, Collier and MacMillan.

Frazier, E.F. (1939). *The Negro Family in the United States*. Chicago: University of Chicago Press.

Frederickson, G. (1976). "The Government Report." *The New York Times Review*, September, 18–22.

Frederickson, G. (1976). "The Gutman Report." *The New York Times Review*, September 30, 18–22, 27.

Fu-Kiau, B.I. (1991). *Self Healing Power and Therapy: Old Teachings From Africa*. New York: Vintage Press.

Gates, H.L. (1994). *Colored People*. New York: Alfred Knopf.

Gibbs, J.T. (1988). *Young, Black, and Male in America*. Dover, MA: Auburn House Publishing Company.

Goodlad, J. (1983). *A Place Called School: Prospects for the Future*. New York: McGraw-Hill.

Goodman, M.E. (1952). *Racial Awareness in Young Children*. Cambridge: Addison Wesley.

Greenberg, B. and Dervin, B. (1970). "Mass Communication Among the Urban Poor," *Public Opinion Quarterly,* 34, 224–235.

Greenfield, P. (1994). "Independence and Interdependence as Developmental Scripts: Implications for Theory, Research and Practice." In P. Greenfield and R. Cocking (eds.), *Cross Cultural Roots of Minority Child Development*. Hillsdale: Lawrence Erlbaum.

Grier, W.H., Cobbs, P.M. (1968). *Black Rage*. New York: Basic Books.

Gurin, P. and Epps, E. (1975). *Black Consciousness, Identity, and Achievement: A Study of Students in Historically Black Colleges*. New York: John Wiley & Sons.

Guthrie, R. (1998) *Even the Rat was White*. (2nd ed.), Needham Heights, MA: Allyn & Bacon.

Gutman, H. (1976). *The Black Family in Slavery and Freedom: 1750–1925*. New York: Vintage Books.

Gynther, M. D. (1972). "White Norms and MMPI's: A Prescription for Discrimination?" *Psychological Bulletin,* 78, 386–402.

Harayda, J. (1987). "How to Be Happy Single," *Essence,* 18(6) (October), 61–62.

Hare, N. (1965). *Black Anglo-Saxons*. New York: Mangi and Mansell.

Harper, F.D. (1981). "Alcohol Use and Abuse." In L.E. Gary (ed.), *Black Men*. Beverly Hills, CA: Sage Publishing Company.

Harper, F.D. (1979). *Alcoholism Treatment and Black Americans*. Rockwille, MD: Department of Health, Education and Welfare, National Institute on Alcohol Abuse and Alcoholism.

Heitler, J. (1976). "Preparatory Techniques in Initiating Expressive Group Therapy with Lower-Class, Unsophisticated Patients," *Psychological Bulletin*, 83(2), 339–352.

Helms, J.E. (1984). "Toward a Theoretical Explanation of the Effects of Race on Counseling: A Black and White Model," *Counseling Psychologists,* 12(4), 153–165.

Herskovits, M.J. (1958). *The Myth of the Negro Past*. Boston, MA: Beacon Press.

Highlen, P.S. and Hill, C.E. (1984). "Factors Affecting Client Change in Individual Counseling: Current Status of Theoretical Speculations." In S.D. Brown and R.W. Lent (eds.), *The Handbook of Counseling Psychology*. New York: John Wiley & Sons.

Hill, R. (1971). *Strengths of the Black Family.* New York: National Urban League.

Hilliard, A.G. (1997). *SBA: The Reawakening of the African Mind.* Gainesville, FL: Makare Publisher.

Hilliard, A.G. (1996). "Either a Paradigm Shift or No Mental Measurement," *Psychdiscourse.* 26(10), 6–20.

Hilliard, T. (1972). "Personality Characteristics of Black Student Activists and Non-Activists." In R.L. Jones (ed.), *Black Psychology.* New York: Harper & Row.

Hines, P.M. and Boyd-Franklin, N. (1982). "Black Families." In M. McGoldrick, V. Pearce, and J. Giordane (eds.), *Ethnicity in Family Therapy.* New York: Guilford Press.

Holloway, J.E. (1990). "The Origins of African American Culture." In J.E. Holloway (ed.). *Africanisms in American Culture.*

Holloway, J.E. (1990). *Africanisms in American Culture.* Bloomington: Indiana University Press.

Hughes, D., Seidman, E., and Williams, N. (1993). "Cultural Phenomena and the Research Enterprise: Toward a Culturally Anchored Methodology." *American Journal of Community Psychology,* 21, 687–703.

Hughes, L. (1954). "Mother to Son." In *Selected Poems by Langston Hughes.* New York: Knopf.

Jackson, B. (1976). "Black Identity Development." In L. Gloubshick and B. Persky (eds.), *Urban Social and Educational Issues.* Dubuque: Kendall-Hall, 158–164.

Jackson, M. (1968). "How I Got Over." In *Mahalia Jackson Sings the Best-Loved Hymns of Dr. Martin Luther King, Jr.* (album). New York: Columbia Records.

Jaynes, G.D. and Williams, R.M. (1989). *A Common Destiny: Blacks and American Society.* Washington, DC: National Academy Press.

Jensen, A. (1969). "How Much Can We Boost I.Q. and Scholastic Achievement?" *Harvard Educational Review,* 39, 1–123.

Jewell, K.S. (1988). *Survival of the Black Family: The Institutional Impact of U.S. Social Policy.* New York: Praeger.

Johnson, J. (1983). "Why Black Men Have the Highest Cancer Rate." *Ebony* (March), 69–72.

Jones, R.L. (ed.) (1996). *Handbook of Tests and Measurements for Black Populations,* Vol 1 & 2. Hampton, VA: Cobb and Henry Publishers.

Kardiner, A. and Ovessey, L. (1951). *The Mark of Oppression.* New York: Norton.

Karenga, M. (1976). *Kwanzaa, Origin, Concepts, Practice.* Los Angeles: Kawaida Publications.

Kambon, K. (1992). *The African Personality in America: An African Centered Framework.* Tallahassee: Nubian Nation Publications.

Karenga, M. (1990). *The Book of Coming Forth By Day.* Los Angeles: Univ. of Sankore Press.

Kerner, O. (Chairman) (1968). *Report of the National Commission on Civil Disorders: U.S. Riot Commission Report.* New York: Bantam Books.

King, L. (1982). "Suicide from a Black Reality Perspective." In B. Bass, G.E. Wyatt, and G. Powell (eds.), *The Afro-American Family: Assessment, Treatment and Research*. New York: Grune & Stratton.

Kluckjohn, F.R. and Strodtbeck, F.L. (1961). *Variations in Value Orientations*. Evanston, IL: Row, Perterson.

Knight, G. (1973). "I've Got to Use My Imagination." In *Imagination* (album). New York: Buddha Records.

Kincaid, M. (1968). "Identity and Therapy in the Black Community," *Personnel and Guidance Journal,* 47, 884–890.

Kuhn, T.S. (1970). The Structure of Scientific Revolutions. Chicago: Chicago University Press.

Kunjufu, J. (1986). *Motivating and Preparing Black Youth to Work*. Chicago: African American Images.

Ladner, J. (1971). *Tomorrow's Tomorrow: The Black Woman*. Garden City: Doubleday.

Leakey, R.E. (1994). *The Origin of Humankind*. New York: Basic Books.

Lerner, R.M. (1986). *Concepts and Theories of Human Development* (2nd ed.). New York: Random House.

Lester, J. (1971). "The Angry Children of Malcolm X." In T. Frazier (ed.), *Afro-American History Primary Sources*. New York: Harcourt Brace Jovanovich.

Lewis, D. (1971). *King, A Critical Biography*. Baltimore: Penguin.

Livermore, M. (1897). *The Story of My Life*. Hartford, CT: ADISA.

Looft, W.R. (1972). The Evolution of Developmental Psychology: A Comparison of Handbooks. *Human Development,* 15, 187–201.

Martin, S. (1997). "Students' Attitudes Toward Four Distinct Learning Orientations and Classroom Environments." Doctoral Dissertation, Howard University, Washington, D.C.

Martinez, J.L. (ed.) (1977). *Chicano Psychology*. New York: Academic Press.

Maryshow, D. (1996). "Perception of Future Economic Success and the Impact of Learning Orientation on African American Students' Attitudes Toward High Achievers." Doctoral Dissertation, Howard University, Washington, D.C.

Mbiti, J. S. (1970). *African Religions and Philosophies*. Garden City, New York: Anchor Books.

McAdoo, H.P. (ed.) (1981). *Black Families*. Beverly Hills: Sage Publications.

McAdoo, H.P. (ed.) (1981). "Upward Mobility and Parenting in Middle-Income Black Families," *Journal of Black Psychology,* 8(1), 1–22.

McAdoo, H.P. (1979). "Black Kinship," *Psychology Today,* May, 67–69, 79, 110.

McAdoo, H.P. (1978). "Factors Related to Stability in Upwardly Mobile Black Families," *Journal of Marriage and Family,* 40, 761–778.

McCall, N. (1994). *Makes Me Wanna Holler: A Young Black Man In America*. New York: Vintage Books.

McCord, W., Howard, J., Friedberg, B., and Harwood, E. (1969). *Lifestyles in the Black Ghetto*. New York: W.W. Norton.

McGuire, W. (1983). "A Contextualist Theory of Knowledge: Its Implications for Innovation and Reform in Psychological Research." In L. Berkowitz (ed.), *Advances in Experimental Social Psychology*. New York: Academic Press.

McLoyd, V.C. (1998). "Socio-Economic Disadvantage and Child Development." *American Psychologist,* 53, 185–204.

McLoyd, V.C. (1991). "What Is The Study of African American Children the Study of?" In *Black Psychology,* (3rd ed.), R.L. Jones, (ed.).

Miller, O. (1997). "Cultural Influences on the Classroom Perceptions of African American Grade School Children." Masters Thesis, Howard University, Washington, DC.

Miller, P.A. (1993). *Theories of Developmental Psychology*. New York: W.H. Freeman and Company.

Mitchell, H. (1989). "The Black Family: Five Generational Model for Continuity and Enhancement." Unpublished manuscript.

Moore, E.K. (1981). "Policies Affecting the States of Black Children and Families." In H.P. McAdoo (ed.), *Black Families*. Beverly Hills: Sage Publications.

Moore-Campbell, B. (1987). "Breaking the Age Taboo," *Essence,* 17(10), 51–52, 108.

Moreland, J.K. (1958). "Racial Recognition by Nursery School Children," *Social Forces,* 37, 132–137.

Moynihan, D. (1965). *The Negro Family: The Case for National Action*. Washington, DC: Office of Policy Planning and Research, U.S. Department of Labor.

Murray, C. and Herstein, R.J. (1994). *The Bell Curve*. New York: The Free Press.

Murrell, S. (1978). *Community Psychology and Social Systems: A Conceptual Framework and Intervention Guide*. New York: Behavioral Publications.

Myers, H.F. (1982). "Research on the Afro-American Family: a Critical Review." In B. Bass, G.E. Wyatt, and G. Powell, *The Afro-American Family: Assessment, Treatment and Research*. New York: Grune & Stratton.

Myers, L.J. (1988). *Understanding the Afrocentric Worldview: Introduction to an Optimal Psychology*. Dubuque, IA: Kendall/Hunt.

Myers, L.J. (1985). "Transpersonal Psychology: The Role of the Afrocentric Paradigm," *Journal of Black Psychology,* 12(1), 31–42.

Myes, H.J. and Yochelson, L. (1949). "Color Denial in the Negro," *Psychiatry,* 11, 39–42.

National Center for Health Statistics (1979). *Health*. Washington, DC: Government Printing Office.

National Commission on Excellence in Education (1983). *A Nation at Risk: The Imperative for Educational Reform*. Washington, DC: Government Printing Office.

Nobles, W.W. (1998). "To Be African or Not To Be: The Question of Identity or Authenticity—Some Preliminary Thoughts." In R.L. Jones, (ed.). *African American Identity Development*, Hampton, VA: Cobb & Henry.

Nobles, W.W. (1986). *African Psychology: Towards It's Reclamation, Reassession and Revitalization*. Oakland: Black Family Institute.

Nobles, W.W. (1985). *Africanity and the Black Family*. Oakland, CA: Black Family Institute Publications.

Nobles, W.W. (1978). African Consciousness and Liberation Struggles: Implications for the Development and Construction of Scientific Paradigms. Presented at the Fanon Research and Development Institute, Port of Spain, Trinidad.

Nobles, W.W. (1978). "Toward an Empirical and Theoretical Framework for Defining Black Families," *Journal of Marriage and Family*. November, 679–688.

Nobles, W.W. (1977). "The Rhythmic Impulse: The Issue of Africanity in Black Family Dynamics." Paper presented to the second annual symposium on Black Psychology, Ann Arbor, Michigan.

Nobles, W.W. (1976). "Black People in White Insanity: An Issue for Community Mental Health," *Journal of Afro-American Issues*, 4(1), 21–27.

Nobles, W.W. (1976). "Extended-Self: Rethinking the So-called Negro Self-Concept," *Journal of Black Psychology*, 11(2).

Nobles, W.W. (1974). "Africanity: Its Role in Black Families," *The Black Scholar*, June, 10–17.

Nobles, W.W. (1972). *African's Philosophy: Foundation for Black Psychology*. N.R.L. Jones (ed.), *Black Psychology*. New York: Harper & Row.

Norton, D.G. (no date). "Black Family Life Patterns, the Development of Self and Cognitive Development of Black Children." In Powell, Yavrstate, and Morales (eds.), *The Psychosocial Development of Minority Group Children*. ADISA.

Nsamenang, A. Bame. (1995). "Theories of Developmental Psychology for a Cultural Perspective: A View from Africa." *Psychology and Developing Societies*, 7, 1–19.

Ogbu, J. (1990). "Minority Status and Literacy in Comparative Perspective." *Daedalus*, 119, 141–168.

Oliver, M. and Shapiro, T. (1995). *Black Wealth/White Wealth*. New York: Rutledge.

Pachter, L. and Harwood, R. (1996). "Culture, Child Development and Psychosocial Development." *Journal of Development and Behavioral Pediatrics*, 17, 191–198.

Palardy, J.M. (1969). "What Teachers Believe—What Children Achieve," *Elementary School Journal*, 69, 370–374.

Parham, T.A. (1994, 1998). Passport to the Future Program—Unpublished Document.

Parham, T.A. (1993). *Psychological Storms: The African American Struggle for Identity.* Chicago: African American Images.

Parham, T.A. (1989). "Cycles of Psychological Nigrescence," *The Counseling Psychologist,* 17(2), 187–226.

Parham, T.A. and Helms, J.E. (1985). "Relation of Racial Identity to Self-Actualization and Affective States of Black Students," *Journal of Counseling Psychiatry,* 28(3), 250–256.

Parham, T.A. and Helms, J.E. (1981). "Influences of Black Student's Racial Identity Attitudes on Preferences for Counselor Race," *Journal of Counseling Psychology,* 28(3), 250–256.

Parham, T.A. and McDavis, R. (1987). "Black Males and Endangered Species: Who's Really Pulling the Trigger?" *Journal of Counseling and Development,* 66, 24–27.

Patton, J.M. (1981). "The Black Male's Struggle for an Education." In L.E. Gary (ed.), *Black Men.* Beverly Hills, CA: Sage Publications.

Pearl, A. and Riessman, F. (1965). *New Careers for the Poor.* New York: Free Press.

Pedersen, P.B. (1982). *Alternative Futures for Cross Cultural Counseling and Psychotherapy.* A.J. Marsella and B.P. Pedersen (ed.), *Cross Cultural Counseling and Psychotherapy.* New York: Pergamon.

Pettigrew, W. (1964). "Negro American Personality: Why Isn't More Known?" *Journal of Social Issues,* 20, 4–23.

Pidgeon, D.A. (1970). *Expectations and Pupil Performance.* Washington, DC: National Federation for Educational Research.

Poussaint, A.F. (1972). *Why Blacks Kill Blacks.* New York: Emerson Hall.

Powell, G.J. (1973). "Self-Concept in White and Black Children." In C.B. Willie, B.M. Kramer, and B.S. Brown (eds.), *Racism and Mental Health.* Pittsburgh: University of Pittsburgh.

Powell, G.J. and Fuller, M. (1970). "Self-Concept and School Desegration," *American Journal of Orthopsychiatry,* 40, 303.

Powell-Hopson, D. and Hopson, D. (1998). *The Power of Soul.* New York: Simon and Schuster.

Pugh, R. (1972). *Psychology of the Black Experience.* Belmont, CA: Wadsworth.

Rainwater, L. (1970). *Behind Ghetto Walls: Black Family Life in a Federal Slum.* Chicago: Aldine.

Ray, E.C. (1989). "Lifestyle: Commuter Marriage: Does It Work?" *Essence,* 19(10), (February), 103, 107–108.

Richardson, E. (1981). "Cultural and Historical Perspectives in Counseling American Indians." In D.W. Sue, *Counseling the Culturally Different.* New York: John Wiley & Sons.

Rogers, C. (1961). *On Becoming a Person.* Boston: Houghton Mifflin.

Rogers, D. (1978). *Adolescence: A Psychological Perspective* (2nd ed.), Monterey, CA: Brook-Cole.

Rogoff, B. and Chavajay, P. (1995). "What's Become of the Research on the Cultural Basis of Cognitive Development?" *American Psychologist,* 50, 859–877.

Rosenberg, M. (1979). *Conceiving of Self.* New York: Basic Books.

Rosenthal, R. and Jacobson, L. (1968). *Pygmalion in the Classroom.* New York: Holt, Rinehart & Winston.

Rothbart, M., Dalfen, S., and Barrett, R. (1971). "Effects of Teacher Expectancy on Student-Teacher Interaction," *Journal of Educational Psychology,* 62(1), 49–54.

Rubovitz, P.C. and Maehr, M.L. (1973). "Pygmalion Black and White," *Journal of Personality and Social Psychology,* 25(2), 210–218.

Semaj, L. (1981). "The Black Self: Identity and Models for a Psychology of Black Liberation," *Western Journal of Black Studies,* 5(3), 158–171.

Schlesinger, A., Jr. (1978). *Robert Kennedy and His Times.* Boston: Houghton Mifflin.

Segall, M.H., Lonner, W.J. and Berry, J.W. (1998). "Cross-Cultural Psychology as a Scholarly Discipline: On the Flowering of Culture in Behavioral Research." *American Psychologist,* 53(10), 1101–1110.

Shade, B.J. (1991). "African American Patterns of Cognition." In R.L. Jones, (ed.), *Black Psychology* (3rd ed.). Hampton, VA: Cobb & Henry.

Shipp, P. (1983). "Counseling Blacks: A Group Approach," *Personnel and Guidance Journal,* 62(2), 108–111.

Smith, E. (1977). "Counseling Black Individuals: Some Strategies," *Personnel and Guidance Journal,* 55, 390–396.

Stacks, C. (1974). *All Our Kin: Strategies or Survival in the Black Community.* New York: Harper & Row.

Staples, R. (1982). *Black Masculinity.* San Francisco: Black Scholar Press.

Sudarkasa, N. (1981). "Interpreting the African Heritage in Afro-American Family Organization." In H.P. McAdoo (ed.), *Black Families.* Beverly Hills: Sage Publications.

Sue, S. (1978). "Ethnic Minority Research: Trends and Directions." Paper presented at National Conference on Minority Group Alcohol, Drug Abuse and Mental Health Issues, Denver, Colorado.

Sue, S. (1977). "Community Mental Health Service to Minority Groups," *American Psychologist,* 32, 616–624.

Sue, S. and Wagner, N. (1973) (eds.). *Asian Americans: Psychological Perspectives.* Palo Alto, CA: Science and Behavior Books.

Sue, D.W. (1981). *Counseling the Culturally Different.* New York: John Wiley.

Sue, D.W., Arredondo, P. and McDavis, R.J. (1992). "Multicultural Counseling Competencies and Standards: A Call to the Profession," *Journal of Counseling Development and Development,* 70, 477–484.

Task Force on Education for Economic Growth (1983). *Action for Excellence: A Comprehensive Plan to Improve Our Nation's Schools.* Denver: Educational Commission of the States.

Thomas, A. and Sillen, S. (1972). *Racism and Psychiatry.* Secaucus, NJ: The Citadel Press.

Thomas, C. (1971). *Boys No More.* Beverly Hills: Glenco Press.

Thomas, G. (1977). *Access to Higher Education: How Important Are Race, Sex, Social Class, and Academic Credentials for College?* Baltimore: John Hopkins Press.

Thomas, W. (1967). *The Thomas Self-Concept Values Test: For Children Ages 3–9*. Grand Rapids, MI: Educational Service.

Washington, E.D. (1932). *Selected Speeches of Booker T. Washington*. New York: Kraus Reprints Company.

Weinberg, M. (1977). Minority Students: A Research Appraisal. Washington, DC: ESDHEW, National Institute of Education.

Wesson, A. (1975). "The Black Man's Burden: The White Clinician," *The Black Scholar*, 6, 13–18.

White, J.L. (1984). *The Psychology of Blacks: An Afro-American Perspective*. Englewood Cliffs, NJ: Prentice-Hall.

White, J.L. (1972). *Toward A Black Psychology*. In R.L. Jones (ed.), *Black Psychology*. New York: Harper & Row.

White, J.L. and Parham, T.A. (1990). *The Psychology of Blacks: An African American Perspective* (2nd ed.). Englewood Cliffs, NJ: Prentice-Hall.

Williams, R. (1975). *Textbook of Black-Related Diseases*. New York: McGraw-Hill.

Williams, R. (1974). *Cognitive and Social Learning of the Black Child: The Survival of Black Children and Youth*. Washington, DC: Science Publications.

Williams, R.L. (1981). *Collective Black Mind: An Afrocentric Theory of Black Personality*. St. Louis: Williams & Associates, Inc.

Wilson, Amos (1993). *The Falsification Of Consciousness: Eurocentric History, Psychiatry and the Politics of White Supremacy*. New York: Afrikan World Infosystems.

Wilson, Amos (1978). *The Developmental Psychology of The Black Child*. New York: United Brothers Communications Systems.

Wobogo, Vulindlela, (1976). "Diop's Two Cradle Theory and the Origin of White Racism." *Black Books Bulletin*, Vol. 4(4), 20–29, 72.

Wylie, R. (1978). *The Self-Concept*, (rev. ed.) (*Vol. 2: Theory and Research on Selected Topics*). Lincoln: University of Nebraska Press.

Wyne, M.D., White, K.D., Coop, R.H. (1974). *The Black Self*. Englewood Cliffs, NJ: Prentice-Hall.

Yalom, I. (1975). *The Theory and Practice of Group Psychotherapy*. New York: Basic Books.

Index